VICKY

VICKY

RUSSELL DAVIES and LIZ OTTAWAY

with a personal memoir by
RT HON. MICHAEL FOOT MP

SECKER & WARBURG
LONDON

First published in England 1987 by
Martin Secker & Warburg Limited
54 Poland Street, London W1V 3DF

Text copyright © 1987 by Russell Davies
Captions copyright © 1987 by Liz Ottaway
Personal memoir copyright © 1987 by Michael Foot

British Library Cataloguing in Publication Data

Davies, Russell
    Vicky
    1. Weisz, Victor 2. Cartoonists – Great
    Britain – Biography
    I. Title   II. Ottaway, Liz   III. Foot,
    Michael
    741′.092′4   NC1479.W4

    ISBN 0-436-44759-2 (paperback)

Typeset in 12/14pt Lasercomp Bembo
Printed in Great Britain by
BAS Printers Limited, Over Wallop, Hampshire

To the memory of Vicky

Contents

Preface

This book has been produced under the auspices of the Centre for the Study of Cartoons and Caricature at the University of Kent at Canterbury. The Centre holds approximately 3400 Vicky originals, drawn mainly for publication in the *Daily Mirror*, *Evening Standard* and *New Statesman*.

The authors' first debt is to Vicky's sister, Elizabeth Weisz, for her kindness and cooperation throughout. We are also grateful for the continuing generosity of the trustees of the Leverhulme Trust. The Vicky material in the Cartoon Centre was originally sorted and catalogued under the terms of a grant from the Trust in 1979. A companion volume on David Low, published in 1985, was produced with the help of a further grant; and a third grant has enabled Liz Ottaway, under the direction of Professor Colin Seymour-Ure, to spend most of her time for several months on the preparation of this volume, with special responsibility for picture research and the drafting of the captions.

In the writing of the narrative text, Russell Davies was often thankful for the groundwork done several years ago by Peter Birks, who in the course of compiling a postgraduate thesis interviewed several intimates of Vicky's who have since died. His notes and transcripts are lodged at the University of Kent. Very many people kindly replied to our requests for information. In particular, we would like to thank Tom Baistow, Michael Foot, Dr Hans Feld, Anthony Howard, Robert Lantz and Stella Richman for extended interviews; and Ronald Searle for kindly putting us in touch with Vicky's second wife, Lucie Gray Mondange, who has been most generous and frank with her memories. The help of K. S. Karol was vital in elucidating Vicky's activity in Paris. In informal interview, Sir Charles Wintour, Lord Cudlipp, Mark Roberts, Nicholas Garland, Peter Noble, Paul Johnson, Wally Fawkes, John Gross, Miriam Gross and Godfrey Smith all provided valuable information; and we are grateful for the material supplied by Rosita Gross, Dr Rachael Whear, Moni Cameron and Alan Mumford. Dozens of correspondents were kind enough to supply revealing anecdotes about Vicky and his work. Those incorporated in the text are attributed, with thanks, in the Notes.

We are especially delighted that Michael Foot agreed to contribute a personal memoir of Vicky.

Among librarians, archivists and curators who allowed access to papers, drawings and newspaper cuttings we are grateful to John Allard and Alan Freeman at the *Daily Mirror*; Laura Berryman and Ted Peacock at the *New Statesman*; Norman Higson at the Brynmor Jones Library, University of Hull; Yael Hirsch at the Ben Uri Art Society; Edda Tasiemka at the Hans Tasiemka Archives; and Jeff Walden at the BBC Written Archives Centre. The Departmental Record Office (Home Office) went to the limits of the permissible in releasing information on Vicky's entry into Britain and subsequent citizenship. In East Berlin, Fräulein Brigitte Weber was instrumental in arranging a visit to the State Library of the German Democratic Republic.

The quality of the reproductions owes much to the skill of the University of Kent's photographer Jim Styles, who always produced the best possible image from an array of cartoons; likewise Gerry Bye, Head of Photography, Cambridge University Library. Our thanks go to Mark Bryant, our editor, for the patient way in which he prepared a complicated set of manuscripts for the press; and also to the designer, Sue Hadden. Elizabeth Weisz, among others, looked over the manuscript in draft; but the authors remain entirely responsible for what appears. We are most grateful to all those who encouraged us.

Cambridge and Canterbury, 1987
R.D.
L.O.

Introduction

Vicky (Victor Weisz) was the best-loved and most fiercely hated political cartoonist of his time. Born in Berlin of Hungarian-Jewish parents, he was compelled by family tragedy to put himself to work in his mid-teens, and he produced drawings almost daily thereafter for the best part of forty years. By conviction he was a humanitarian and an emotional, uncalculating Socialist. He did not greatly care to distinguish between political and economic dictatorship; so that while his deepest contempt was reserved for the world's Fascist despots, some of whom survived him, he also feared and resisted the power of a clumsy and bullying America.

Saved by his Hungarian passport from early disappearance in Hitler's concentration camps, Vicky left Germany and settled in London. Almost at once, under the tutelage of the *News Chronicle* Editor, Gerald Barry, he set out programmatically to learn the British way – of politics, humour, sport, literature and graphic art. His success in carrying through this process of auto-acclimatisation is one of the more inspiring legends of twentieth-century British journalism.

Vicky himself was inspired, as all young cartoonists necessarily were, by the example of the great David Low, some of whose rhetorical flourishes and running characters Vicky openly adapted to his own purposes. But their styles never seriously overlapped, Low gradually taking on the stolidity of a distinguished veteran, while Vicky, under the noisy influence of Richard Winnington, began to release the full energy of his natural volatility.

His output as a contracted political cartoonist came to be associated chiefly with four papers: the *News Chronicle*, the *Daily Mirror*, the *Evening Standard*, and the *New Statesman*. Less well known are his six-year stint for *Time and Tide*, and his pseudonymous work, as 'Smith', pocket cartoonist of the *Chronicle*, and 'Pierrot', who interpreted the French scene to readers of *L'Express* in Paris. In the last fifteen years of his life Vicky again built on the experience of Low by securing himself the nearest thing to complete freedom of comment that a cartoonist can reasonably desire under British law. Indeed, every daily-paper cartoonist's ideal conditions of work were those enjoyed by Vicky in the 1960s.

Yet in 1966 this pre-eminent craftsman died by his own hand – the most shocking death of this kind since the presumed suicide of Gillray 150 years before. It would be impertinent to state baldly why Vicky was impelled to take this terrible step. Many contributing factors suggest themselves, not least sheer exhaustion after decades of daily invention, and Vicky's perennial insomnia. By his own report, Vicky at the end was living with his political conscience twenty-two hours a day. He mentioned fears of the loss of professional powers, and difficulties in his fourth marriage; and then, as ever with Vicky, there was the political situation. Ever since Aneurin Bevan had gone over to Labour's pro-nuclear faction in 1957, Vicky had felt increasingly isolated on the left wing of a party which in fact he never joined. By castigating the ineptitudes of the Macmillan and Home governments, he was able to divert himself, but in 1964 he came face to face with disillusion – the face of Harold Wilson, which he was bafflingly unable to draw. The performance of Wilson's government heaped professional agonies upon him. These were not metaphorical pains. 'Poor Vicky,' as his friend James Cameron wrote in a stricken memoir for the *Standard*, 'he really meant it.'

Vicky was a melancholic, but only in the drawings colleagues designated as his 'Oxfam style' was this side of his nature made manifest. When not dwelling on man's inhumanity to man, he was splendidly inventive, with a marvellous knack of converting a topical craze – be it for Davy Crockett hats or Graham Sutherland portraits – into political metaphor. It is hard on Vicky that he is best remembered for 'Supermac', an intended satire on personality cultism which accidently gave the cult a focus. There was so much more to Vicky than that. He knew his cartoon history, and came close to reintroducing into Britain's rather thin-blooded modern politics the beefy flavour of authentic pre-industrial disrespect.

His stylistic influence lives on in the work of his avowed devotee Nicholas Garland of the *Independent*. Sadly the two men never met. On a visit to the Côte d'Azur, Garland once spied Vicky typically engrossed in hilarious conversational combat, but was too shy to interrupt. The dialogue they never had perhaps may be discerned at times in Garland's own productions.

Vicky's help through the 1970s would have been invaluable – to newspaper readers, to an impoverished cartooning community, and particularly to Socialists, still locked in debates that were current in his lifetime. This book tries to explain what Vicky did, and why he is so much missed.

A Personal Memoir
Rt Hon. Michael Foot MP

He had become my closest friend, and I thought I knew almost
everything about him. Over the last years right up to two days
before his death, the intimacy had seemed to grow; whenever
we met, we could resume an argument, almost in the middle of
a sentence. He was a comic genius, gifted beyond measure with
the power to laugh at the world; yet not so far beneath the surface
a sense of tragedy, associated as I supposed with his Jewishness,
had always been there. Somehow I had not applied this to him
personally. Then one cold afternoon, Charles Wintour, editor of
the *Evening Standard* at the time, rang up and told me he was
dead. I had barely understood at all. Despite occasional conversa-
tions on the fringes of the subject, I had no comprehension of
how near his mind was to the end of its tether.

We had fixed a standing Monday lunch date at a Fleet Street
restaurant or pub – starting originally at the old Wellington and
moving to Mario's halfway up Chancery Lane – for all of us an
entrancing moment in the week, always guaranteed to be lit up
by some new expression of Vicky's charm. One person in that
regular company did at least comprehend more than the rest of
us – James Cameron; truly Vicky's closest kindred spirit over a
number of decades. Their response to events was continuously
and uncannily the same. They often found themselves, in
Cameron's phrase, 'poised between hilarity and despair'. Incred-
ibly for two such complicated anatomies, their hearts beat as one.
Being the only two real artists in our company they shared too,
I believe, the fear that suddenly they might awake to find the
gift gone or rapidly fading. The apprehension might seem especially incredible in Vicky's case when he would turn up in the
New Statesman offices each Monday with such a superfluity of
ideas; enough to have given the editor a choice between several,
enough to prove afresh each week that the source of his genius
was as potent as ever.

For Vicky, James Cameron always was the prince of modern
journalists, the reporter who could best place each individual scene
and spectacle in the world-wide drama. Since his death – twenty
years after Vicky's, amazing to relate – no successor has been able

to do so well what he could do: to relate our individual agonies or absurdities to a much larger humanity. And he placed Vicky's own death amid that drama too: for Vicky was a casualty of the Vietnam war and its associated enormities, including the sophistries with which those much nearer home, within his own adopted country and his beloved, wayward Labour movement, excused their part in the horror. And if he had lived, which of us would have escaped the lash?

The few, the happy few, for whom friendship with Vicky was the greatest uncovenanted blessing ever bestowed upon us, would happily take the risk. He could offer moments of rich enjoyment – for example, when, feeling we were not being properly served in El Vino's he put the landlord's bowler hat on his little head and strutted along the bar apologising to customers – or those long, loving evenings of reconciliation among his argumentative friends in his elegantly furnished Wimpole Street flat, when his wife, Inge, showed how well she could meet his standards of cooking and when he whipped the cream and demanded proper acclamation for his skill. Was he truly happy then? It was hard not to believe so, although another impression might be gained if one dared to disturb him at the Regent Street Quality Inn where he would normally have his insomniac breakfast and reach anew for his cudgels and his victims. He studied the newspapers with a diligence which made him as well-informed as any editor, and much better than most. And nothing, no distraction whatever, would be allowed to shake his crusading spirit.

He was a twentieth-century Don Quixote and he honoured the mournful knight just as Heinrich Heine, fellow artist, fellow Jew, and kindred spirit, had done before him. Heine wrote:

> My colleague mistook windmills for giants; I, on the contrary, see in our giants of today only ranting windmills . . . I must constantly fight duels, battle my way through untold misery, and I gain no victory which has not cost me something of my heart's blood. Night and day I am sorely beset, for my foes are so insidious that many of them, whom I have dealt a death-blow, still show the semblance of life and appear in all shapes and molest me day and night. What agonies I already have had to endure from these perfidious ghosts!

And that was Vicky too. He had painted a Daumier-like painting of his knight-errant, and was justly proud of the technical skill it displayed; wherever he moved, it was given the pride of place on his wall. No doubt was possible; his Don Quixote was a tragic figure. Yet, naturally enough at those lunches, the hilarity quickly subdued the despair, and it was not until after his death that a conversation with Inge cast a most curious retrospective glance on their therapeutic effects. Whenever I had sought, born, blind, boneheaded optimist that I was, to cheer him in his most despondent moments, he would come home to dinner more despondent than ever. But when Jimmy Cameron had been there, to deepen the darkness from the outset and at every turn in the argument, the balm would take effect and he would return with a renewed light in his eye, the same indeed which, if only I had had the sensitivity to see it, had helped to shed a few gleams into Jimmy's hell. James Cameron, like Vicky, was sometimes derided for his Don Quixotism. Perhaps this was the only form of journalism fully suitable for the age of Auschwitz, and Hiroshima, and Vietnam, and Afghanistan and all such horrors. Together, the two of them, Vicky and Cameron, lifted the old trade to a new level.

In Vicky's Valhalla, we should note, one name stood higher even than Don Quixote – that of Heinrich Heine himself. I remember telling him how I had first encountered his hero; how a copy of *Heinrich Heine: Works of Prose* had arrived from New York at the *Evening Standard* office in 1943; and how a week or two later – with no wartime or other excuse – we had reprinted for sheer delight the poet's prose portrait 'The Late Dr Ascher': how exciting it was to receive in response the letters of Jewish refugees who had found shelter on our shores. They had brought with them their portable Heine just as Heine had once described the Bible as their portable homeland. Vicky could finish the story of Dr Ascher in his own words, or often with his own pen, for Heine's portraits were brilliant caricatures ready-made, and thereafter Heine was never long absent from our debates and disquisitions. No too sharp distinction need be drawn between Heine and Vicky. They shared so much: their Jewishness, their agnosticism, their anarchism, their insomnia, their primitive socialism, their mixture of gravity and gaiety in the same smile and the same tears, their refusal to make obeisance before any authority in this world or the next, their love of the countries of their adoption, their allegiance to an international faith which would embrace all mankind and womankind. I had been introduced to Heine through translations of his prose exquisitely done but, I suppose, lacking in the last touch of perfection. Vicky had drunk his poetry with his mother's milk and his family's agony when Hitler was engaged in the vain task of stamping out the work of the most

xv

popular poet since the Psalmist. Page after page from Heine awaken memories of Vicky: and no one ever showed such recompense to his master, accepting his verdict.

Cold and shrewd philosophers! How compassionately they smile down at the self-tortures and crazy illusions of poor Don Quixote; and in all their school-room wisdom they do not mark that his very Don Quixotism is the most precious thing in life — that it is life itself — and that Don Quixotism lends wings to the whole world, and to all in it who philosophise, make music, plough and yawn!

Vicky made himself the best cartoonist in the world, the one proper successor to David Low, a student and example of the greatest tradition of caricature. It could be argued that others might equal or occasionally surpass him in draughtsmanship, but he more than restored his pre-eminence with his humour, his fertility, his diligence, his political insight and instinct. Few observers have ever studied the English political scene with more persistence and acumen. He knew every corner of the workshop, every twist in the game, every shade of character. In this sense his equipment as a cartoonist was unique. It is hard to believe that any of his famous predecessors, Gillray, Rowlandson and the rest, understood the internal operations of British politics as Vicky made it his business to comprehend them.

Of course, this extraordinary knowledge was not easily acquired. If he had not been a genuis anyhow, he would have become one by taking pains. When he arrived in London in the thirties and got a job on the *News Chronicle* he had none of the uncanny understandings of English habits, pastimes and idioms which became one of his strengths. He set about learning them, by reading and listening and through the range of his all-perceptive eye. Gerald Barry was his first editor and mentor, and Vicky was always eager to acknowledge the debt. Richard Winnington, and later James Cameron and Tom Baistow, were his intimate journalistic confederates. Somehow the greatest days of the *News Chronicle* were associated with Vicky, and when he left — after some of his cartoons had been refused publication by Barry's successors — the Liberal journal seemed preparing for its own doom.

Then came more strained and strenuous years on the *Daily Mirror*. Here freedom was complete. Vicky had won the opportunity to say exactly what he wished to a vast national audience. But year by year his own doubts and anxieties tortured him, to the

Vicky depicts the sometimes volatile relationship between himself and his friend Michael Foot in this drawing of the two men standing on soapboxes shouting at each other. The legend reads, 'Dear Michael, I'm sorry I lost my temper last night. Hope to see you soon. Yours, Vicky.'

amazement of his employers and friends. Somehow he needed to preach to the unconverted; somehow he needed to awaken his enemies. He sought a new context for his message, and found it in the *Evening Standard*, signing a contract guaranteeing him freedom more secure than any cartoonist before him, even Low, had ever had. Little Vicky had become an independent power, almost the Fifth Estate of the Realm.

Most men who wield such power become corrupted, but here was one of his secrets. He was incorruptible, the most incorruptible man I ever knew. Neither money nor other material offerings could sway him from what he considered the course his conscience dictated. All the other more subtle seductions were equally pushed aside, rejected without reckoning. He could not be bought, brow-beaten or bulldozed. He stood against the world, the proud unshakable anarchist who knew there was a force more explosive than bombs and who, knowing so well how power corrupted others, stayed miraculously immune himself. Above all, he had an abiding compassion, drawn from his heart and nurtured by his love of music, literature and beauty. Some of his victims might find the claim baffling, but if ever they dared breathe a word of dissent, a host of *their* victims from the underworld of the defeated, the forgotten and the maligned, could rally from the depths to defend their champion.

Vicky felt for those who suffered, the casualties of war, poverty and persecution, as if the strokes fell across his own back. 'No one ever lost an inch of sleep from any public worry,' said Dr Johnson. Vicky utterly disproved the thesis. He hardly had a full night's rest for most of his adult life, and one cause of his unsettled mind was undoubtedly that he felt more sharply than most of the human race. He had no armour to protect himself against twentieth-century horrors. Someone once wrote of Shelley that he was one of the rare beings for whom the thought of the suffer-ing of his fellow men was intolerable. Vicky had the same feeling of love and pity for his fellow men:

Me – who am as a nerve o'er which do creep
The else unfelt oppressions of this earth.

Some part of this universal quality, of course, he owed directly to his Jewishness. He made a notable addition to the immeasurable debt which the British people owe to the Jewish people. When the Jews were driven out of Spain, a Turkish Sultan was alleged to have said: 'What, call ye this Ferdinand wise, he who depopu-lates his own country in order to enrich mine?' What riches Vicky brought to our shores and how splendidly he dispensed them! It was a good day when he arrived. It was even better, the day after and thenceforward, when he resolved to take us at our best liberal word – when he assumed that he would have the right to say what he thought, though the heavens fell and however much all the undercover totalitarians and skin-deep democrats might scream. Curiously, the little Hungarian became a great English patriot, upholding the finest traditions of this land, our most precious treasures of free speech, free thought, the right to laugh at the mighty, the duty to appease the pains of the weak. He could put us all in our places. 'You're a Scot, you're English, you're Welsh – I'm the only one here who's really Brrritish' –

he would roll a Germanic 'r' slyly – 'I've got a document to prove it.' Karl Marx said he wanted to put little Heine in his pocket and bring him to London. For us, the miracle had happened.

He was truly one of that most exclusive company: a comic genius, like Heine himself, like Cervantes, like Jonathan Swift or Charles Dickens or Charlie Chaplin or Groucho Marx. He could not look out upon the world without seeing it perpetually shifted from what the rest of us would regard as normal. Applied to the world at large, these men can be the saviours of our sanity. Applied to the stage covered by political caricature, the service may be even swifter. The exposure of the absurdities, the pretensions, the falsities of political man can start to restore our health. So sure did Vicky's combined observation and touch become that the performers seemed almost to be obeying his instructions, conforming to his specifications. It is hard to recall the world, say, of Macmillan and Butler and De Gaulle and Khrushchev without seeing them now, first and foremost, through Vicky's eyes just as the world of Baldwin and Chamberlain, and Hitler and Mussolini can be recollected best through those of David Low, and just as we may peer back into the combats of earlier political centuries through the eyes of Gillray and Daumier. Somehow the very greatest cartoonists catch the spirit of the age and then leave their own imprint upon it; they create political heroes and villains in their own image; they teach the historians their trade and warn the best of them against the fatuities of hindsight; they practise a form of journalism more potent than anything even the greatest practitioners with words may achieve. The weapon, wielded by few masters, is the most deadly in the whole armoury of political controversy. Those who possess it in this measure may destroy by ridicule – the only instrument, said Byron, which the English climate cannot rust.

Yet by some extraordinary fate it is also decreed that those who train themselves to wield this power must ensure that it is accompanied by something else, by a tragic sense too. If the capacity to ridicule, to wound, to kill, is exercised without mercy, without reference to any other larger aims, it will soon pall or lose it sharpness. It is no accident that the satirists in other fields have served a serious purpose. It is necessary for the great cartoonist, as for all other true artists, to pour his whole heart and soul and spirit into the task, even if he may run the risk, as poor Vicky did, of draining it altogether.

When he died tributes flowed in from all over the world to Vicky the artist, the incomparable master of political humour, and some of us in Fleet Street bowed our heads in remembrance of the most lovable companion we had ever known. But the proper thoughts of Vicky at the end, the proper epitaphs, can best be given in the words of Heine. I select four extracts. The middle two, portraying what Heine said to his maker from his bed of torture, harshly apposite though they are, might be thought too finally sombre. So the first recalls the Creed, every phrase of which Vicky would relish reciting, and the last recalls the political commitment which I am sure he would acknowledge. The middle two, the devastating two, are given in the German in which Vicky would be proud to recite them, with the translations contained in Professor Prawer's *Heine's Jewish Comedy* just below.

I already believe the main things in the Bible: I believe that Abraham begat Isaac and Isaac begat Jacob and Jacob, in his turn, begat Judah; and I also believe that Judah came in unto his daughter-in-law by the way to Timnath. I also believe that Lot had a drop too much in the company of his daughters. I believe that Potiphar's wife kept pious Joseph's garment in her hand. I believe that the elders who surprised Susannah in her bath must have been *very* old. I believe, in addition, that the patriarch Jacob cheated first his brother and then his father-in-law, that King David arranged a good posting for Uriah, that Solomon got himself a hundred wives and complained afterwards that all is vanity. I also believe in the Ten Commandments and even keep most of them: I do not covet my neighbour's ox or his maidservant or his cow or his ass. I do not labour on the Lord's sabbath; and to make quite sure – for no one can know exactly which day of the week the Lord rested on – I often remain idle the whole week through . . .

O Gott, verkürze meine Qual,
Damit man mich bald begrabe;
Du weisst, ja, dass ich kein Talent
Zum Martyrtume habe.

Ob deiner Inkonsequenz, o Herr,
Erlaube, dass ich staune:
Du schufest den fröhlichsten Dichter und raubst
Ihm jetzt seine gute Laune.

Der Schmerz verdumpft den heitern Sinn
Und macht mich melancholisch,
Nimmt nicht der traurige Spass eine End',
So werd' ich am Ende katholisch.

Ich heule dir dann die Ohren voll
Wie andre gute Christen –
O Miserere! Verloren geht
Der Beste der Humoristen!

[O God, shorten my agony
so that I can be buried soon;
you know that I lack the talent
to be a martyr.

Permit me, Lord, to express astonishment
at your illogicality;
you created the merriest poet, and now
you rob him of his cheerfulness.

Pain dulls my gay serenity,
and makes me melancholy;
if this sad jest does not finish soon
I'll turn Catholic in the end.

Then I'll wail into your ears
like other good Christians.
O Miserere! the world is losing
the best of all humorists!]

Woran liegt die Schuld? Ist etwa
Unser Herr nicht ganz allmächtig?
Oder treibt er selbst den Unfug?
Ach, das wäre niederträchtig.

Also fragen wir beständig,
Bis man uns mit einer Handvoll
Erde endlich stopft die Maüler –
Aber ist das eine Antwort?

[What is to blame for this? Could it be
that God is not altogether all-powerful?
Or does He make the mischief Himself?
Ah – that would be base.

Thus we question without end,
until a handful of earth
is at last stuffed into our mouth to silence us –
but is *that* an answer?]

Vicky on that last night might have spoken in such terms, but
it was not for him nor for Heine his whole fate:

xxi

I doubt that I deserve the laurel wreath, for poetry has always been merely an instrument with me, a sort of divine plaything. If you would honour me, lay a sword rather than a wreath upon my coffin; for I was, first of all, a soldier in the war for the liberation of humanity.

Vicky and Heine, divinely gifted, haters of tyranny, lovers of peace, belonged to the same army.

'Big Heads and Little Legs' 1

Vicky was born in what is now West Berlin, at 14 Regens-burgerstrasse south of the Kurfürstendamm, on 25 April 1913. In Britain a matter of days before, a group of Fabians including Sidney and Beatrice Webb had begun to publish a magazine called the *New Statesman*, in which Viktor Weisz was destined to figure, forty years on, as a most distinguished contributor.

His parents were Hungarian Jews. Isabella Weisz, née Seitenbach, and her husband Dezso (for the Germans' benefit, Desiderius) spoke Hungarian between themselves and held Hungarian passports, but on their honeymoon they had fallen in love with the Black Forest resort of Pforzheim. Two of their three children were born there, before business considerations took the family to Berlin. The children, Oskar (born April 1909), Elisabeth (born December 1910) and little Viktor were brought up as German speakers only. Hungarian nationality involved the nuisance of applying annually for permission to reside in Germany, but the family was to be grateful later for the measure of protection afforded by their foreign papers.

The young Weiszes were striking children, dark, compact, and

2 Family portrait, Berlin, *c.* 1916

A pleasing family group taken when Vicky was three years old. He is the youngest and sits on his father's knee. Oskar stands in the middle with Elisabeth on his right. The physical similarity between Vicky, his sister and mother is striking.

I

facially almost fierce in repose, though gifted each with a marvellous sudden grin. An interviewer writing of Vicky in the last months of his life remarked that when the cartoonist smiled for the first time during their encounter, 'it was like all the lights in a building being turned on simultaneously'.[1] Elschen, Vicky's sister, still displayed this happy faculty in 1987.

Family photographs record the Weisz children's participation in the normal juvenile jollifications – fancy dress, swimming, cycling – though it is plain from a picture of Viktor and his bike that he would have needed to go carefully in such thick and powerful spectacles. At the age of six or seven he had contracted a disease he remembered as scarlet fever (perhaps more likely measles, which carries a heavy risk of ocular damage if the patient is exposed to too much light), and this left him permanently short-sighted. The affliction probably intensified the independent concentration which his mother early noted in him; while other children played marbles, 'Viki' (as the family spelt his name) would be found sitting by himself on the floor, engrossed in drawing with his crayons.

His size, too, set him apart. He was always tiny, a fact which

3   Chess players, Berlin, *c.* 1920

In later life, playing chess and attending concerts of classical music, at the Royal Festival Hall in particular, were the only two relaxations Vicky ever allowed himself. Here he seems to be remonstrating with his sister and, judging from the chessmen lying beside the board, he appears to have the stronger game position.

2

4 Early oil painting, 1924

This juvenile piece was painted when Vicky was eleven years old. He has signed it using the German spelling of his surname: Weiss (the family later used the Hungarian form: Weisz).

exaggerated his nervous intensity – and no doubt did much to occasion it in the first place. Schooldays drew attention to his unwelcome uniqueness. 'I think I was the smallest boy that school had ever seen,' Vicky estimated. 'I had a special bench made so that my feet would reach the floor . . .' But he was alert, lively and, as events were to indicate, perhaps a touch belligerent in compensation. 'As a matter of fact I think I was a very precocious, a rather awful child.'[2]

Already marked out as a talented draughtsman, the boy formed an early ambition to be a painter, and at the age of eleven he began a course of private tuition with an artist called Tennstedt.[3] An instinct for design, at least, was part of the family tradition, for Desider Weisz was a jeweller and goldsmith by trade, responsible for the design of his own wares. But the combination of smallness and aesthetic preoccupations is not a propitious one for

3

a schoolboy, and Viki was obliged to take steps to protect, both literally and symbolically, his reputation among his peers. 'The toughest thing I could do would be to take up boxing, and I joined a Jewish boxing club, Maccabi, in Berlin. And became, sort of technically, a good boxer.'[4]

There must have been a good deal of flair and spirit to go with the technique, for Viki seems never to have suffered in the ring. Elisabeth Weisz watched her brother box on a weekly basis and enjoyed the experience enough to form a lifelong enthusiasm for ringcraft. Viki retired from pugilism at thirteen, after damaging a finger in training; but having won the 'All-Berlin Championship for Boys under 90 lb', he had made his point. Late in life he apologised for having shown proficiency in the sport ('I rather hate boxing and I think it's a bad thing'),[5] and this was the protestation of a man who knew the ignoble art to be indefensible according to his own best humanitarian standards. Declarations of principle, however, did nothing to discourage him from using

5   Young boxer, Berlin, *c.* 1924

Vicky, now wearing spectacles and flanked by two much larger and older boys, gives no hint of his frailty, only lack of stature. He was a member of Maccabi, a Jewish boxing club in Berlin, until he retired from the ring at the age of thirteen having already won the 'All-Berlin Championship for Boys under 90 lb'.

the ring as a hilarious metaphor for political combat. The groggy victims of the 'straight left' he advocated are drawn with relish.

Despite Viki's personal victories, the stately progress of the Weiszes from year to bourgeois year was not as secure as it seemed. Desider Weisz had all the makings of a highly prosperous citizen, and his photograph suggests a kindly and comfortable man with time to indulge his children. A Hungarian poem he wrote to Isabella during the days of their courtship was preserved by the family. But within Mr Weisz was a weakness that would prove abruptly fatal. He was a gambler, of the addictive kind. On a losing streak, he showed himself ultimately prepared to wager not just his own money but the family's goods. Near the end, even Isabella's jewels went – a doubly shaming loss for a dealer in that commodity.

The last calamitous risks were taken on behalf of Desider Weisz's firstborn, Oskar, whose ambition it was to be a furrier. A fur-factory was established, but when it failed, the paterfamilias was left with no refuge from despair. He retired to the factory office, where, fortified by a bottle of spirits, he shot himself through the mouth. His daughter believed that his last communication was a telephone call to her, advising against what he saw as an unwise liaison with a Frenchman. It was Oskar who summoned the police when his father did not come home from work. Desider Weisz was a fastidiously neat person, and that morning, Oskar now recalled, he had not bothered to shave.[6] He died in his forty-fourth year.

It was August 1928. Viktor Weisz was only fifteen; but with Oskar entangled in their late father's affairs, and the trainee milliner Elisabeth fully occupied in consoling their mother, it was upon Viki that the burden fell of maintaining the family. Their accommodation shrank by stages, from a handsome seven-room apartment in the Bayerischer Platz to three rooms in the Brandenburgische Strasse; but it was not long before earnings began to come in. Energetically hawking his caricatures around Berlin's papers on a freelance basis (a German middleweight boxer was his first sale), Viki was taken up by the *12 Uhr Blatt*, a mildly radical journal which for a time represented a haven for anti-Hitlerians. Here young Weisz was accepted as a very junior member of the graphic department. 'They gave me,' he later recalled, 'long trousers and regular working hours.'[7] Indeed, the story is told that he turned up at the Charlottenburg office in short pants on the first day, and was sent away to buy the distinguishing uniform of the adult male.

6 '*Gute Besserung*', unpublished, Berlin, 26 May 1934

Vicky had been working for *12 Uhr Blatt* for six years in 1934. In this delightful colour drawing he hopes his brother Oskar will 'Get well soon' and recover fully from his appendicitis. He signs using the family's nickname for him – Viki. (Many people who knew Oskar have said of him that he *enjoyed* bad health.)

In his mid-teens, Vicky (it seems appropriate henceforth to salute him with the name that made him famous in exile) was a professional cartoonist. The only advice he was given as he began was to draw 'men with big heads and little legs' – '*Männer mit jrosse Köppe und kleene Beeneken*' in the atrocious Berlin Cockney of his boss, Rolf Nürnberg. Vicky started out in the sports department. Was he not, after all, a famous boxer? Athletics, tennis, boxing itself – it was varied and pleasant work, quite enough to occupy Vicky's time. But Hans Tasiemka, who ran the *Feuilleton* arts section, had his eye on Vicky, and managed after considerable striving to persuade him to divert some of his attention to the performing arts.[8] The most effective lure proved to be theatrical first nights, which delighted Vicky, and whose flavour he must already have caught, for he was present at the première of Brecht's *Dreigroschenoper*: this took place on 28 August 1928, less than a fortnight after the suicide of Dezso Weisz.[9]

It would have been astonishing if Vicky, hauled untimely out of school and denied the luxury of a period of contemplative mourning, had not been starstruck. His work was his escape from care. With sketchbook in hand he was suddenly a professional participant in the famous Berlin theatre world, assured a front seat not only at avant-garde productions but at the music-hall and cabaret. He was encouraged, even to some extent empowered, to gain admission to the dressing-rooms, there to perfect a likeness; and one of these incursions supplied Vicky with a story which till the end of his life he continued to tell with pleasure. He had achieved an entrée to the dressing-room of Adele Sandrock, a big star in Germany at the time; but when she understood his purpose, she took violently against it. 'I hope you are not *caricaturing* me,' she bellowed, in what one German account of the story calls a *Feldwebelstimme*, a parade-ground voice. 'Caricature is an invention of *Bolshevism!*'[10]

Vicky revelled in this denunciation. The idea that merely by wielding his pencil he had conferred a kind of political status upon himself was deeply appealing. He was not a Communist in any official sense – throughout his career he guarded his freedom of comment by refusing to join any political party – but in the sharply polarised politics of Berlin he belonged unquestionably, like nearly all non-religious Jews, to those who maintained a faith in socialist internationalism. In practice this entailed a friendly interest in the Communist International. The artist Käthe Kollwitz, another non-joiner, had declared in 1927 that the events of the previous ten years in Russia seemed to her 'to be comparable in greatness and far-reaching significance only to the great French Revolution'[11]; and indeed, it was virtually impossible to anchor oneself against the treacherous tides of Nazism without holding to some such grand idea.

Käthe Kollwitz was more important to Vicky than he generally acknowledged. When asked to recall his early influences, he generally nominated the major graphic artists of the *Simplicissimus* school: Karl Arnold (from whom Vicky took a particular shape of hand, heavily hanging and gnarled, which he commonly attached to suffering figures – even, on one occasion, Hitler)[12]; or 'that great humanist, the cartoonist Heinrich Zille', whose name, Vicky found on his return to Germany in 1947, 'is still revered by many Berliners of middle age. Living in the working-class district of Berlin amongst the people he loved, he caught their wisecracks about life in the slums and put them down on paper. I still remember a drawing of a family sitting at their meagre dinner and father fishing an insect from his plate, saying, "Well, better a fly in the soup than no meat at all." That is a typical Berlin remark . . .' Another cartoon that stuck in his mind also concerned food. It depicted, he said, 'a gluttonous, bull-necked German surveying the left-overs of a gargantuan meal, lighting

7

7A '*Die Toten von Dortmund*', *Simplicissimus*, 2 March 1925 by Karl Arnold

7B '*Eine deutsche Mutter*', *Simplicissimus*, 21 January 1924 by Käthe Kollwitz

Simplicissimus, a weekly paper, first appeared in Munich on 1 April 1896. It was the first publication of its kind to combine literature and art and was especially innovative in its use of artistic styles. Contributors were committed to producing 'combatant art review without political tendencies' for 'people who long for education'. They aimed to expose and denounce militarism, social excesses and exploitation of the defenceless.

Accustomed as we now are to its format, it is hard to appreciate how daring the compositions were. Karl Arnold's colour drawing, 'The Dead of Dortmund. And why did *they* have to face their judge?', shows a two-dimensional style reminiscent of poster-art while Käthe Kollwitz's charcoal drawing, 'The German Mother', introduces another entirely individual tone. Neither drawing had any accompanying text; humour would have been inappropriate. The influence of Käthe Kollwitz on Vicky's later work is marked. He often used her starving-mother-with-children compositions.

Die Toten von Dortmund

„Und warum mußten fie vor den Richter treten —?!"

a cigar and saying: "I'm as full as a pig. The question is, what to eat now?"[13] Vicky had evidently studied volumes of *Simplicissimus* far older than himself, for that cartoon appeared in 1907.

But when it came to stylistic influence, it was from Käthe Kollwitz that Vicky borrowed most. He took, indeed, an entire genre, the most direct inspiration for which seems to have been one of Kollwitz's very few *Simplicissimus* drawings: '*Eine deutsche Mutter*', published on 21 January 1924. This is a sombre charcoal in which the thin, draped figure of the starving mother huddles close to her two hollow-eyed children – a girl in the immediate foreground, and behind her a boy whose beseeching or accusing gaze is directed straight at the viewer. This composition, in recognisable variations, became a fixture in Vicky's later repertoire. Time and again, his refugees and victims of war fall into this stylised Kollwitz posture, with one or other of the children awakening the guilt of the reader with his eyes. Inevitably there are differences in emotional texture, for the adumbrated pain appears to lurk

8

Eine deutsche Mutter

CAMPBELL AUF DER AVUS

In May 1932 Sir Malcolm Campbell
became the first driver to reach
250 mph. Breaking his own land-speed
record of 246.09 mph set the previous
year, he was driving one of a long
series of *Bluebird* cars – this particular
one powered by a Napier Lion aero-
engine. ('*Avus*' means 'motor road' –
*Automobil-Verkehrs-und-Ubungs-
Straße*.)

within Kollwitz's charcoal, while Vicky's inks make a more chal-
lenging statement; but the group effect, give or take the urchin
cuts or 'nappy' negroid hair of Vicky's children, and the often
oriental cast of their features, is remarkably similar.

This tableau was the one piece of the German art-heritage that
Vicky exported wholesale. Its reappearances in his British output
were not, it must be said, received with enthusiasm by colleagues.
Even close friends felt a 'preachy' quality in the design, and complained (on surer ground here perhaps) that Vicky's inventiveness
evaporated when he faced the worst of human sufferings. From
time to time, it must indeed have seemed that his mother-and-

children were a stock response; but for him, the image must have represented a kind of *ne plus ultra*, a vision which said all that he could bear to say on the matter. The first formative impression made on Vicky by Kollwitz's version must have been very deep.

Little of this was of immediate application to the job in hand at the *12 Uhr Blatt*. Vicky was much too variously busy to impose an all-purpose style upon himself. He drew to suit the subject. Malcolm Campbell, the speed-record seeker, loomed through a blizzard of dashing lines in his car, the 'Bluebird'. Max Schmeling, the national hero, World Heavyweight Champion of 1930, whom Vicky knew, was gradually reduced through long practice to a simple design of square-toothed grin and flowing eyebrows

SCHMELING

9 'Schmeling', *12 Uhr Blatt*, 21 June 1932

'Schmeling will win this evening's World Championship in New York', boasts the headline. In the event, the challenger Jack Sharkey was awarded an unpopular decision in their fifteen-round contest for the World Heavyweight Boxing Championship. The majority of the 72,000 spectators at Madison Square Garden preferred to think that 'Der Max', as he was affectionately known, was still the champion.

11

like the f-holes in a 'cello. A cartoon record of the latest Wimbledon tennis news is rendered in flat-footed stick figures whose comical stride owes much to the cinema animations of the period. Arts subjects were treated with a contrasting care. Advertising a broadcast by the orchestra leader Béla Dajos in 1929, Vicky drew the violinist in compressed, cameo-like form, as though fashioning a piece of his late father's jewellery. It was competent work, but too defensively wrapped within itself to suggest anything of the later Vicky. As though in acknowledgement of this, the signature is a curlicued 'V. Weiß'.

He was sometimes obliged to go to extreme lengths to obtain a 'sitting', or the necessary equivalent thereof. Resourcefulness was tested to the limit when General Balbo, the aviator and pioneer Fascist, arrived in Berlin and declined to receive journalists. Vicky promptly secured himself a temporary job as a bell-hop in Balbo's hotel, cartooning his victim on a shirt-cuff while awaiting his orders for room-service. If Vicky was shy, it was a selective shyness, which failed notably to impair his willingness to confront subjects with his interpretation of them and to request the endorsement of a signature. The habit got him thrown out of more dressing-rooms than Adele Sandrock's, for his drawings were designed to succeed on their own eccentric terms, and not as repositories of flattery.

One reaction to his early work did succeed in disconcerting Vicky, and it occurred at the office. He had developed an occasional style by which familiar and fashionably elegant subjects could be rendered in just a few decorative curves, producing in successful cases an effect which bordered pleasingly upon the abstract. It was a manner he was capable of reviving, in the cause of nostalgia or deliberate archaism, much later in life – as in his *New Statesman* Profile portrait of Edith Sitwell. But at the end of a week in which he had produced such drawings for the *12 Uhr Blatt*, Vicky was shocked to discover his pay-packet drastically slimmed. It was, the management assured him, a matter of simple productivity ratios. Fewer lines, less pay. You couldn't expect to get away with so much less visible output for the same money. Whether this adjudication, traced to its source, would ultimately have proved to be a tease, one cannot tell. Vicky always told the story with the astonished laughter of one who continued to believe it.

He had the great good fortune to be surrounded already by a number of lifelong friends, who would share with him the arts-world gossip at the Insel and the Schwannecke and the Roman-

Dame Edith Sitwell

Vicky

10 Edith Sitwell, *New Statesman*,
23 January 1954

Dame Edith Sitwell was well-known
for her poetry but more so for her
resemblance to the Plantagenets. This
rather static portrait, which
accompanied an article entitled 'Queen
Edith', projects well her beautifully
chiselled, mask-like face and hooded
eyes. Without reference to any bodily
form, her thin hand floats in the air,
dominated by a large ring.

isches Café, and would one day share his exile. Hans Tasiemka,
his bureau chief from 1930 to 1933, would re-emerge as founder
and proprietor of the remarkable Tasiemka Archive of press
cuttings, operating from a house in North London. A fellow
journalist, Paul Markus, known by his initials as 'Pem', would
run a newsletter through which Anglo-Jewish refugees from the
Continent kept in touch. Bernard King, with whom Vicky had
attended classes at the Berlin Kunstakademie, became a colleague

of his in the art department of the *News Chronicle* (where Vicky continued to call him 'Herr König').

One of Vicky's closest friends was Robert Lantz, later an enormously influential agent for writers and actors in New York. They first saw each other at the Metropol-Theater, where Vicky, sketching in a stage-side box, was miffed to observe in the opposite box another young man apparently doing the same. This was Robby Lantz, who, it was revealed the following day when they accidentally met, was actually writing a review. Having established that their territories did not overlap, they struck up an alliance which renewed itself in London.

All these men were about to have to make a new accommodation to the future. Since 1928 Vicky had campaigned in his cartoons against the Nazis as often as he was able. He had made himself conspicuous enough to be in danger if ever Hitler came to power. Twenty years later he recorded how he had felt, as a radical socialist and a Jew, on the fateful 30 January 1933:

> I sat in the newspaper offices of the *12 Uhr Blatt* . . . and stared at my empty drawing-board, unable to collect my thoughts. My mind was filled with forebodings. I went out into Berlin's streets. Thousands of Nazi swastikas and old Nationalist black-white-red flags decorated the houses and enthusiastic Nazis were making their way to the centre of the city to see their Führer. They cheered him wildly as he drove to the Presidential palace. But there were those Berliners whose sullen, grim expressions spoke as loudly as the shouts of *Heil Hitler*. Rumours of an impending general strike call by the Communist Party to the trade unions swept the city – but Wedding, the 'Red Core' of Berlin, remained tensely silent, and there were only a few minor clashes.[14]

Vicky made his way home, he said, with the shouts of '*Deutschland Erwache!*' still ringing in his ears.

> That evening, Hitler put on a top hat and tails and with his colleagues, among them Herr Hugenberg, the industrialist and director of the Ufa film company, went to the premiere of a film. I did what was to be my last anti-Nazi cartoon to appear in Germany, depicting the Führer and his Ministers entering the cinema. The caption was based on a well-known German advertising slogan: 'And in the evening to the cinema . . .' The title of the film was *Morgenrot* – Dawn.

On that same evening in London, Vicky could not resist point-

11 'Vicky, by Sacha Guitry', *Sunday Dispatch*, 24 October 1937

Aged twenty-four, Vicky went to Paris to draw the renowned and well-respected French actor, director and dramatist, Sacha Guitry, and got himself drawn instead. This lightning sketch suggests a slightly bashful young man – it is undoubtedly Vicky – with round spectacles, dark eyebrows and long hair brushed back from his face.

VICKY, BY SACHA GUITRY

ing out, 'a farce about cricket, *A Bit of a Test*, had its first night at the Aldwych Theatre'. The one aspect of the British temperament he could never accept was its willing immersion in local trivia, at the expense, inevitably, of international politics.

Within weeks the Nazis had engineered the Reichstag fire, freedom of the press was abolished, and the twenty-year-old Vicky lost his job. His home was subject to Gestapo searches. Only his Hungarian passport saved him from early deportation to the concentration camps. The *12 Uhr Blatt* was taken over, as *Der Spiegel* later put it, 'by Goebbels' chauffeur'.[15] Whatever work Vicky obtained must have been private and anonymous. Thirty years later, Pem reported finding ('*in einer Berliner Bar am Lehninerplatz*')[16] a guest book in which whole pages were covered with wonderful caricatures by Vicky; so it may be that he sustained himself for a time as a 'lightning-sketch artist'.

There was plainly no future for Vicky in Germany. By January

1934 he was in Budapest, trying his luck in his country of nominal origin. But his minimal Hungarian permitted neither explanation nor negotiation; and expatriate Berliners like Nicholas Vilag (then a journalist, later a gallery-owner in London) proved unable to help. Vilag, in fact, annoyed Vicky by advising him to get out of Hungary as fast as possible, before the Nazis seized control there too. Vicky's movements thereafter are mysterious. He was back in Berlin by 26 May 1934, for his brother was recovering from appendicitis there, and Vicky made a dated drawing of the convalescent scene (signing it 'Viki'). But then he disappears again. Home Office papers record a brief initial visit to the UK in June 1935. Vicky must have spent a good deal of time in Paris, for he came away with a useful command of French and an 'instant' caricature of himself by Sacha Guitry. Receiving Vicky in his studio, the dramaturge seized his sketchbook and turned artist into model.

Though Isabella and Elisabeth Weisz had resolved to stay and sit it out, trusting in their passports to protect them, Oskar had now moved to England. His friends in the fur trade had rallied round to act as his guarantors, and he was now in a position to do the same for his brother. Vicky arrived in London on 9 October 1935. It was recorded as 'A business visit'. He applied to the authorities — as the Weiszes had always been obliged to do throughout their lives — for permission to stay. He never regretted it.

'Is Vicky a Man or a Woman?' 2

His old Berlin associates were surprised to see Vicky in London, but did their best to make him welcome. Robby Lantz fixed him a few days' lodging with a Mrs Novakovsky in Golders Green. All arrangements were necessarily temporary, for no one could count on his right to remain in Britain. Lantz himself had entered on a three-day permit; he later enjoyed the dubious luxury of re-applying every sixty days. A veteran lawyer called Ernest Gambs processed a great number of these pleas from an office in Great Russell Street, earning widespread gratitude among an emigré community largely unable as yet to cope with English-language documentation.

One condition under which the British authorities granted extensions to the residence permit did happen to favour Vicky. Permission to stay was normally granted so long as the applicant took no 'employment'. This term, however, was interpreted by

12 Untitled, *New Statesman*,
19 February 1955

Anthony Eden, 1st Earl of Avon
(1897–1977), succeeded Churchill as
Prime Minister in 1955. Following the
nationalisation of the Suez Canal in
1956, he launched an offensive against
Egypt which received worldwide
condemnation. Eden resigned in 1957.

17

the Home Office (and a certain generosity on their part was acknowledged here) in the narrowest way, so that numerous contractual circumventions of the problem became possible: retainers, *ad hoc* fees, even certain forms of self-employment would raise no dangerous objection. To a freelance artist like Vicky this was excellent news, for it meant that a way of life perfectly natural to his profession was sanctioned by the system.

His position was further secured by the intervention of a two-man team of sponsors, Peter Witt[1] and Victor Creer. Witt was another ex-colleague from Berlin. He later became a successful theatrical agent in the United States. Creer became a company chief in the British electrical trade. But in the 1930s both men were operating on the fringes of the British film industry. Together they set Vicky up in business as 'Vicky Publications Ltd', paying him a retainer of £4 per week.

MR ROOSEVELT

13　'Mr Roosevelt', *Evening Standard*, 7 February 1936

1936 was re-election year for Franklin D. Roosevelt, the thirty-second President of the United States. Facing an increasing Republican backlash he was none the less confident. His 'New Deal' policies, designed to reduce record unemployment and help America recover from economic depression, were proving successful and his efforts to cultivate the image of an approachable, homely man – holding frequent press conferences and broadcasting 'fireside chats' on the radio – paid dividends.

18

Witt also managed to find an office for Vicky, with the not unmemorable address of 7 Park Lane. Photographs taken there suggest that with its sloping ceilings it was not much more than a garret, but at least it sounded a moderately prestigious one.[2] A curious advantage to Vicky was the proximity of Speakers' Corner. To see this literal enactment of freedom of speech in progress delighted him, and he liked to say that the soap-box orators and their hecklers provided him with the most concentrated English-language studies he ever undertook. Home was a short walk away in Gloucester Place – though it was only a one-room flat, shared with brother Oscar, who was beginning to work up an impressive line in hypochondria.

All things considered, Vicky made an exceptionally prompt start in British journalism. And he began – this seems rather poignant now – at the very same place where he finished: in the Londoner's Diary column of the *Evening Standard*. Eventually this

14 'The Marx Brothers in *A Night at the Opera*', *Evening Standard*, 29 February 1936

The film *A Night at the Opera* (released in 1935), was the Marx Brothers' most popular production despite Harpo's role being weakened and the absence of Zeppo (who had left the act in 1933 after the making of *Duck Soup*). Most of the action takes place on board a ship as the three Brothers (left to right – Harpo, Groucho and Chico) at first wreck, and then help an opera company.

space would enclose his famously caustic fabulations of Macmillan, Home and Butler. Early in February 1936 it was Roosevelt and Lloyd George who occupied Vicky's pen and brush – just small caricatures or 'studies', as the caption sometimes had it. In that first month, Vicky also tackled Sir Austen Chamberlain, Gil Robles the Spanish Rightist, Toscanini, Jack Hulbert and Jack Buchanan, Rabindranath Tagore, Anthony Eden, Tolstoy, the Marx Brothers (in 'A Night at the Opera'), and a plump Adolf

19

15 'Herr von Ribbentrop, Germany's Ambassador-Designate in London', *Daily Telegraph*, 12 August 1936

The appointment of Joachim von Ribbentrop (Hitler's foreign-policy adviser) was welcomed as a means of improving lines of communication between the British and German governments, but there was no acknowledgement of the possible danger of the man's fierce adherence to Hitler's expansionist policies. (In 1939 von Ribbentrop would negotiate a German–Soviet Treaty of Non-Aggression which enabled the Nazis to invade Poland – an act which precipitated the Second World War.)

HERR VON RIBBENTROP

Hitler ('Herr Hitler's latest photographs show that he is putting on flesh').[3] The *Standard* was certainly testing Vicky's range. These early efforts were kept and pasted in an album, Herr Hitler being noticeably omitted.

During these early months of his second career, Vicky made fullest use of his freelance liberty. Through his agents, he made himself known as a young man with a ready-made reputation, and several newspapers bought his work. The *Daily Express* took the occasional celebrity caricature, and the *Standard*, once Vicky's first burst was over, often featured a Saturday tableau in which Vicky depicted Hollywood stars in the costume of their latest film release. The great attraction of *Standard* appearances was that they yoked Vicky's work to that of the great David Low, whose pre-eminence among political cartoonists he was now beginning to appreciate.

There was no outlet at first for Vicky's own political opinion, which was in any case seriously under-informed. He had arrived in England knowing the names of only three British politicians – Baldwin, Churchill and Chamberlain – and it would be some time before he felt at home with the political usages and customs underpinning even this meagre gallery of reputations. Nor was continental news easy to come by; the exiled Berliners learnt it piecemeal and belatedly from odd copies of a Viennese newspaper passed around.[4] For Vicky, whose addiction to news was already well established, it was a torture thus to be starved of information.

He later became notorious for working in the heart of the right-wing 'enemy camp'; but he had done so from the start. The 'Peterborough' column of the *Daily Telegraph* took caricatures, starting in August 1936 with Von Ribbentrop, the German Ambassador. Drawing a Nazi for the *Telegraph* sounds in retrospect like a definition of uncongenial work for Vicky, yet he continued to enjoy, in a manner of speaking, the hospitality of the *Telegraph*'s pages right up to the spring of 1941, when the *News Chronicle* acquired his exclusive services.

His best contacts were still in the film business; so when a new monthly magazine called *World Film News* was launched in the spring of 1936, it was natural that Vicky should be taken on, especially as the first editor, Hans N. Feld, was himself a refugee from Germany.[5] Boasting the 'support and goodwill' of Eisenstein, T.S. Eliot, André Gide and H.G. Wells, among others, and a roster of correspondents which named the likes of W.H. Auden, Alistair Cooke and Graham Greene, *World Film News* was topped off by a board of Controllers including John Grierson, Alberto Cavalcanti and Basil Wright. But somehow this all-star assembly did not cohere on the page. For a magazine devoted to the visual arts it was very literary in style and lacking in strength of design – as were the Vicky cartoons it enclosed. In a monthly series called 'Cockalorum', Vicky took on the impossible job of dramatising the points currently at issue between the financiers, writers, directors, censors and performers who all had their hands on some portion of the film-production process. In attempting to do justice to this multiplicity of interests, Vicky merely reproduced the chaos in another form. But at least these were, in their way, fully-wrought 'situation' cartoons, presenting their own landscape and prominently copyrighted to 'Vicky Publications'.

After a twelve-month run he withdrew from *World Film News*, which had already undergone a great many design and management changes, and would continue to do so. Several Vicky drawings were opportunistically reprinted, some more than once, but by the middle of the second year of publication, the magazine's texts were striking the odd note of xenophobic rancour ('Aliens Stifle British Talent' claimed 'British Film Man') which must have made him glad to have moved on.

A LA RECHERCHE DU TEMPS PERDU

16 '*A la recherche du temps perdu*', *World Film News and Television Progress*, April 1936

World Film News was edited by Hans Feld who had come to Britain in 1935 (aged thirty-three) from Prague where he ran an anti-Fascist monthly called *Die Kritik*. For every Vicky cartoon printed in *World Film News* Feld paid him £5. This cartoon shows Alexander Korda (seated behind his desk), producer of the 1936 Futurist film, *Things to Come*, and H.G. Wells who wrote *The Shape of Things to Come* (1933), the prophetic novel on which the film was based. Korda's film, which was not well received by the critics, contains a series of vignettes which chart the world at war and the aftermath of destruction. The portrait of Henry VIII is a reference both to what has been seen as a bygone 'golden age' and a reminder of the chaos that was a result of the Tudor king's divorce from his Spanish queen, Catherine of Aragon.

His next monthly-magazine connection came on a publication still more notable for the discrepancy between its portentous titling and its unprepossessing appearance. *Headway*, 'A Monthly Review of the League of Nations', was a rather thin, archaic-looking pamphlet which habitually ran a reprinted cartoon by Low or Bernard Partridge as its cover illustration. In December 1936, however, an original cover drawing was commissioned from Vicky, and a great oddity it proved to be, with its Pan-like devil figure playing the pipe of 'hate' amid swirling mythological mists and waters.

Almost everything is wrong about the drawing, yet something satisfactorily pagan, some whiff of the real medieval evil, hangs

LORD NUFFIELD

17 Lord Nuffield, *Tatler*, 17 November 1937

William Richard Morris, 1st Viscount Nuffield (1877–1963), launched his first car, the Morris Oxford, in 1913. The Cowley followed in 1915 and by 1925 the 'bull-nose' Morris cars outsold all other makes in the U.K. The first of the classic Morris Minors, designed by Alec Issigonis, was produced in 1949. Lord Nuffield was also known as a philanthropist particularly in the field of medicine and founded Nuffield College, Oxford.

about it just the same. *Headway* was not discouraged. It used Vicky a few more times the following year, and almost solidly throughout 1938, when *Headway Towards Freedom and Peace* became the title. Vicky's commitment to those very ideals kept him in touch with *Headway* until the spring of 1939, though when it came to policy on Germany, his line was very far from the 'peace-at-all-costs' to which the League's conformists clung. To supply illustrations for equivocating articles like 'Adolf Hitler: This Man of Good and Evil Genius' must have tested his patience severely, especially when he saw himself captioned in such neutral terms as 'a continental artist to whom the great popular orator on the public platform was long a familiar figure'.[6]

BREACHES OF THE PEACE?

Sir Oswald Mosley was wearing a new uniform—black, military-cut jacket, grey riding breeches and jack boots. He had a black peaked military hat, and a red arm band.
Cartoon by Vicky.   —DAILY TELEGRAPH, October 5th, 1936

18 'Breaches of the peace?', *Time and Tide*, 10 October 1936

In 1932 Sir Oswald Mosley founded the short-lived British Union of Fascists (BUF) known as 'Blackshirts' because of their uniforms. Anti-Semitic in their views and imitative of both Mussolini's fighting Fascists (also called 'Blackshirts') and the German Nazis, they numbered 20,000 at the height of their activity.

Happily, Vicky's escape from enforced neutrality had already been made. Just a year after his arrival in Britain, his tour of self-advertisement had taken him to the offices of *Time and Tide*, the 'independent, non-party' weekly founded and edited by Lady Rhondda. Early in October 1936 Malcolm Muggeridge wrote an article on Sir Oswald Mosley for which Vicky supplied an illustration of the British Fascist leader in giant baggy riding-breeches. This was the beginning of an association with *Time and Tide* that would last until the end of 1943. Running weekly from mid-1937, it was among the longer stints of Vicky's career, and one of the least-remembered.

Memoirists like Muggeridge have generally looked back on *Time and Tide* with more amusement than respect, on account of the undoubted prevalence of large tweedy ladies in the organisation. (Muggeridge's friend Hugh Kingsmill was responsible for the celebrated judgement that Lady Rhondda, 'though not quite a *grand prix* bore, was a perfectly respectable yeoman bore'.)[7] But in the late 1930s, at least, the paper offered a rather lively forum for the exchange of liberal opinion – feminist within the limitations of the time, and affording space both to conventional parliamentary socialists like Ellen Wilkinson MP and to radical iconoclasts like George Orwell. Into this range of opinion Vicky fitted extremely well; and the more regularly he worked, the better his chance of finding a consistent political style.

His first big feature, in the Coronation Number of 1937, was a 'Parliamentary Tour, personally conducted by Ellen Wilkinson', in which early versions of Anthony Eden and Stafford Cripps appear. Vicky hits off Eden quite well, by dint of borrowing the fiercely rhythmical line of R.S. Sherriffs. His Lloyd George, on the other hand, owes something to David Low, though not more than was owed by most contemporaries. A month later, Vicky had a series of fantasy predictions ('What Next?') accepted, and from then on he was a fixture in the magazine, whose Diary he illustrated from its inception in October 1937. Pseudonymously written by persons dangerously assigning themselves the names of winds ('Sirocco', 'Sou'Wester', 'East Wind' and so on), the Diary fell back gradually into the hands of the meteorologically impartial 'Four Winds', who was Lady Rhondda herself.

Nothing comes as a greater relief to a freelance than a bread-and-butter job, a continuum of work. But at *Time and Tide* Vicky's opportunities to escape from the Diarist's choice of subjects were few and far between. What he needed was some relief for a pent-up ego. He achieved it in a rather startling direct

The Baldwin Face, near view . . . which crisis etched which wrinkles ?

Ll.G. . . . so much more interesting now . . .

19A 'The Baldwin Face, near view . . . which crisis etched which wrinkles?', *Time and Tide*, 8 May 1937

19B 'Ll. G . . . so much more interesting now . . .', *Time and Tide*, 8 May 1937

These caricatures of Stanley Baldwin and David Lloyd-George respectively are two of a number that illustrated an article entitled 'A Parliamentary Tour, personally conducted by Ellen Wilkinson, MP'. Wilkinson was writing a summer recess guide to absent politicians to compensate for, as she says, the House of Commons not really 'doing its duty by the Coronation visitors'. 'Monarch, Court and Peerage are putting on a good production. The Commons have closed their doors. No performance in the duration. Americans are in despair.'

20 'What next? 1. Russia', *Time and Tide*, 19 June 1937

Stalin succeeded Lenin as Chairman of the Politburo in 1924 by securing enough support within the party to eliminate other rivals – Trotsky included – who disagreed with his theory of using socialism in the Soviet Union as a base from which communism would spread. During the 1930s he instigated 'purge trials' to rid himself of opponents in the government and army. His tyrannical rule, the 'cult of the personality', was eventually denounced after his death. This drawing is the first in a series entitled 'What Next?'

WHAT NEXT ?
1. Russia

Stalin arrests himself for plotting against his own life, spying for Fascist Powers and being a Trotskyist

therapeutic contrivance: a little cartoon-strip starring himself.[8] (Those theorists who interpret shyness as a form of inverted arrogance have an interesting case-history in Vicky.) It was the *Sunday Chronicle* (later the *Referee*, and later still absorbed into the *Empire News*) which took the strip on late in 1936, introducing it without pre-announcement and reaping a large number of letters 'saying how much our readers enjoyed the first adventure of the solemn little man with the spectacles and the comical curl'. Vicky 'has struck a new note in strip cartoons,' ran the claim. 'The figure he has created – the man who finds a crazy way out of his troubles – is . . . just Vicky, drawn in his own likeness.' Goggling eyes; a fiercely arched eyebrow; balding in front, arty

26

fronds of hair behind; and a stubbly jowl – these indeed remained the central features of Vicky's view of himself, though in these years of his youth there is a more combative jut to the chin, and a more svelte rhythm to the double-breasted suit, than Vicky ever claimed to affect in later life.

The 'plot-lines' of a three- or four-frame strip are hardly likely to bear much re-examination, but it is interesting to see Vicky playing on the fringes of Surrealism: peeling off convict-stripes to convert a white horse into a zebra, or watering the flowers in a patterned carpet to grow a bouquet for his *innamorata*. These are really tiny storyboards for animation sequences in a style nearer Max Fleischer's than Disney's.[9] The narrative gag, however, never came easily to Vicky, and a survey of his output of one-off joke cartoons (contributed sundrily to the *Sketch*, *Lilliput*, *Men Only* and others) reveals many duplications and re-runs of ideas pioneered in the 'Vicky by Vicky' strip, minus the participation of the authorial character.

21A   'Vicky . . . keeps his head', *Sunday Chronicle*, 4 October 1936

21B   'Vicky . . . says it with flowers', *Sunday Chronicle*, 25 October 1936

These slightly off-beat 'Vicky by Vicky' cartoon strips were published nearly every week in the *Sunday Chronicle* from September 1936 to April 1937. They appeared without any advance publicity and were very popular with readers. Vicky never drew anything like this in style again.

NO, FOR THE THIRD TIME, THIS *ISN'T* TOOTS!

BALLOON BARRAGE

22A 'No, for the third time, this ISN'T Toots!', *Lilliput, c.* 1939

22B 'Balloon barrage', *Men Only, c.* 1939

Vicky never found it easy to produce one-off jokes and gags and was often repetitive in the use of his material. The *Lilliput* drawing is only one of many jokes depicting statuesque women in uniform. The *Men Only* drawing is a delightful one, in colour. The joke is a simple one but well-constructed and, unusually for Vicky, it has no caption. Barrage balloons (known as 'Blimps') were used during the Second World War as a means of foiling low-flying enemy aircraft and were particularly effective at night.

If there is an autobiographical strain in the strips, it surely centres on Vicky's turbulent amours, in the course of which, to use the extreme terms one strip employs, he is always either terminally smitten by love, with a pistol to his head, or turning the aggression outward and shooting his girlfriend's portrait to smithereens. Vicky's emotional needs did not go unnoticed by the *Sunday Chronicle* readership, for he received many invitations from ladies. In March 1937 there was even a proposal of marriage, to which the paper gave prominence. 'I sensed that you need sympathy,' wrote a lady from Southport, 'that you wanted mothering. Since then I have watched your drawings. They reveal the real you . . . and now more than ever I feel that you are in need of companionship. I am forty-five and have a modest income . . .'

So did Vicky. Spurning the lure of Lancashire, he went instead to the *Sunday Dispatch*, as illustrator of a gossip column, 'Almost in Confidence', compiled by the Marquess of Donegall. The arrangement lasted only a few months, during which most of

Vicky's effort was expended on rather soulful pastel portraits of aristocratic young ladies. Here was an odd way of life indeed, a veritable *vie de bohème* . . . eating his daily 'Lyons Steak' for one-and-a-penny at the Corner House at Marble Arch,[10] then adjourning to the Park Lane studio to immortalise some fashionable beauty. That some sittings did take place at the studio is suggested by a photograph dated November 1937, in which an almost parodistically languid model poses for her portrait.

Publicity was being generated on behalf of Vicky's imminent exhibition, his first, to run at the Lefevre Gallery during November and December. The *Sketch* carried a double-page spread of celebrity caricatures from the show, which was attended by at least one of its victims – the former Minister of Transport, lately transferred to the Ministry of War. As the Marquess of Donegall related it: 'Coming out of Vicky's exhibition in King Street, St

23 At work, 7 Park Lane, London W1, November 1937

Vicky poses for a publicity photograph in his Park Lane studio in front of completed caricatures and portraits of Flora Robson, Jean Harlow (who had died on 8 June) and Katharine Hepburn.

James's, I ran into Hore-Belisha and Lord Gort, walking to the War Office. So I dragged the Minister and the new Chief of Staff in to have a look at Vicky's exhibited cartoon of Hore-Belisha done as one of his own beacons. "Very good," Hore-Belisha said, "is Vicky a man or a woman?"' Vicky cannot have greatly relished the anecdote, but any publicity helped.[11]

A regular job on a daily paper still eluded him. In October 1937 he had landed a series with the *Daily Mail*, but it ran only till Christmas and was stylistically null. 'Funny Figures' was nothing more than an assemblage of stranger-than-fiction statistics, set out in boxes and decorated with skimmingly 'instant' drawings – rather less polished than Vicky's sports cartoons in the *12 Uhr Blatt*. Some of the information purveyed was of glancing personal interest to Vicky ('In Vienna there are 121 women to 100 men' . . . 'A normal person turns and tosses in bed from 20 to 40 times a night'), and a little of it was even mildly propagandistic at the expense of the *Mail*'s entrenched conservative beliefs ('The aggregate age of the 27 English High Court judges

MR LESLIE HORE-BELISHA

24 'Mr Leslie Hore-Belisha', *Sunday Dispatch*, 5 December 1937

Hore-Belisha was Minister of Transport from 1934 to 1937 in the coalition National Government of Ramsay MacDonald, Stanley Baldwin and Sir John Simon, during which time he gave his name to the beacons that marked pedestrian ('zebra') crossings.

25 'Funny Figures', *Daily Mail*, 10 November 1937

This drawing is No. 9 in a series of seventeen which ran twice weekly from 12 October to 8 December 1937. The whole series is nothing more than a collection of statistics, such as '"Left" and "Right" shoes were not made until the 19th century' and 'In the 17th century a pound of tea cost £10'. The illustrations that accompany these facts are somewhat uninspired.

APRIL FOOL!

26 'April Fool', *Daily Herald*, 1 April 1938

Chamberlain's appeasement policy was designed to pacify Germany and Italy, while allowing time for Britain to rearm against the possibility of a European war. However, his meekness in the face of Italy's violation, in Spain, of the Non-Intervention agreement between the principal European powers – Britain, France, Germany and Italy – meant he fell into the trap Mussolini had laid for him. While pretending Italy was keeping to the agreement, Mussolini was able to build up his forces in the Mediterranean.

is 1701 years' . . . 'The Great War cost England on an average £6,000,000 per day'). But this was not work that challenged either Vicky's pen or his intellect, and with a bizarre parting flourish – 'The British Army uses 11,650 horses, 818 mules, 1 donkey and 1 ox' – it lapsed.

In January 1938, the venerable Will Dyson, cartoonist of the *Daily Herald*, died. His job, on a radical paper with certificated sales exceeding two million, was widely coveted. The fact that Dyson had first drawn for the *Herald* as long ago as 1913 strongly suggested that for the right man, there was a job here for life. So the chance that fell to Vicky fell also to Kem, Blix, Hagg, Teg, Boyle, Stocks, Hynes – any number of aspiring monosyllables – plus Sceptimus, Houghton, Aki, Tom Cottrell, George Whitelaw, Sherriffs, and others. Each was given a week to prove himself on the page. Vicky's turn came at the end of March.

Inevitably he muffed it: not visibly worse than most, but just about averagely. The one stroke of luck he enjoyed – having 1 April as the last day of his cartoon week – was thrown away on a cartoon employing no fewer than eight identifying labels, plus caption and signature: an overload of information clearly betraying the artist's anxiety. Apart from his unconfident handling of characters, Vicky was still uncertain of the number of dimensions he was working in. This was not a problem normally posed by his half-tone celebrity portraits, which, even when shaded to accommodate a suggestion of roundness and 'body', worked equally well when considered merely as patterns of pigment, flat emblems of a face. But given a large setting, or even just a room, in which to situate patently 'unreal' figures, Vicky was perplexed as to how rigorously to apply the known rules of perspective, depth and shadow.

31

No cartoonist ever finds an invariably foolproof way of solving this problem (unless like Saul Steinberg he is not a cartoonist at all but a kind of mental geographer, with his own completely personal maps to draw). Yet Vicky did eventually arrive at a triumphantly high ratio of success. His policy, formed quite possibly without a conscious search, seems ultimately to have been to treat the foreground of a cartoon roughly as he would the visible portions of a theatre stage, adding set-dressing in approximately the normal theatrical measure. There are famous exceptions, but on the whole the less there is in the way of a far-receding background, the more Vickyish will be the cartoon. When problems of depth arose, in other words, the cartoon rectangle (when Vicky kept to the classic shape) was treated rather like a proscenium opening, and 'stage-depth' was invoked. That this

27 'Joe Kennedy', *Courier*, Summer 1939

Joseph Kennedy, father of John F. (thirty-fifth President of the United States and first Roman Catholic to hold that office), was a millionaire banker and US Ambassador to Britain in the late 1930s. Vicky drew a total of eight coloured portraits of leading international politicians and three in black and white of newspaper barons. These were published in four issues of *Courier*, a magazine which had a very short life. Beginning in the winter of 1937 and published quarterly, it ceased when war was declared in September 1939.

scheme of things was never far from Vicky's mind is indicated by the number of cartoons he drew in which the proscenium arch does appear. He often depicted his victims as actors and music-hall artistes, particularly in the later years when the conviction was strong upon him that most of the world's statesmen were 'merely players'.

After the *Daily Herald* disappointment (George Whitelaw got the job), there was no immediate prospect of Vicky's grappling

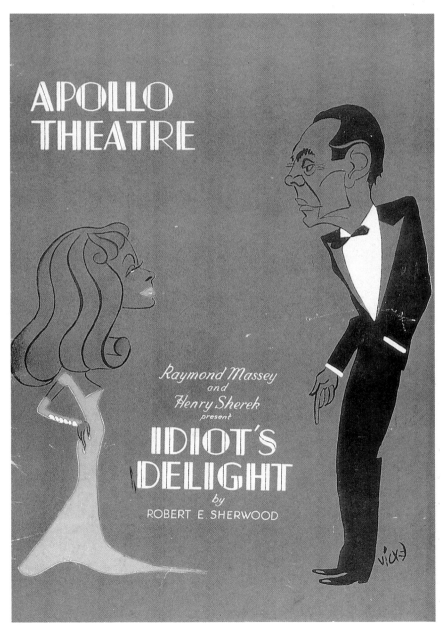

28 Programme cover for *Idiot's Delight* by Robert E. Sherwood at the Apollo Theatre, London, starring Raymond Massey and Tamara Geva, March 1938

Written in 1936, this play reflects the anti-war sentiment that was growing in the United States in the mid-1930s. Sherwood wrote in the play's postscript that '. . . decent people don't want war . . . They fight and die . . . because they have been deluded by their exploiters, who are members of the indecent minority.' The overall sentiment of the play is that human conflict is largely the fault of those who make it possible – the weapons manufacturers. Instinctively one feels Vicky concurred.

with such problems on a daily basis. He was back on the freelance round. There were some enlivening novelties to cope with, like colour work for *Courier*, a citizen-of-the-world travel publication foreshadowing today's in-flight magazines. Vicky had also worked in colour on theatre programmes, when the impresario Henry Sherek took a shine to him and gave him decorative programme-covers to do for the revues at the Dorchester, just down the road from his studio. For another Sherek co-production, *Idiot's Delight*, a play starring Raymond Massey at the Apollo Theatre, he designed a rather striking coloured cover, but only half of it – the female lead, Tamara Geva – is in his own tradition: the figure of Massey is strongly influenced by the crisp heraldic brushwork of Sherriffs, whose theatrical portraits were a weekly feature of the *Sketch*.

When one is a mimic and a chameleon by temperament, there is always a danger one may never acquire one's own 'voice'. Such a danger certainly threatened Vicky in 1939. When in doubt, he gave people approximately what they already knew. He had secured commissions for book-illustrations; and in, for example, *Outrageous Rhapsodies* (1938), a book of very light verse by G.W.L. Day (who was to produce a couple more such for Vicky to adorn), he had kept pretty much to the style he was slowly refining in *Time and Tide*. What this meant, however, was that the most successful drawing in the book proved to be a pastiche, offered 'with apologies to Mr Ernest H. Shepard'. Now Shepard was not an easy man to emulate, with his wispy, flyaway line yet curious strength of composition; but Vicky's pen catches his mood of berserk Edwardianism perfectly. There was something to be proud of here, and something to be worried about, for Vicky was almost too open to influence. In *Home Truths* (1939), a comic rhymed alphabet by William Douglas-Home, the Vicky illustrations lean more to the neatly marshalled school of Fougasse. The surest way to please was to 'fit in', and here was Vicky doing it.

His morale, always destined to fluctuate, hit some low points in the immediate pre-war months. Late in 1938 for *Time and Tide* (which had become increasingly preoccupied with 'The Jewish Question') he drew a cartoon in which 'the non-Aryan' faced a set of doors marked severally 'Art', 'Commerce', 'Professions', 'Immigration' and 'Suicide'. 'Suicide' is the only door open. Vicky himself had already passed through the 'Immigration' door, but two of his family had not.

Two things chiefly sustained him in this time of tension. One was the relationship with Lucie Johanna Bolien, a refugee from

29 'The comical economist', in *Outrageous Rhapsodies* by G.W.L. Day, London, Herbert Jenkins, 1938

Outrageous Rhapsodies was Vicky's first commission to illustrate a book by G.W.L. Day. Two others followed in 1940 and 1948 – *We Are Not Amused* and *Sigh No More, Ladies*. Vicky's style at this point was still evolving and these commissions did not present much opportunity for experimentation. All three volumes are well stocked with illustrations (*We Are Not Amused* has fifty-one). Gerald William Langston Day was a writer of light-hearted verse and short pieces of social satire. Other volumes by him include *Libellous Lyrics on Superior People* (1937) and a biography, *The Life and Art of W. Heath Robinson* (1947).

THE OPEN DOOR

30 'The open door', *Time and Tide*, 22 October 1938

The accompanying 'Time-Tide Diary' piece written by 'East Wind' asks 'What do the Nazis intend with their unfortunate Jewish citizens?' Jews were now excluded from professions and business and a newly instigated ban existed against 'semi-professions, including commercial travellers and salesmen'. The 'Immigration' door is partly opened, albeit inwards, with barbed wire blocking the exit – 'Suicide' is the only way for the non-Aryan.

Germany like himself, and an actress, like so many of the ladies he had admired since his short-trousered days. At thirty, she was five years older than Vicky. They were married on 18 April 1939 and lived in an apartment block in St John's Wood. As a partnership it did not last long, foundering early in the war, but as a friendship it survived. Lucie remained on good terms not just with Vicky but with his second wife (another Lucie, another actress) and later with all the Weiszes, particularly Vicky's mother. (Later Lucie married a prosperous businessman and moved to Littleborough in Lancashire, where the Weisz clan visited her.) No doubt the marriage had been something in the nature of a mutually protective alliance. In only one respect could it have made a really lasting difference to either life. Lucie did at one stage become pregnant, but the child was lost in a bad miscarriage. To his later wives Vicky always insisted that there would be, must be, no children.[12]

Then there was the matter of Hitler. Professionally, and as the Germans say 'world-historically', Vicky was almost eager for the confrontation he knew to be inevitable – as eager as a war-hater could be. He hated the clash of ignorant armies (Japanese atrocities against China had already drawn from him his first compassionate cartoons in the Kollwitz style, done for *Time and Tide*) but in order to dispose of Hitler an exception had to be made.

31 Lucie Johanna Bolien, *c.* 1938

Lucie Johanna Bolien was Vicky's first wife. They were married on 18 April 1939, when she was thirty years old and Vicky was twenty-five, at the Marylebone Registry Office in London. She was a German speaker who had been an actress but evidently never pursued a serious career in Britain. This photograph was taken at the London Studios, 259 Oxford Street.

"I am the greatest German that ever lived"—
Hitler to Schuschnigg at Berchtesgaden, 1938.

NAZI NUGGETS

"We know where we began, but only God knows where we will end one day."—Dr. Goebbels in "Im Spiegal von Freund und Feind."

"The German people know that Hitler is their father, and they feel safe."—Dr. Ley, addressing Germans at Stuttgart, August 30, 1938.

Vicky, the famous artist, is illustrating these true sayings of Nazi leaders.

32 'I am the greatest German that ever lived', *Time and Tide*, 9 September 1939

Vicky compares Hitler's intellectual stature with thinkers from the past – Lessing (dramatist and critic), Goethe (poet and dramatist), Dürer (painter and engraver), Beethoven (composer), Luther (religious reformer) and Mendel (Austrian botanist). He consistently used outline only to indicate when people were dead and drew personalities different sizes when making comments about their relative power and influence.

33 'Nazi nuggets', *Daily Mirror*, 2 September 1939

This short series (only three) would probably have been dropped even if war had not been declared, because of its lack of variety, but it is interesting to see Vicky billed as 'the famous artist'.

Vicky was familiar with all shades of British opinion on the matter. He had worked for newspapers which had promoted Appeasement. *Headway*, the League of Nations magazine, had limply hazarded that '1939 can be a peace year'. *Time and Tide*, interestingly, had no such illusions. 'We Need Churchill', an editorial headline demanded in May. 'We Still Need Churchill', it insisted in July, adding with a fine foresight, 'We may find our-selves at war by September'.

When September came, Vicky had a new little project on the go: 'Nazi Nuggets', for the *Daily Mirror*. He had read widely in the literature of Nazism and kept notes of incriminating speeches. In the coming years this store of quotations would come in useful, but as 'Nazi Nuggets' they were soon superfluous. 'We know where we began,' ran Nugget No.2, quoting from Dr Goebbels, 'but only God knows where we will end one day.' The following morning, war was declared. Three days after that, Vicky's series was discontinued. This could have been a disaster – if he had not recently found the means by which his future would be assured.

Vicky's War

On the face of it, to be an irregularly employed graphic artist of German birth and Hungarian citizenship was no enviable destiny in the England of September 1939. But Vicky's personal outlook was more secure than he probably realised. Maintaining his luck with sponsors, he had recently found his most powerful ally yet in Gerald Barry, editor of the *News Chronicle*. Acknowledged by Vicky at the height of his fame as 'the man who really made me, in a way, what I am today',[1] Barry had been editor of the amiable, Liberal, libertarian *Chronicle* since 1936. The paper was owned by the comparatively passive Cadbury family, though on the Board there lurked a few 'interventionist' remnants of the merger that had created the title – notably Sir Walter (later Lord) Layton. Barry, however, was a fierce resister of pressures from upstairs, and took a pride in protecting his staff.

The *Chronicle* was committed to no regular cartoonist on the eve of war. Richard Winnington was employed to supply illustrations in several genres on demand. Within a few years he would achieve a near-unique fame as a film critic who illustrated his own column with caricatures of the stars. For cartoon comment, Barry

34 Gerald Barry (1898–1968)

Gerald Barry was Editor of the *News Chronicle* from 1936 to 1947 and a director of the *New Statesman*. He was knighted in June 1951 for his services as Director-General of the Festival of Britain, a post he held from 1948 to 1951. In 1939, under Barry's tutelage, Vicky had begun the long process of familiarising himself with the British, their politics and their literature. He started this task by reading Shakespeare, Dickens, Lewis Carroll, the *Oxford Book of Verse* and *Punch*.

35 Vicky at work in the *News Chronicle* offices in Bouverie Street, London EC4, *Picture Post*, 31 March 1951

Pensive, Vicky sits hunched on a chair, poised to break the blank surface of his drawing-board. He had got into the habit of drawing more than one – often as many as three – cartoons per day. Labouring to keep up with the changing news in the world, he demanded of himself a personal comment on each development.

relied on contributions from irregulars, notably Willi Wolpe, another 'friendly alien', who drew under the pseudonym of 'Wooping'. From time to time, simultaneously emphasising his interest in graphic work and his international outlook, Barry would feature a sizeable gallery of recent political cartoons bought in from all over the world, not excluding Germany – a useful service both to his readers and to the ambitious Vicky.

'Vicky turned up in my office one day (in 1939, I think),' Barry recalled, 'suggesting himself through his agent as cartoonist for the *News Chronicle*.' Either Witt or Creer, evidently, was still active on Vicky's behalf, and for a reason Barry's account makes clear.

> His English was then almost as funny as the cartoons he brought under his arm: but he plainly possessed a wholly insufficient

understanding of our manners and habits of thought to make a cartoonist for a popular British daily [the *News Chronicle* had a circulation of about one and a half million copies]. Yet with the outstanding talent his drawings revealed it would have been a blunder to turn him away. So we paid him a retainer and started him off on a prolonged, patient process of conditioning.[2]

Vicky's own idea, Barry related, was to start off by reading the works of Shakespeare; but the editor counselled that Dickens should take precedence; 'and before Dickens, *Alice in Wonderland*, and the back numbers of *Punch* and *Wisden*; and visits to the Derby and the dogs and to the theatre and the Oval and White Hart Lane – and above all, hours and hours in the stupefying boredom of the gallery of the House'.[3] It was a wonderful gamble by Barry, and an expression of faith in Vicky's diligence and powers of absorption.

Of all Barry's recommendations, Vicky seems to have resisted only the visit to the cricket ground; for in 1953, on an outing to Lord's with George Mikes, he claimed to be witnessing the first run he had seen in his life, and to be puzzled by the fact that with two batsmen running only one run was scored.[4] Cricket was perhaps the one area in which Vicky made a really obstinate show of incompatibility with the natives. When, in his *New Statesman* years, he was persuaded to take up the bat himself, in the annual grudge match against *Tribune*, he generally appeared with his pads on upside down and never made more than an elegant 2.

Several of the Barry suggestions passed straight into Vicky's repertoire. Dickens, perhaps, did not offer such fertile territory as the editor had hoped. Vicky did make repeated use of some irresistible tableaux like Oliver Twist's 'Asking for more', but on the whole his instinct in favour of Shakespeare was vindicated. His many versions of the *Romeo and Juliet* balcony scene featured some of the most frightful-looking Juliets ever cast, General Franco being perhaps the outstanding instance. But *Alice*, and the drawings of Tenniel, remained among his favourites to the end. The lovely interplay between comic hallucination and severe Victorian hatching in Tenniel's work never lost its appeal for Vicky. Sometimes one senses that, stuck for an idea, he simply trotted out a Tenniel (again the mimic, relying on a sure-fire laugh); but the look of these near-engravings is so satisfying, and Lewis Carroll's text so full of teasingly hollow utterances waiting for political allusion to occupy them, that readers surely never begrudged Vicky this seeming fixation.

HAROLD IN BLUNDERLAND

36A 'Harold in Blunderland', *Daily Mirror*, 20 February 1956

36B Cheshire cat, *Evening Standard*, 13 April 1964

Lewis Carroll's *Alice in Wonderland* was among the first books that Gerald Barry recommended to Vicky in 1939 when he embarked on his survey of English literature. Throughout his career, Vicky habitually returned to reinterpreting Sir John Tenniel's drawings. Harold Macmillan was Chancellor of the Exchequer in Eden's government from 1955 to 1957. During this time, gold and sterling reserves fell alarmingly as a deficit in international payments developed and the inflation rate spiralled.

Alec Douglas-Home succeeded Macmillan as Prime Minister in October 1964. He had no distinctive personal impact, and if his emergence as leader was seen as something of a victory for the right wing of the party, it was only in contrast to such progressive figures as Butler and Maudling (see also **149**).

For some years, 'Curiouser and curiouser', with Alice's feet receding from her sight as her neck grew, earned repeated appearances, as was to be expected with everything from prices and incomes to defence expenditure 'going up'. Later, Tweedledum and Tweedledee took over as favourites, when the policies of Right and Left, or Britain and America, were culpably difficult to tell apart. When some new threat of war or destruction was in the air, the arrival of the monstrous black crow, ensuring that the twinned parties 'quite forgot their quarrel', was a bonus. In use to the very end of Vicky's career, the Tenniel genre probably struck its last renewed inspiration in 1964, when Douglas-Home, doomed to electoral defeat, appeared as the fading grin of the Cheshire Cat.

While assimilating these beloved texts and characteristic flavours of Britain (a parallel genre was Victorian Painters, whom Vicky guyed remorselessly from 'Bubbles' to 'The Stag at Bay'), he continued to produce work for publication. No exclusivity clause was attached to his retainer, so Vicky returned for a while to his old haunts. For the comparative sparsity of his appearances in the *Telegraph* he was not compensated by any great variety in the subject matter; Peterborough kept calling for new versions of Roosevelt's election opponent, Wendell Willkie. But the freelance grind would soon be at an end.

Gerald Barry arranged quite carefully for his protégé to grow

40

THE SMILE

37 'The smile', *News Chronicle*, 4 December 1942

Transfixed, Hitler gazes at an enigmatic Stalin portrayed as the 'Mona Lisa'. Behind the Soviet leader lie the ruins of the German attempt to capture Stalingrad. In all, 70,000 German soldiers died during the campaign, which ended in February 1943, and 91,000 were taken prisoner.

WE MUSTN'T STAND IN A CROWD, IT'S TOO DANGEROUS

38 'We mustn't stand in a crowd, it's too dangerous', *Time and Tide*, 27 January 1940

Vicky's tiger, with the word 'Aggression' instead of stripes, has a Hitleresque quiff. Its tongue hangs out in anticipation of a satisfying meal as it stalks the neutral countries. However, aggressive behaviour was not just the preserve of Germany at this time. Russia's fears of German influence had led to that country's invasion of Finland the previous November.

into the job, giving him a confidence-inspiring burst of appearances in the first month of war and then settling for a trickle of gag-cartoons as the autodidactic 'conditioning' process got under way. Vicky found Women in Uniform a useful theme – indeed, large women in general seem to have caused him considerable dismay, and his husbands, more often than not, were half the size of his wives. Vicky himself was just an inch or two over five feet in height.

If Barry was keeping an eye on Vicky during this period (and a correspondence in *Time and Tide* suggests that he had become a close reader of that magazine),[5] Vicky was taking careful note of the *Chronicle*'s output – and to an almost reprehensible degree. After three months of war, Barry called for a bumper edition of the paper's 'As They See It Abroad' cartoon feature. Among ten syndicated cartoons reprinted, one from Melbourne showed a tiger whose stripes spelt out the word 'Aggression'; another, from Milan, carried the caption 'Hurry up and comb your hair. Here comes the RAF taking photographs!', while a third from Paris, entitled 'Inscrutable', took the form of a photomontage converting Stalin into the Mona Lisa. All three ideas would soon reappear in the work of the magpie Vicky. His Stalin Mona Lisa ('The Smile') numbered among his most famous wartime productions – though his comment on Russia's enigmatic foreign policy is enhanced by the additional figure of Hitler, gazing at the 'painting' in a fascination paralleled according to reports at the time by his real-life adoration of Leonardo's original (which, it was erroneously rumoured, had been removed to Berchtesgaden).

For a few months, *News Chronicle* readers lost sight of Vicky. Those who knew him to be Berlin-born might reasonably have assumed he had been interned (as 'Wooping', for example, was)[6] under the disastrous 'Collar the lot' policy of sequestration of aliens. But here again his Hungarian citizenship had spared him, for Hungary stood nominally aloof from the war until invaded

SEYSS-INQUART: WEERBARSTIG?...DAN ZAL JE MIJN WARE GEZICHT ZIEN!

39 *'Sabotage in Nederland', Vrij Nederland*, 24 August 1940

On 10 May 1940, the German Army began a powerful and ruthless attack on Holland. After the city of Rotterdam had been laid waste, Hitler placed Holland under the rule of Artur von Seyss-Inquart, a man noted for his Nazi zeal who in 1938 had helped to hand over his native Austria to the Third Reich. The friendly mask hides his terror face. The caption reads, 'Resist my system?... Then you will see my real face!' (The wording in the cartoon itself is: 'Get rid of Hitler – Free Holland!'; 'Death penalty on grand scale for sabotage'.)

43

by Germany. Had Vicky's passport been German, no amount of evidence of his anti-Nazi activities would have saved him from at least a temporary incarceration in the transfer camp at Huyton. Luckily, he was free to intensify those activities – which he did, when Holland was overrun in mid-1940, by contributing cartoons to a magazine for the Dutch nationals and resisters abroad, *Vrij Nederland*. Since the address of this publication was 7 Park Lane, it may very well be that Vicky handed over his studio to the Dutch staff when he moved to his desk at the *Chronicle*. He drew for them, adding inscriptions in Dutch, until after a few months native Dutch artists became available to take over the job (in styles that were strikingly old-fashioned by comparison).

It was in *Time and Tide* that he registered his reactions to the great events of 1940. He never missed a week, and thoroughly exploited the opportunity of testing the strategies of design and metaphor he would need as a daily-paper cartoonist. The 'Aggression' tiger made an early appearance. Advertisements for Shell petrol, Guinness and Johnny Walker whisky were studiously

IMPENETRABILITY! THAT'S WHAT *I* SAY!

40 'Impenetrability! That's what *I* say!', *Time and Tide*, 9 March 1940

In spring 1940, US Under-Secretary of State, Sumner Welles, travelled as a special envoy to Italy, Germany, France and Britain for the sole purpose of informing President Roosevelt of conditions in Europe. He hoped to be able to discuss at least a reduction in what he called 'innumerable artificial barriers to the restoration of peaceful trading' but found a situation of pessimism on the part of the French leader, Blum, a determination to destroy the Nazi system on the part of Churchill, and aggression from Hitler. He truly was walking on eggs.

NOW, GENTLEMEN, LET'S DISCUSS PEACE

adapted. Vintage cars chuntered into view, conveying Vicky's disapproval of outdated ideas and 'old crock' personnel. Sumner Welles, Roosevelt's envoy, is seen producing the good old curate's egg – having mastered such clichés, Vicky was understandably over-fond of them for a while – and it is Welles who inaugurates the Tenniel series by appearing as Humpty Dumpty.

Vicky produced some strikingly confident work during these critical months. His 'Now, gentlemen, let's discuss peace', in which the negotiators all have gun-barrel heads, is a memorable composition, though not original: a version of the same idea had been produced for the *St Louis Post-Dispatch* in 1938 and widely syndicated.[7] Any expression of tight national resolve tended to bring out Vicky's now emphatic admiration for the *Standard*'s David Low. 'Christmas 1940', in which a lone sentry guards a

41 'Now, gentlemen, let's discuss peace', *Time and Tide*, 16 March 1940

Vicky often used this theme of depersonalised gun-barrel heads to depict militarists. Two of the men wear wing-collars – an item of dress associated especially with Neville Chamberlain, who in 1938 had described the Munich Agreement (signed by himself, Daladier, Hitler and Mussolini) as securing 'peace in our time' but which it soon became clear was merely putting off the day when Hitler would start his war. This cartoon is a statement of general hopelessness and lack of confidence in the negotiation process.

45

CHRISTMAS 1940

VERY WELL, ALONE

British cliff, is plainly Vicky's homage to Low's 'Very well, alone' of the previous June. But the charge, to which Vicky's friend James Cameron lent support, that Vicky's style in these years was 'clearly under the total domination of David Low' seems harsh. One has only to look at the work of a contemporary like Wyndham Robinson of the *Star*, whose style really did contain almost no element that Low had not pioneered, to see how far from slavish were Vicky's emulations of the master. Even when he aimed at the full production-number effect of Low — so many of whose cartoons seem to record scenes from a preposterous international pageant — Vicky found himself resisting the broad, conforming rhythms that Low used to give heavy lateral movement to his compositions. Vicky was helplessly dedicated to the knobbly uniqueness of individuals. It was the single most important reason why he gradually abandoned the brush in favour of the pen — for in its very scratchiness, the nib confirmed his commitment to those capering, antic elements in the human personality which cannot be absorbed into mass movement, in cartoons or in life.

David Low was himself suspicious of Establishments, yet he managed to become one, in his own person. Here at least was an aspect of the great man's achievement that lay well beyond the scope of Vicky's desires. If there came a moment when he ceased to worry about Low's pre-eminence, it was probably on

COME INSIDE AND SHUT THE DOOR, STANLEY, THAT NOISE MAKES ME FEEL QUITE FAINT

42A 'Christmas 1940', *Time and Tide*, 7 December 1940

42B 'Very well, alone', *Evening Standard*, 18 June 1940 by David Low

42C 'Come inside and shut the door, Stanley, that noise makes me feel quite faint', *Morning Post*, 31 July 1933 by Wyndham Robinson

Two weeks after the evacuation of the British Expeditionary Force from Dunkirk (codenamed 'Dynamo'), Low's soldier displays defiance in the face of that near disaster. He is the propagandist's archetypal brave British 'Tommy'. By way of contrast, in this stylistically uncharacteristic cartoon, Vicky's soldier is patient and melancholy. The euphoria that followed the 'miracle of Dunkirk', when more than seven times as many men returned alive as was expected, had by now abated. 'Christmas 1940' is an example of Vicky's respect and admiration for David Low, but he was clearly not influenced by Low's artistic style. Low always used a brush to create his long unbroken calligraphic lines, Vicky used a pen. On the other hand, 'Come inside . . .' shows how dominant Low's work was over Wyndham Robinson's style.

15 February 1946, when, as he wrote to his wife-to-be, the actress Lucielle Gray, 'The funniest thing happened with my cartoon this morning. Low came out with nearly [the] same cartoon – the same caption – I'm sending you both with this letter – you can then see for yourself – I'm very flattered and feel rather proud about it.'[8] The cartoons were urging an end to the wheat and cereal famine, with the world's Ministers sitting up on clouds, and the caption 'Now let's get down to earth'. An unexceptional production for both men, but an epiphanic moment for one of them.

Barry eased Vicky back into the *News Chronicle* in December 1940, increasing the dosage month by month until, in May 1941, the new cartoonist was appearing every day. Cut to six pages in 1940 'by order of the Paper Controller', the *Chronicle* was soon reduced to a four-page sheet, so that to have a contribution published at all became a kind of honour; yet Vicky held his place. Gerald Barry was not a connoisseur of puns, but tolerated some gruesome wordplay (like the 'Vichyous Circle' of French affairs) for the sake of the momentum they helped to create in his employee's work. Vicky responded exuberantly to the challenge of daily production, maintaining a bubbling scorn which disguised the sense of tragedy more natural to his temperament. Creations like 'Undertaker Adolf', with his slogan (adapted from the old ice-cream carts) 'Stop me and Bury One', may even have caused some of the more staid readers to elasticate their tastes a little.

NOW, LET'S GET DOWN TO EARTH

COME DOWN TO EARTH

43A 'Now, let's get down to earth', *News Chronicle*, 15 February 1946

43B 'Come down to earth', *Evening Standard*, 15 February 1946 by David Low

By coincidence both Vicky and Low alight on the same subject for their cartoons. Even content is similar – the labelling of 'famine', the spectre of hunger and foreign ministers in, one could say, another world. Ernest Bevin holds the 'Resolution on wheat & cereal famine' paper. Low is the more extreme in showing a skeleton but Vicky's realism is more shocking.

James Cameron, who was devoted to Vicky but naturally preferred the work he produced later, in the years of their friendship, once wrote that Vicky 'like everyone else in those days . . . oversimplified Hitler'.[9] Whether Vicky deemed such a thing possible is doubtful. Certainly he had no reason to do justice to the Führer's complexities when his simplicities were already intolerable in themselves. Facially and physically, Hitler presented himself to the world as a cartoon-like figure to begin with, so there was little to be done with him except to maximise the commonplace meanness of his features and triangularity of his nose. More productive were Goering, with his Wagnerian girth and absurd self-satisfaction; and Goebbels, whom Vicky continued to render as a scuttling, baboon-like creature with huge ears – the nearest Vicky came to returning Nazi race-rhetoric in kind. It was Goebbels who trespassed on Vicky's territory by claiming that 'British caricatures of German types are insulting, because they are no longer truthful.' Vicky depicted him putting this regrettable state of affairs to rights. The German High Command was a group of men to whom Vicky would have relished bidding a personal farewell, but when the time came the opportunity was denied him. He could experience the Nuremberg Trials only through

UNDERTAKER
ADOLF & Co

'STOP ME
AND BURY
ONE'

FOR BRITANNIA

. . . AND WHEN I WANTED TO LAY IT OUT THE CORPSE HIT ME

the medium of the newsreels, and the court-room sketches of David Low.[10]

Stalin was always more problematical. Even before Germany invaded Russia, Vicky was under pressure to flatter the Russian leader. George Bernard Shaw (along with J.B. Priestley possibly Vicky's most often caricatured civilian subject in this period) wrote to ask the *News Chronicle*: 'Cannot our caricaturists find something more plausible than the long-discarded uglifications of Ramsay MacDonald to represent Stalin? They were not in the least like MacDonald, and they are wildly unlike Stalin, who is much the handsomest of all the present rulers of Europe.'[11] Vicky, who beneath his perplexity over the Russo-German Pact was as anxious to believe in Stalin as anyone, duly provided four Stalins in advancing stages of beautification. Three weeks later, Hitler's armies set off for Minsk. 'Germany has not got a dog's chance,' commmented G.B.S.[12]

The war on the Eastern Front occasioned some of Vicky's least characteristic work. Concerned to pay appropriate tribute to the

44 '. . . and when I wanted to lay it out the corpse hit me', *News Chronicle*, 23 May 1941

Goering (head of the Luftwaffe) and Hitler react to their failure to break Britain from the air during 'the Blitz' of London and other major cities. The Germans had suffered severe losses because Britain had been able to build on her daylight air superiority by using radar at night.

45 James Cameron (1911–85)

James Cameron was one of the most
influential and widely travelled foreign
correspondents of his day – specialising
in the Middle East and Asia. Lord
Beaverbrook once praised him as
someone who wrote the grim hard
truth from the heart. Vicky was his
best-loved friend. They shared concern
about ordinary people, horror at social
injustice, and fear of, as they saw it,
man's imminent destruction by
nuclear weapons. (They were both at
the meeting in 1958 which saw the
birth of the Campaign for Nuclear
Disarmament (see also **132**).)

46 'All my own work', *News
Chronicle*, 26 April 1943

Fanatical arch-propagandist Josef
Goebbels redraws (from the left)
Goering, Himmler (head of Gestapo),
von Ribbentrop, Hitler, a Gestapo
officer, a German worker, a
Wehrmacht infantryman and an SS
officer. The German eagle is behind.
The repression of the German worker
by gagging is the most striking
element in this cartoon, which is
notable for its sympathy with him. He
becomes an heroic figure in the
'revised' version, the others merely
smile.

ALL MY OWN WORK

50

47 George Bernard Shaw, in *Profiles and Personalities* by Peter Noble, London, Brownlee, 1946

George Bernard Shaw (1856–1950) had a very caricaturable face. His white whiskers, the lively wrinkles around his eyes and his ruddy complexion combined to confirm him as a man with a great sense of fun. This is one of many portraits of G.B.S. that Vicky drew.

51

Russian people's defence of their land, he adopted the solemn vocabulary of Soviet symbolism: giant hands shaking; great fists clenching and crushing; an open palm lifting up the 'Flower of Russia's Youth'; a Red Army soldier writing 'A New Chapter' in a book called *The Russian Glory*. What was heartfelt in these images was buried in the 'official', commemorative style. Cartoons in praise of individuals never did come easily to Vicky, as he admitted, and his temperament was even less well suited to generalised heroics. Any hint of muscularity – even the yeoman

48 'The sacrifice', *News Chronicle*, 13 July 1942

July 1942 marked the halfway point in the siege of Leningrad at the northern end of the Russian front. To the south fierce fighting was taking place as the German Army made an assault on Stalingrad. Hitler's plan to move up the Volga and thereby cut off Moscow was ill-conceived and doomed to failure. This cartoon pays homage to the heroism and tenacity with which the Red Army defended its homeland.

THE SACRIFICE

STRUGGLE FOR LIFE

muscularity of popular resistance – was somehow death to his inspiration. Possibly it reminded him of the rhetoric of Fascist sculpture. So in his salutes to the British war effort, Vicky did not enjoy his finest hour. When he drew a brawny merchant sea-man wrestling with a Nazi shark ('Struggle For Life'), the image did not even raise the comforting echoes of national stereotype that accompanied his Russian statements.

Two general weaknesses marred Vicky's wartime work. One was a habit – difficult to resist amid the dramatic light-and-shade of worldwide conflict – of filling out the frame with deep and not always shapely shadows, in ink or blue-black crayon. These gave his cartoons prominence amid the greyness of the page, but cluttered many otherwise satisfying compositions, and left them with an oily texture. An equally pervasive fault, the effect of which cartoonists are always inclined to underrate, lay in Vicky's lettering, which having lost its obviously 'continental' flavour had not yet acquired new and consistent forms. His inscriptions would remain faintly provisional and unconvinced for the best part of another decade, until quite suddenly, assertiveness and consistency

49 'Struggle for life', *News Chronicle*, 30 June 1942

Another heroic cartoon but one in which the point is slightly laboured. The swimmer is just too muscular and the shark has not one but two swastikas. From the point of view of Allied seamen, the German U-boats were monsters of the deep that lay in wait for their prey and attacked without warning. Their tactics of 'wolf-pack' hunting had met with considerable success in the first six months of 1942, and until June 1942 U-boat commanders considered it safe to surface at night. They had not reckoned on the Allied aircraft carrying radar – in two months twenty-seven were sunk, most by sudden air attacks.

53

VICKY'S WEEK-END FANTASIA

'OH GOODY! IF THEY DOUBLE THE PRICE OF MEAT, WE'LL GET A 1/8d RATION!'

'T.V. NOTHING – SPEND A WEEK-END IN THE DOME OF DISCOVERY FOR SLIMMING'

'THESE LADY CRICKETERS AT LORDS ARE ALREADY PRODUCING SERIOUS SOCIAL REPERCUSSIONS'

'PARDON ME, IS THIS THE QUEUE FOR THE SOUTH BANK, BATTERSEA PARK OR ANTONY AND CLEOPATRA?'

WE'RE HELPING THE RUSSIANS SPLENDIDLY BY KEEPING THE GERMANS GUESSING *WHERE* WE'LL INVADE THEM IN 1943!

50A 'Vicky's Week-end Fantasia', *News Chronicle*, 19 May 1951

50B 'We're helping the Russians splendidly by keeping the Germans guessing *where* we'll invade them in 1943!', *News Chronicle*, 28 August 1941

Vicky developed the idea of the 'Week-end Fantasia' early on in his career with the *News Chronicle* and it was a feature which lasted until he left the paper in 1953. It appeared every Saturday, like David Low's 'Topical Budget' in the *Evening Standard*. The influence of Low's most famous invention, Colonel Blimp, is plain in both these drawings. Vicky often drew reactionary clubmen – as here discussing women cricketers at Lords – and faceless stupid people, such as Colonel Too-Little and General Too-Late, voicing absurd, topsy-turvy ideas.

arrived together. Thereafter, Vicky's boldly brushed-in capitals numbered among the most confidence-inspiring attractions of his style.

An early innovation which lasted not just through the war but to the end of Vicky's term at the *News Chronicle* was his 'Weekend Fantasia', drawn for the Saturday edition.[13] Its content, social observation zanily intermingling with political allusion, recalled Low's 'Topical Budget' for the Saturday *Evening Standard*; but whereas Low had commanded (in every sense) a whole page, Vicky had just four or five tiny frames to work with, usually in a vertical-strip format. Though the space was small, however, four or five solid ideas were needed to fill it, an obligation which eventually became burdensome to Vicky, and even in the short-term obliged him to resort to some recycled Low-isms. The 'Fantasia' frequently played host to irate clubmen, their utterances pre-

. . . NON AVETE DA PERDERE ALTRO CHE LE CATENE

51 '. . . *non avete da perdere altro che le catene*', *News Chronicle*, 27 July 1943

The conclusion of the campaign in North Africa left the Allies with powerful forces available for further offensive action. The time was not right for an invasion of France, but an attack on Sicily and Italy offered an alternative. This cartoon was later prepared as a propaganda leaflet but was never dropped. The drawing was printed in black and white surrounded by a magenta border and on the back was a proclamation from the Supreme Commander of the campaign, General Eisenhower. The caption reads '. . . you have nothing to lose but your chains' and the falling sheet of paper says 'Honourable surrender'. The Sicilian offensive dealt Mussolini a mortal blow and it became evident after his fall on 25 July that Italy was about to surrender.

fixed with a 'Dammit, sir . . .' whose indebtedness to Colonel Blimp's 'Gad' could scarcely be disguised. Vicky also conceived a tribe of literally faceless reactionaries and bureaucrats which likewise recalled Low, as did the names, if not the configurations, of the old-school war-lords 'Colonel Too-Little' and 'General Too-Late', with their pin-striped ally 'Mr Can't Happen Here'.

While learning on the job, Vicky was gathering a minor reputation as a prophet. The eye of posterity spots this perhaps too easily (there was no particular reason to applaud Vicky at the time for his 1945 cartoon in which a family shows itself prepared to live in a tent as long as they can keep their television set); but he did enough to keep the *News Chronicle* alert to this aspect of his talent. A cartoon called 'A Tale of Two Cities' was reprinted early in 1943 to show how accurately Vicky had foreseen the battle for Leningrad. More immediately gratifying was 'The Maltese Cross' of April 1942, which had Hitler blinded by the radiance of the island's emblem. A week later, when King George VI awarded the George Cross to Malta 'to honour her brave people', Vicky's drawing took on the character of a prediction. Perhaps more satisfying to Vicky personally was a 1943 cartoon addressed to the Italian people and captioned 'You Have Nothing To Lose But Your Chains'. Within days it was reprinted in translation and prepared for dropping over Italy as a leaflet by the Allied air forces.[14] Vicky, who had an exhibition running just then at the Modern Art Gallery in Charles II Street ('all proceeds go to the Stalingrad Hospital Fund'), must have felt that he, like the Allies, was winning at last. He continued to fund a hospital bed till the end of the war.

It was not until early in 1944 that he took his first holiday since the outbreak of hostilities. The readership was left not entirely bereft of amusement, for Richard Winnington had been running his self-illustrated film column for some months past. On the first Saturday of Vicky's absence he produced his famous drawing of James Cagney in *Johnny Vagabond*, positively jumping off the page. Winnington was an important presence in the long glass-walled Features Room on the third floor of the *Chronicle* building in Bouverie Street, and his most direct influence was exerted upon Vicky. Very exacting in pursuit of a likeness, Winnington would sometimes improve a finished drawing by pasting on to it a superior version of the head – a practice which Vicky preferred to avoid, but which he ceased to disdain.

In point of style, Winnington favoured a frankly nibby kind of pen-work, leaving evidence of swiftness and even violence in the drawing. This favoured a sense of movement, which Winnington could capture with remarkable economy. He passed these virtues on to Vicky in a curious atmosphere of affectionate hostility. Winnington was a kind man but a naturally combative conversationalist. Advice from him generally took the form of a noisy rebuke, scarcely softened by the invariably suffixed epithet 'Cock'. At some level, too, there was no doubt an undercurrent of real resentment in Winnington's remarks, for Vicky had moved in on his territory at Features, and was proving more versatile than his colleagues had expected. Where Winnington was surest of his ground was in his native Englishness. 'You clever bloody foreigners always get it wrong about the English,' he is remembered as barking at Vicky. 'Ernie Bevin should be batting at wickets *chalked on a wall* and not on the bloody playing fields of Eton.'[15] Since this story is told by Tom Baistow, who did not join the *Chronicle* staff until after the war, the suggestion is that Winnington had been dishing out this kind of encouragement for some years past. That the two men's mutual respect survived the strain was partly attributable to the compatibility of their politics. Winnington, like several others in the *Chronicle*'s orbit, had been a member of the Communist Party (and indeed was supplying a simultaneous film column to the *Daily Worker* under the pseudonym 'John Ross'); but he was no more a doctrinaire 'hard' leftist than Vicky was. The appalling variety of man's inhumanity to man provided them with enormous common ground, over the cultivation of which they argued ceaselessly.

The *News Chronicle*'s Liberal line was expounded partly by Gerald Barry's editorials (in which Carroll's Alice again stacked

52 'James Cagney in *Johnny Vagabond*', *News Chronicle*, 29 January 1944 by Richard Winnington

Richard Winnington worked on the *News Chronicle* for ten years from 1943 until his death, producing an influential film criticism column accompanied by his own satirical caricatures. He and Vicky had a mutual respect and admiration. Of all the people in their particular group at the *News Chronicle* Vicky took most notice of Winnington and the comments he often made on his ideas – both visually and politically. Winnington was a stickler for accuracy. However, his practice of re-drawing when the cartoon was not quite right, and then gluing the new version over the old, was not one that Vicky copied to any great extent.

DRAWN BY VICKY

"MILITARY IDIOTS, WITH JUNK FROM THE DECADENT DEMOCRACIES, TO SEE THE FUERHER"

100 CARTOONS FROM THE "NEWS CHRONICLE"
FOREWORD BY A. J. CUMMINGS

53 'Military idiots, with junk from the decadent democracies, to see the Fuerher [sic]', cover illustration for *Drawn by Vicky: 100 cartoons from the* News Chronicle, London, The Walding Press, 1944

General Eisenhower (left) and Field Marshal Montgomery knock at the door of the Siegfried Line, the last defensive barrier of the Third Reich. The door is opened by Field Marshal Model. Prior to this point there had been some conflict between the Allied leaders: each was convinced that his particular strategy would be the one to bring the war to an end, and Montgomery wanted a single ground commander – himself. It was Eisenhower's 'broad-front' strategy of two simultaneous thrusts, one at Strasburg, another in the Ruhr, which was put into effect, as opposed to Montgomery's 'single punch' attack on Berlin.

up a respectable tally of appearances) and partly by the political correspondent A.J. Cummings, father of Michael Cummings the by no means Liberal cartoonist. When Vicky's first cartoon collection (*Drawn by Vicky* (1944)) was published, it was Cummings Snr. who provided the Introduction. He applauded Vicky's 'enthusiastic appreciation of Hazlitt, whom he regards as our greatest essayist', and pointed out Vicky's 'ability to catch and reflect a popular mood . . . whether he shoots at Diehardism in a domestic controversy or at the criminal obsessions of evil men in the bitter conflict now drawing to a close'. Cummings was not keen to identify the rising 'popular mood' of the moment as Socialism, but concentrated instead on the area where he and Vicky could readily agree: the Beveridge Report. An impeccable Liberal, Sir William Beveridge was completely acceptable to Cummings – and to Vicky, who regarded the 1942 Report on Social Security as the first large and necessary step in the direction of welfare socialism. Vicky drew frequent cartoons on the subject, emphasising delays and highlighting any attempt to take the governmental scissors to Beveridge's proposals. One drawing, a Guinness spoof worded 'My Goodness, My Beveridge' drew a 'Salute to Vicky' in the letters column from Sir William himself. Vicky chiefly liked him for his declaration that there must be 'no

54 'My goodness, my Beveridge', *News Chronicle*, 27 May 1944

The Beveridge Report was one of four independent consultative documents dealing with the problems of post-war reconstruction in Britain. Although the Commons approved its general principles of 'social security', they merely welcomed it as an aid for further discussion, later short-circuiting Beveridge with their own White Paper on full employment. It became clear that the general public were not to expect too much, initiative and competition would be encouraged, and that in order for a social security plan to operate effectively there must be full employment. 'My Goodness, My Guinness', was a famous, long-running advertising slogan. The cartoon is a fairly faithful copy of a Guinness poster, with Beveridge replacing the figure of a zoo keeper.

55 'Is this a human being?', in *9 Drawings by Vicky (Scenes in an Indian famine)*, London, Modern Literature, 1944

The drawings for this book were not made from life but are Vicky's terrible imaginings. He remained haunted by such images throughout his life. Periodically, he forced himself to try to come to terms with his horror of social injustice by drawing what he considered to be the worst, but this never seemed to help him purge himself. (See also **108**.)

IS THIS A HUMAN BEING?

peace with the Giant Evils', which were identified as Idleness, Squalor, Disease, Ignorance and Want. This sentiment matched Vicky's precisely, provided that the emphasis fell ultimately on Want. When Air Raid Precautions had been introduced in 1939, Vicky had drawn a poor citizen asking 'Why A.R.P.? Is it more cruel to bomb them than to let them starve?'[16] After five years of war he still felt the same.

The kind of concern Vicky felt about world famine now seems normal and laudable. It has even become, in a rather disgraceful sense, fashionable. But in Vicky's lifetime, his horror at the waste of life was seen as a kind of morbid fixation, deplored by even his closest colleagues, who saw it as their duty to jolly him out of it. Yet down to the last month of his life, Vicky felt driven to give graphic expression to feelings which his intimates found

60

embarrassing and even 'soppy'. He himself acknowledged that he was operating in dangerously grim territory. 'Grim', in fact, became a code-word for the genre in negotiations between Vicky and Gerald Barry, who dreaded such submissions and resisted them whenever possible.

Just before Christmas 1944 Vicky published the most coherent of his 'grim' productions: a pamphlet entitled *9 Drawings* (on the subject of the famine in India). The interplay of drawings and words is startling, for the texts are gathered in from a strange variety of sources, including St Luke's Gospel, Alfred Adler, Clement Attlee, Blake, Shakespeare, nursery rhymes and, of course, Lewis Carroll. Yet one's reaction to the book is inevitably ruled by the impact of the artwork, as Mulk Raj Anand,[17] the Indian novelist and critic, admitted in his Introduction. This contained as careful a justification of what later came to be known as Vicky's 'Oxfam Style' as has yet been constructed. 'Unlike the art of his daily cartoons, where he is still evolving a style to suit his uncanny insight,' Anand noted, 'in the kind of picture reproduced in this book he has already achieved a masterly convention of his own.'

Anand surely discussed with Vicky his German influences – and was perhaps put gently off the scent, for he remarks that 'what he shares with Käthe Kollwitz is only a common ground, because he is not as heavy as she is . . . And his line does not exploit the exaggerated lasciviousness so popular in Germany during the Weimar Republic'. The latter assertion is true enough, but the relative heaviness, or not, of Kollwitz's work is very much a matter of one's personal reaction to her cloudy charcoal medium. Something about this suggested line of influence seems to have met with Vicky's resistance.

Anand stresses that these are not eyewitness drawings but Vicky's 'imaginative realisation of India's despair . . . they evidence to a sensibility which has been deeply stirred by the great hunger on the continent of Europe and is well aware of China's legions of dead through starvation of the last few years'. Edging closer to the heart of the difficulty these drawings present, he goes on:

> in terms of pure draughtsmanship they show that Vicky has become the line that he draws . . . the occasional brush work with which he deepens the shadows shows that he has sensed the movements of rotting flesh and congealing blood . . . he gathers the weakness, the ignorance, the filth, the squalor and the triviality of life into an aura of sympathy which creates

56 'Götterdämmerung sweepstake', *News Chronicle*, 28 April 1945

This cartoon is a joke in pardonable bad taste. The precise outcome of the 'twilight of the gods' was as follows: Hitler committed suicide on 30 April; Goering was captured by the Allies, was found guilty at Nuremberg and sentenced to hang (he committed suicide in his cell); Goebbels committed suicide before he could be arrested; Himmler committed suicide when captured by the Allies before he could be tried; von Ribbentrop was found guilty at Nuremberg and was hanged; and Mussolini was shot by his own countrymen.

beauty out of insufferable putrescent ugliness. And thus he transforms the spectator's emotion into a peculiar strength of thought.

Though its very defensiveness betrays the expectation of an adverse first reaction to Vicky's 'grim' style, this was a thoughtful apologia, with which many at the time found themselves in agreement. The *Daily Worker*'s reviewer confessed that *9 Drawings* 'moved and angered me more than anything has done for a long time'[18]; and the *New Statesman*, 'haunted' by the images, felt that the accompanying quotations 'could be more bitter than they are without missing their mark'.[19] But a weary public, intent on making an end to the war, had little energy left over for such a struggle with its conscience. In March 1945 *Reynolds News* reported that 'Vicky's nine drawings of the Indian famine . . . can still be

GÖTTERDÄMMERUNG SWEEPSTAKE

Put X in column you fancy opposite criminals	Killed in battle	Captured by Allies	Committed suicide	Shot by Allies at sight or escaping	Killed in air raid	Murdered by Nazis	Killed by non-Nazis or prisoners	Alive in German-held territory	Escaped to neutral territory	Found in mental home	Believed alive, whereabouts unknown	Any other idea

How will the Nazi leaders meet their end? What will be their fate by May 30, 1945? Suicide? Capture? Death in battle? Alive in the Redoubt? Here is an opportunity for you to use your ingenuity. Put a cross opposite each criminal under the column of your choice, then cut the puzzle out and check your guesses on May 30. No prizes except your own self-satisfaction

obtained. I don't have to say more, have I?' Nothing more was heard of the little book.

While he had campaigned for months against the complacency of those who claimed at various points that the struggle was all over bar the shouting, Vicky too looked forward to the peace. He did not give way to optimism until 31 March 1945, when in a 'Weekend Fantasia' he depicted himself parading down the street with a sandwich-board reading 'No, it WON'T be long now' – and causing an onlooker to faint with shock. Vicky had been a Second Fronter since 1942, recommending a 'Victory Drive' towards Berlin well over two years before the D-Day landings. Now he could drop such militaristic incitement from his repertoire.

He had found other ways of preparing for the moment of triumph itself, addressing home-front issues which less committed observers might have preferred to leave in abeyance until the score was settled with Germany. As early as 1941, before America's entry into the war, Vicky greeted a £3 minimum-wage settlement for agricultural workers with a salute to the shades of the Tolpuddle Martyrs ('What you sowed, we are reaping').[20] Later, when the Beveridge proposals were in the air, he agitated on behalf of the Labour rank-and-file for a Social Security system. Any radical proposal of which he approved, or any campaigning speaker – like Herbert Morrison, who gave a series of Saturday afternoon addresses in 1943 – was shown being greeted with a Blimpish chorus of 'Feller's dangerous! He's talking *Socialism*!' In moments of angry impatience with Labour politicians, Vicky would depict the supposed Socialists themselves uttering this alarm-call. Perhaps he sensed already how hard a job it would be to keep some of them away from the middle of the road.

Vicky took scant professional notice of VE Day. Having allowed himself one moment of triumphalism – a 'Götterdämmerung Sweepstake' in which readers were invited to guess which of the several available uncomfortable fates might befall each Nazi leader – he shifted quickly into electoral gear. As he correctly diagnosed, there was not all that much to be done except to ensure that Winston Churchill's reputation as a wartime leader was carefully detached from his peacetime potential. Churchill himself helped by mounting the absurd 'Gestapo' campaign against Labour – a gift to the comic fantasist. Labour came in on a landslide in spite of the *News Chronicle*'s advice to 'Vote Liberal'.

Vicky's glee was much moderated by the prospect of having to caricature Clement Attlee on a regular basis. His 'Open Letter'

57 Untitled, *News Chronicle*, 3 May 1945

Vicky sits on the pavement, reduced to begging. His wartime personalities are all gone and he has to start again. There is no real sense of regret; Vicky moved quickly away from the war in Europe onto the subject of the next political battle in Britain – the 1945 general election. This first post-war election was held on 5 July 1945 – the Labour Party won by a convincing margin.

to Attlee,[21] beseeching the addition of 'props, distinctive personal touches' to the Prime Ministerial demeanour, betokened a not entirely pretended panic. It was perfectly true that Attlee's public persona was self-contained to a terrifying degree; it trailed absolutely no interesting superfluities within the cartoonist's grasp. But then Vicky always dreaded the prospect of working up a new cast of characters. In the last days of war he had depicted himself as a destitute pavement-artist, all his Axis 'favourites' having gone at a stroke. The 'Open Letter' format was to become a habit with him. He greeted most new leaders with it – it was a way of announcing himself, of declaring open season, of adjusting his sights. But behind the manoeuvre lay real fears. In his early thirties, Vicky was already beginning to speak of his dread of waking up with a mind bereft of ideas; his sleep, poor since boyhood, was now bad enough to require medicinal enhancement. Less pressingly, there was Vicky's apprehensiveness lest he come up against a political face he could not 'get'. As a matter of fact, one such was elected to Parliament in 1945, though it was twenty years before James Harold Wilson began to cause real trouble.

Less worrisome, for a change, was Vicky's personal life, which had re-established a kind of equilibrium after the break-up of his marriage to Lucie. At the studio of a well-known artist and gallery-owner, the imposingly rotund Jack Bilbo,[22] he had met another Lucie, the red-haired daughter of a Liverpool fruit-merchant. Lucie Gray was a student at RADA, and a part-time model for some quite prominent artists, like Matthew Smith.[23] Volatile and independent by temperament and quite as radical as Vicky in politics, she was a talented actress who entered the profession with the suitably embellished given-name of Lucielle. She began to share Vicky's life, the liveliest social parts of which revolved around Alec Clunes's Arts Theatre Club and the Players' Theatre (where the actor Leonard Sachs teased Vicky unmerci-

58 Lucielle Gray and Vicky, London, *c.* 1945

A suitably dramatic photograph of Vicky and his second wife by John Vickers, who specialised in taking photographs of theatre personalities, musicians and composers. Lucielle Gray was an established actress who was to spend the winter of 1945/46 on an ENSA tour of the Continent. Their daily letters from this period give great insight into Vicky's working life.

fully, getting a regular earful of Vicky's now excellent English in return). When Vicky got really low, Robby Lantz, now working at Columbia Pictures, took him to the Windmill Theatre, where they sometimes attended what were laughingly called 'the dress rehearsals'.

In one area of his life he was suffering great anguish. By moving to Hungary, his mother and sister had put themselves temporarily beyond the scope of Hitler's genocidal ambitions. But as the war progressed, it became increasingly obvious that Hitler would occupy Hungary, putting Jewish citizens in terrible danger. Isabella Weisz got out in time, granted an exit visa on grounds of her advancing years. No such privilege was extended to Elisabeth. She was rounded up and twice put on transports bound for death camps – Dachau and Ravensbrück. Miraculously, she escaped twice, and was finally imprisoned in a smaller camp, between Vienna and Wien-Neustadt. Liberation came only just in time for her. Helplessly delirious from starvation and typhus in the chaos of the German collapse, she was crawling along the side of a road when a Russian transport picked her up. The outlines of this horrifying story were known to Vicky, but his sister never told him the details, and he never asked to be told. There was a sense between them that it would be too much for him to bear.

What he could do in 1945 was to begin the desperate process of trying to bring his sister to England. By the time she was able to communicate again with the outside world she was in Budapest, which under Russian domination might at any time be closed off from the West. Elisabeth was in poor health, had no work, and despised the Hungarians, who at several points in her appalling experience had treated her callously. Communications with Budapest were so bad that for some time the most efficient conveyance was a courier; journalists working for the *News Chronicle* took parcels on Vicky's behalf, enabling Elisabeth at least to pay her room-rent with cigarettes. The aftermath of the war was full of more frightening realisations for Vicky than he had ever experienced during the conflict itself. *Aftermath* would be the title of another of his 'grim' booklets, to be published the following year, and which now, in this black time of sickening anti-climax and anxiety, he began to compile.

He had worked for Britain, maintaining the morale and resolve of some millions of readers, throughout the Blitz and the flying-bomb attacks. In recompense, the 'gods of the copy-book headings' sent him a letter, dated 26 July 1945, from the 'Trading With The Enemy Dept.', a government office in Kingsway, WC2. Replying nominally to the Chief Accountant of the *News Chronicle*, who had written 'on behalf of Mr Victor Weisz requesting permission to send financial help to his sister in Budapest', the functionary stated: 'I am directed by the Controller-General to inform you that the Department is not aware of any method of providing financial assistance for persons resident in Hungary, other than those who are British subjects. It is regretted, therefore, that in the absence of an authorised scheme of individual remittance, the Dept. is unable to assist.'

Nothing could have been more mincingly calculated to remind Vicky, without ever quite saying the words, that cartoons or no cartoons he was himself an alien still.

The Worst Winter   *4*

In mid-November 1945, Lucielle left on an ENSA tour of the Continent, as part of the troupe performing *Strange Orchestra* by Rodney Ackland.[1] While Vicky could not bring himself to find out very much about the play, he felt sure that Lucielle would return a 'riper and more experienced actress'. He did not mention the 'testing of the relationship' that is often a useful by-product of such separations; but the six months that followed certainly did test Vicky. By the spring he was remarking that 'all in all it was the worst winter ever for me' (a judgement he might have held in reserve if he had foreseen the Great Freeze of 1946–7).

The couple evidently promised to exchange letters on a daily basis, or as near as could be managed, and Vicky, a letter-writer neither by training nor by inclination, kept nobly to the plan. Odd dates were missed, but there were compensating days when two and even three letters were entrusted to the erratic mails. Lucielle was often a town or two ahead of the system, yet Vicky's epistles must have caught up with her in the end – for it is thanks to the correspondence Lucielle preserved that the winter of 1945–6 comes down to us as the most intimately documented period of Vicky's working life. Moreover, since the *News Chronicle* offered a notably stable working environment, the routine aspects of this admittedly fretful winter can be taken as typical of Vicky's whole first decade as an established Fleet Street cartoonist.

To begin with, he embarked on his winter bachelordom in a state of feud with Dick Winnington. 'Well, darling,' Vicky told Lucielle in an early letter, 'this is Friday afternoon at the *Chronicle* and you know what that is. Everybody shouting, drawings fighting each other and Dick and I of course still not speaking to each other.'[2] The cause of this particular quarrel is now lost. There were several such over the years, the tendency to squabble being exacerbated on Winnington's side by an enthusiastic intake of lunchtime beer.

The manner of their reconciliation this time, however, is interesting as a rare example of the healing power of politics. Vicky had been looking forward eagerly to a London showing of D.W. Griffith's film *The Birth of a Nation*, from which he expected both

59 Self-portrait as an Englishman, unpublished, 25 November 1945

Vicky added a poignant postscript to the letter that contained this drawing: 'Barry [the editor of the *News Chronicle*] has heard about my naturalisation. It seems I've got to take my place in the queue . . . And I saw myself already like this . . .' In later life, he was able to say, 'I myself do not look upon myself as a foreigner . . . when I talk . . . I do not say "they", I say "us".' (This is a nice giveaway of his foreignness – he should say 'we'.)

an enlargement of his cinematic education and an immersion in the movie's 'large humanity and love', as promised by the respected critic Dilys Powell. But at the mid-December press show, Vicky suffered a dreadful shock. 'Never in my life,' he wrote to Lucielle, 'have I seen a filthier, cruder film, full of violent race prejudices . . .' Barely managing to sit through the Ku Klux Klan sequences, Vicky at last was entirely repelled. 'Shortly before the end, when Christ appeared, I couldn't stand it any longer and walked out.' It was while he was fuming in the vestibule that Winnington also emerged. 'I want to break an eight weeks' silence,' he said, 'just to tell you how shocked I am about this film, Cock.' The normal give-and-take was restored from that moment. But in his letter, Vicky was typically unable to enjoy the relief, writing as he was 'still in white hot anger' over the stance of Griffith's film.

Vicky's own sense of racial alienation was still easily aroused. When Lucielle told him how conspicuous she felt under the eyes of the Europeans, he replied in a bitter postscript: 'Now you know what it means to be a B. foreigner. They've been looking at me like this ever since I can remember.' A later letter's postscript records the failure of her attempt to reassure him: 'Of course everyone sees that I'm a foreigner – my face is my uniform.' A fresh disappointment underlies these bleak remarks. The Home Secretary had just announced that naturalisation procedures were to be resumed, and Gerald Barry had written immediately to advance Vicky's claims. The applicant was overjoyed. 'So darling,' he wrote to Lucielle, 'you may have left a dirty foreigner but you may come back to a real Englishman – and will I be English, by Gad! That'll be one life ambition of mine fulfilled.' He celebrated with drawings of himself as a pukka Englishman, checks and moustaches and all; but it soon became clear that the excitement was very premature. He must take his place in the queue – 'a long queue', he confessed.

Powerless to accelerate the process of his own acceptance, Vicky now began to be bombarded with disturbing communications from his sister Elisabeth, who was stranded in murky Budapest, as ignorant of the language as Vicky had been a decade earlier, and as bereft of work and money. Cabled messages of support were no substitute for the nourishment, hope and medical assistance Elschen needed after her terrible experiences. She, having no other possibility of escape from her 'home' country (Hungarian papers being now a liability), increased the moral pressure on Vicky throughout the winter.

His mother and brother, meanwhile, apart from acting as local reminders of Elschen's anguish, made their own direct claims on his energies. Isabella Weisz was now established in Cleveland Mansions, W9, where a natural bewilderment at her transplantation can only have been intensified by the company of Oscar. Vicky's brother was spiralling painfully towards a divorce from his wife Hedi, and an affair he embarked upon in compensation came to a similarly dismal end, provoking an outbreak of hypochondriasis. Vicky was always able to joke about his brother, especially when a real illness gave him the upper hand ('Oscar . . . looks quite jealously at me lying in bed – poor chap, he's got no complaint at the moment'); but Oscar and Mama together

SO THIS IS WHAT WE FOUGHT FOR

60 'So this is what we fought for', *News Chronicle*, 16 November 1945

Civil war in India between Hindu and Moslem factions seeking self-government and independence from Britain was threatening to explode. In this cartoon the racist and class-conscious attitudes of British women appal Indian soldiers decorated for their bravery. (A group of FANYs had walked out of a dance in Calcutta because Indian ATS were present.)

were almost more than Vicky could bear on his invariable weekly visits ('these Saturday afternoons with my family depress me more and more . . . these two seem to have a remarkable gift for making the worst of everything').

Small wonder that Vicky's morale at work took some alarming dips over the winter months. He began defiantly enough in November with a strong anti-racist cartoon about an incident in Calcutta where some First Aid Nursing Yeomanry personnel allegedly walked out of a dance 'because Indian WAACs were present'. Vicky's caption – 'So this is what we fought for' – brought many letters of praise for his courage; others suggested less unpleasant interpretations of the story; and one message, 'signed by about twenty "Boys from Burma" threatened me with violence if I didn't apologise to the FANYs . . . Well, I didn't apologise, and am still alive, I think . . .' This was the sort of opposition Vicky thrived on. Gratification of a more conventional kind was supplied by a cartoon on a football theme, starring a

YOU'RE NOT PLAYING AGAINST A REPRESENTATIVE TORY TEAM, SIR!

team of Herbert Morrisons, when the victim put in a request for the original.

But space was very tight in a four-page paper, and good ideas seemed often to be turned down for no better reason than that Vicky had 'overdrawn his quota'. He had perfected not just the idea but generally the artwork as well by the time the adjudication came through, and this depressed him. He tried to celebrate Lucielle's birthday in early December by writing her letter on a poster-sized sheet. Alas, there'd been no room for that day's cartoon and Vicky could not hide his despondency. 'I feel absolutely superfluous these days, they don't really care . . . Anyway, I feel I've got a double reason to take to the bottle tonight . . . I shall drink as many Scotches as I can get – and like 'em.'[3]

Then, just as abruptly, things began to improve again. Vicky could not find a hat to fit his tiny head (size 6). When Ian Mackay put out a jocular appeal in his column, Vicky ('isn't it awful?') was obviously flattered as well as embarrassed. Office solidarity blossomed in the bitter cold. A.J. Cummings 'raised hell' and got the management to switch on the central heating, despite the fuel shortage. Vicky reported 'quite a lot of love', no less, 'between Dick and myself'. He was much taken with the charm of the drama critic, Alan Dent, to whom he now worked as provider of the weekly first-night caricature.

To cap it all, the editor suddenly became more receptive. Vicky was already 'overdrawn' when he submitted a cartoon on the

61 'You're not playing against a representative Tory team, Sir!', *News Chronicle*, 22 November 1945

Labour's Deputy Prime Minister, Herbert Morrison, prior to 'kicking off' a series of nationalisation acts to extend public ownership of industry, presents a united team to a Conservative Party that lacks leadership. The crowd call for Anthony Eden and Winston Churchill while Oliver Lyttelton appeals. (The Tories had lost badly in the General Election that July.)

62 '"All art is useless" – Oscar Wilde', unpublished, 5 December 1945

This sketch, done in watercolour, is one of a group of four that decorate the left-hand side of a poster-sized birthday letter to Lucielle (the sheet measures 58 × 43 cm). The other sketches show Vicky toasting Lucielle with scotch; Lucielle being marched along by two soldiers; and Vicky standing alone. Vicky chides himself for turning a merry letter into a moaning one – his main complaint being that David Low had been sent by the *Evening Standard* to Berlin to cover the Nuremberg trials while the *News Chronicle* would not let him go.

theme of the new and disastrous film *Caesar and Cleopatra*. To his amazement, Barry 'jumped at it'. Vicky was still enjoying the moment, feeling 'elated' (he often wrote Lucielle's letters in his office while waiting to know his fate), when a summons to the Editor's office interrupted him. When he returned it was with great news:

> O darling . . . I'm just back and I'm very happy. He said it was about time that I got a new contract. So he offered me a three years' contract and a quite substantial increase in salary – but it's really not only that – it's the nice things he said about my work which made me really happy.

From this peak, of course, Vicky fairly rapidly descended. Lucielle had been away four weeks 'and it feels more like four years'. Sir Oswald Mosley held a Fascist meeting which dismayed him; he had expected it, but not so soon after the war, nor so openly. By the time he received his Christmas bonus of £50 he was heading downhill fast again ('anyway £25 of it goes to the tax collector'). Lucielle by now was in Germany, which in itself

gave Vicky 'a queer feeling'. His Christmas wishes were not, and could not be, heartfelt ('I don't believe in it . . . you know the nearer Christmas gets the gloomier I get').

A present of a book of R. Taylor's *New Yorker* cartoons came with a timely and felicitous inscription from Alan Dent, 'To Vicky, my *News Chronicle* complement, who writes so very much better than I can draw.' Vicky had just written a defence of Picasso for the paper, after a public attack on the painter's reputation by Mrs Michael Joseph, daughter of the Pre-Raphaelite William Holman Hunt. 'As a rule, artists take no offence at these explosive reactions to their work,' Vicky wrote in his unsigned article. 'Indifference is much more disagreeable.'[4] His command of English was indeed excellent by this stage. He retained only a partiality for certain continental conditional tenses ('if you would have come', and so on), which stayed with him to the end of his career, sometimes necessitating additional tinkering with his captions.

Christmas Day, as Vicky almost required, was solitary and doleful. His Christmas dinner consisted of a grapefruit, provided by Oscar, a tin of Heinz beans, two fried fresh eggs, and some bacon ('I used nearly all my butter ration'), with an orange for dessert. If it sounds more pitiful than it was, in the context of the 1946 shortages, it was still not the meal of a man with even half of a £50 bonus in his pocket.

Two evenings later, Vicky sat in the bar of the Grove Hall Court apartment block and sank ten whiskies. More of his letters had gone astray. He was at the bottom of a depression exaggerated, as he would soon discover, by illness. Like many depressives, Vicky was sometimes oversensitive to the state of his health, and then again equally liable to blame his mind for bad feelings with physical causes. On this occasion he struggled on too long. His letters made increasingly doomy reading. For Lucielle's edification he invented a Gallup Poll 'to discover if the public would rather be alive or dead', revealing that '35% favour living, 23% wish to die, and 42% Don't Know'. He also sent an account of

> a frightful nightmare – the first one for many weeks. I witnessed a hanging (I don't know who it was) and said to the hangman that the man wasn't dead . . . they laughed and said 'He's dead alright!' – the man really seemed dead – but suddenly turned his head slowly – smiled at me and started to argue with his executioneers [sic].

Only the sight of a catastrophically hung-over Dick Winnington on New Year's morning cheered him: 'his eyes were just little slits. I pasted up a picture of Ray Milland in *Lost Weekend* on the wall in front of Dick's desk and told him to look in the mirror – he did and gave me a sweet-sour smile.'

A few days later, the combination of racking back pains and influenza finally put Vicky out of action. Fortified by a phone call from Lucielle, and doses of 'M & B' – a prototype sulpha drug – from his friend Dr Nicholls, he resolved to give in with grace to his indisposition, allowing his beard to grow (it took half an hour to shave off when the time came) and ceasing to insist on taking his own letters to the pillar-box at the corner of Abbey Road. A tottery recovery was soon made. Gerald Barry, anticipating it, had left word at the *Chronicle* not to let Vicky in; but as the invalid explained to Lucielle, quoting Lenin, 'there is no fortress that a Bolshevik can't storm', and in mid-January he penetrated the Bouverie Street citadel, to learn from Ian Mackay that dozens of cartoonists had been round looking for a job – 'and I'm not even dead yet', Vicky added. On the 18th – the forty-fifth birthday of his friend Pem – Vicky drew his first 'Fantasia' for three weeks. Dr Nicholls had given him some tablets to cheer him up, promising that 'the whole world will look rosy' after a single pill. To Vicky, everything looked 'just as grey as before'. So much for Benzedrine.[5]

Though the *News Chronicle*'s centenary celebrations were now in progress – the design of their anniversary notepaper was much derided by Vicky – Gerald Barry was not around to share them, suffering as he was from 'delayed shock' after a car accident. His subsequent travels on the Continent, part recreation, part reconnaissance (it was fashionable for editors and columnists to bring back their 'impressions' of war-blasted Europe) meant a long absence overall, and a removal of his fine regulating instinct. The struggle for space became more ruthless. Meanwhile, Lucielle had her own problems. *Strange Orchestra* had never been a hit with its garrison audiences, and now it was withdrawn, leaving Lucielle the option of carrying on only in a piece called *Britannia of Billingsgate*.[6] To Vicky's ear, the title told all. He seriously suggested she should resign – a not entirely disinterested proposal. When she decided to stay on, he was as supportive as he could be without claiming the merit of seriousness for *B. of B.*, as they called it.

They had taken to numbering their letters, and on Vicky's side the tally would comfortably exceed one hundred. The drawings with which he invariably closed were delightfully done, in coloured inks and paints, depicting usually Vicky himself in some attitude or situation pertaining to the letter – or sometimes an imagined Lucielle with her superb red hair. An overly solicitous side of Vicky irked her from time to time – he seldom failed to ask 'How are you?', and frequently exhorted her, in the idiom of the classic Jewish momma, to 'Eat!' On the more practical side he also despatched small parcels of luxuries, like Horlicks, coffee and cigarettes, though a request to go under the counter for chocolate noticeably embarrassed him and he would not at first comply with it. Lucielle's professional insecurities were always answered by Vicky in terms of 'experience' and 'broadening'. Whether he was totally convinced of her professional future one cannot be sure. Another of his recounted nightmares suggests that perhaps he was not: 'For some (undreamt) reason you were imprisoned in a military "Glasshouse" and the next morning they executed you – I tried to stop them but couldn't and had to watch . . .' It is a perfect metaphor for her stage-work, with the glasshouse – simultaneously a prison and an exposed place – as the theatre, the critics as the executioners on the morrow, and Vicky helpless in the stalls.

In politics, however, the pair were well attuned. That Lucielle was as fiercely anti-Nazi as Vicky is shown by a letter the *News Chronicle* published in mid-February. Signed 'Lucie Gray' and addressed as from St John's Wood, it noted that the London Symphony Orchestra had invited Wilhelm Furtwängler to conduct in London, and questioned the appropriateness of the invitation in view of the fact that Dr Furtwängler had been 'appointed Prussian State Councillor by Goering in July, 1933'.[7] An editorial note commented that there 'does seem a case for making Furtwängler undergo a period of penance'.[8] Vicky reported a divided reaction among readers, some asking 'who is this self-righteous woman who would stand up to the Nazis', while others agreed with Lucielle and congratulated her. Vicky was sending the *Chronicle* daily by letter-post. Evidently Lucielle did more than merely check on his cartoon.

Fan-mail for Vicky was on the increase. Profile-writers were showing an interest in him. Frederic Mullally set about preparing one for *Tribune*.[9] Peter Noble, dining with Vicky to research the relevant chapter of his *Profiles and Personalities*, took the opportunity of persuading his victim to illustrate the book (where, yet again, drawings of Priestley and G.B.S. were called for). In his day-to-day work, however, another 'bad patch' was in progress. Vicky suspected 'a big movement going on, high up, very high' to restrict his *News Chronicle* space. No doubt the influence of Sir Walter Layton was more evident with Barry still away. At all events, a two-column width was proposed for Vicky's efforts, a scheme he found insulting and absurd. His inventions were now frequently, and in his view conveniently, deemed 'too savage' or 'vicious'. He did not particularly deny it, but explained, reasonably, 'that's the mood I'm in'. If he produced two ideas, the 'funny' one was always taken in preference to the 'grim' one Vicky favoured. It was a victory for him when anything 'grim' sneaked through the editorial defences.

For a while, a real danger arose that Vicky would come to despise the word 'funny' altogether. 'A political cartoonist,' he assured Peter Noble, 'is not a comic artist.'[10] The *Chronicle* management disagreed. The readership was left in no doubt of these struggles, for Vicky dramatised them in a particularly bleak cartoon of late February. In a vertical format familiar from the Saturday 'Fantasia', it begins at the top with the editor's arm issuing peremptorily from his office door with the order 'Go on, do something funny!' The affronted cartoonist itemises a few increasingly mirthless suggestions (the disarray of the United Nations;

76

A CARTOONIST IN SEARCH OF A JOKE

64 'A cartoonist in search of a joke', *News Chronicle*, 20 February 1946

Mistrust abroad despite Foreign Secretary Bevin's efforts, post-war shortages and continued austerity at home – Vicky could find nothing that would satisfy his editor's order to 'do something funny'. He complained to Lucielle, 'I'm working on a big cartoon which they think is funny – perhaps you'll see it in the *Chronicle* – if it ever appears. Anyway – what a job to be funny' (*c.* November 1945).

65 'Come on, boys, here's another one that Hitler missed', *News Chronicle*, 25 March 1946

Civil servants dressed in stone-age clothes, with prehistoric mentalities to match, prepare to demolish John Nash's Regent's Park Terrace. (The critic Robert Lynd had already commented two days earlier on the prevailing mania, as he saw it, for demolishing beautiful houses to make way for flats.) As part of an essential post-war plan to build and rebuild houses to a higher standard, the Labour government had completed over 200,000 houses the previous year.

COME ON, BOYS, HERE'S ANOTHER ONE THAT HITLER MISSED

food and housing; famine, crash, disaster, strike) and places his own figure at the side of each frame, laughing ever more maniacally, until in the last frame we see only a gravestone marked 'Here lies a cartoonist who saw the funny side of life.' Lest we should mistake these deadly ironies for hilarity, the whole assembly is captioned 'A Cartoonist in Search of a Joke.'

Unwary of the Ides of March, Vicky now sprained his ankle while running for a No.9 bus. In time, he came to see the injury as beneficial, since it obliged him to take a taxi to work – one morning he shared a cab with Ian Mikardo MP, who also lived in Grove Hall Court – and he enjoyed seeing the spring at work in Regent's Park. Gradually his spirit began to thaw out again. The returning Gerald Barry banished the possibility of the two-column cartoon for good and all. Through Elizabeth Frank of the *Chronicle*'s arts staff, he met an Australian actress and dancer with whom he shared some evenings in the theatre and at the bar – just often enough to keep Lucielle's anxiety level matched to his own. Robby Lantz, at the time, was deeply smitten with Moira Shearer, so ballet occupied more than its usual share of the two men's leisure hours.

Work, as ever, did most to bring about the upswing. A prominent Spanish surgeon working in Oxford, Dr Trueta, wrote to thank Vicky 'in the most moving terms' for a cartoon about Franco. 'These things give me back my confidence that, sometimes at least, I'm doing a worthwhile job.' When a demolition squad of property developers suggested knocking down one of London's damaged Nash terraces instead of renovating it ('Come on boys, here's another one that Hitler missed!'), Vicky was again pleased with his response because 'I feel this is one of the more useful cartoons'.

An opportunity even arose to do something mildly 'grim', when Dr S.W. Jeger MP (husband of the subsequent MP Lena, later Baroness, Jeger) returned from the Continent with a pamphlet about conditions in Austria, the attraction to Vicky being Jeger's intention to 'debunk' the then-current horror stories about rape atrocities perpetrated by the Red Army. Vicky supplied an inky impression of refugees gathered under the statue of Franz Schubert; and Jeger repaid him by putting in a word with Chuter Ede, the Home Secretary, on behalf of Elisabeth Weisz. It was the first step in a process which would finally bring her, in the autumn of 1947, to the safety of Britain and the care of her family. She entered – such were Britain's requirements of a concentration-camp victim – on a 'Domestic Service Permit', which allowed her to be somebody's maid.

Gerald Barry readily consented to Vicky's little freelance outing for Dr Jeger: 'Oh good, Vicky, you can get rid of your starving people and I don't need to look at them'. The spring publication of Vicky's book *Aftermath* confirmed that the public felt much the same. In spite of some respectful capsule reviews, including

NO PROMISED LAND

an enthusiastic one from David Langdon in *Cavalcade*, the compilation had no mass appeal. 'I feel about *Aftermath* and its "reception" the same as you,' Vicky confided to Lucielle, 'but didn't expect anything different – so I'm not disappointed at all.'

In truth, the effect of Vicky's one-and-sixpenny booklet is crushingly cheerless. A humanitarian and piercingly compassionate message is put over, remarkably, in such a way as to make mankind seem irrecoverably unblest. The treatment begins to seem pitiless in a different sense. Drawings in boiling black inks and charcoals alternate with impeccably depressing quotes from the British press, chiefly from the autumn of 1945, when the postwar revelations of present dearth and past frightfulness were at their most profuse. The figure of the Wandering Jew is reprinted from the *Chronicle*, and typical of the newly-minted works is one featuring two waifs and the caption 'They're working on a bomb that will *only* kill women and children.' The whole production – down to its wretched Austerity paper, which Vicky knew would work against him – penetrates somewhere beyond pessimism. This is not cartoon as propaganda, or even as comment; it is cartoon as lamentation. If you wished to make out a case for the validity of this genre, you could not hope for a more wholehearted attempt to record in pen-strokes the deathly enormity of events – or a more difficult text to live with.

Vicky put it all behind him with the aid of some liver injections from the ever-solicitous Dr Nicholls. The ankle healed, and Vicky drew himself throwing the stick away. At work he felt benign enough, when Dick Winnington was stuck for a joke, to make him a gift of one – 'a really good one, good enough for the *New Yorker* . . . sometimes I feel that he doesn't deserve it'. Then, to Vicky's joy, the *Chronicle* sent him to Stratford-upon-Avon with

66 'No promised land', *News Chronicle*, 20 September 1945

Vicky often had trouble getting Gerald Barry to pass his 'grim' cartoons for publication in the *News Chronicle*. This drawing of the rootless Jewish refugees in the immediate post-war period is an exceptional one that *did* appear. It was included subsequently, together with brand-new drawings, in Vicky's book *Aftermath* (1946). Vicky welcomed the opportunity to draw whatever he wanted, believing that a cartoon was a signed statement of principles.

67 Stratford-upon-Avon sketch, *News Chronicle*, 23 April 1946

Vicky was pleased to be able to see Shakespeare's birthplace: he had been reading Shakespeare since 1939 on his editor's recommendation. He wrote to Lucielle, 'My Stratford drawings are going in tomorrow . . . we compromised at 2½ [columns] for Henley Street with His birthplace – I think [smaller] would have killed it, it's such a delicate drawing' (22 April 1946).

69   35 Welbeck Street, London W1

On Lucielle's return from the Continent, she and Vicky continued living in his flat at Grove Hall Court, prior to moving to a larger flat in Welbeck Street. They married on 20 September 1947, later separating in 1951.

68   'Farewell – my pen –', unpublished, 13 May 1946

Lucielle was to leave Europe to come home on 18 May 1946. This last letter was No. 160 (the couple's personal total was 110 as they had only been numbering their letters since January 1946). Vicky wrote, 'Let's hope this swan-song letter will just get you'.

'Jock' Dent. 'I'm excited today . . . I've always wanted to see Stratford.' In the event, it was a rushed visit, and Vicky was unimpressed by the Memorial Theatre ('red bricks – oooh! . . . it looks more like a factory doesn't it'); but his line-drawings of the town's monuments evidently impressed colleagues who had grown used to him as an exponent of grotesquerie, and had forgotten the delicacy of which he was capable. He sent the page to Lucielle. 'It had really a remarkable success and everyone is congratulating me – including Dick.' Lucielle had just been in Berlin, where Vicky had jovially imagined her placing a plaque, 'VICKY WAS BORN HERE', on 14 Regensburgerstrasse. 'How strange,' he remarked after his Stratford jaunt, 'that you're travelling about Europe with my suitcase and I'm with yours.'

At last her tour was nearing its end. She sent Vicky a book of Leonardo drawings, which he loved though they made him realise 'my miserable limitations'. Alan Dent sent a birthday telegram to 'my dear indispensable Vicky' – adjectives well calculated to please him. Compliments on his Stratford drawings continued to come in: 'nice backhanded ones too – [saying] that they were very much better than my political cartoons'. He now remembered to tell Lucielle that while in Stratford he had met Peter Brook, the 'child prodigy' director, 'and he inquired after you'. He had also prepared the ground with the actor/director

Farewell — my pen —

82

83

Alec Clunes, a friend from the Arts Theatre Club, who had promised to audition Lucielle on her return.

Soon she was as close as Calais. Vicky fretted to cross the Channel, but his naturalisation had still not come through. 'So – no travelling.' Faintly apprehensive of her reception, Lucielle wrote to say that she hoped she wouldn't 'disturb' Vicky.[11] 'You're a bad girl to write such a thing,' he replied roguishly, 'and you disturb me *frightfully*!' It was his 110th letter, 'and the last one'. He concluded it with a drawing of himself casting away the pen that had made of him, temporarily perhaps but much to his astonishment, a letter-writer.

On Lucielle's return they lived together, first at Grove Hall Court,[12] then at a fine flat in Welbeck Street. They were always happy in each other's company; but the end of their story was not a happy one. They were married on 20 September 1947, after which Lucielle began to sense it was a mistake. She had never intended to marry, and now felt trapped at home and thwarted in her work, where her turbulent temperament brought her into conflict with some unsympathetic elders of the profession. In 1951 she chucked it all in and escaped to France. Returning after a year in hopes of making a new start, she let herself in at 35 Welbeck Street with her old keys. When Vicky came home he was furious and threw her out. ('Quite right too – I would have done the same,' she reflected later in life.)[13] He had the lock changed the next morning. They were officially divorced long afterwards, on 23 July 1957.

'The Editor Regrets'   5

His 'worst winter' offered Vicky remarkably little to look back on with professional satisfaction. When in 1952 he came to make a selection of his post-war *News Chronicle* work, published as *Stabs in the Back*, he picked out just one solitary cartoon from his Lucielle-less months, and that a rather unexceptional composition ('Mr Smith Goes To Washington') in which the Food Minister, Sir Ben Smith, visits America to seek a fairer distribution of the world's supplies.[1]

In this Vicky was a little hard on himself, but not altogether wrong. Some of the liveliest ideas that occurred to him – 'Viki', the child cartoonist, with his nursery scrawl; a reinterpretation of Rembrandt's 'The Anatomy Lesson'; a crew of Martians rushing panic-stricken around their planet crying 'Woe! Woe! The Humans are coming!' – were all later recycled or revisited in more emphatically designed forms. The Labour government was as yet preoccupied in locating the reins of power rather than manipulat-

'I AM NO ART CRITIC' – Mr Bevin

70 '"I am no art critic" – Mr Bevin', *News Chronicle*, 16 April 1946

Vicky had written to Lucielle on 12 April, 'My answer to the newly formed "British League for Sanity in Art" [this was anti-Picasso] is "Vicky's League for Insanity in Politics".' He thus drew himself carrying a 'Down with Realism' placard. Foreign Secretary Ernest Bevin ponders a representation of the dissection of the post-war world in which he figures.

ing them. As Mullally pointed out in his *Tribune* profile of Vicky, the electoral defeat of the 'Westminster reactionaries', which 'set the Right-wing cartoonists off on a bogey-man hunt, left the radicals sparring quite as ineffectually at thin air . . .' Vicky had his private version of the same thought: 'It seems to be getting more and more difficult to find something to get one's teeth into – something with a bite, I mean – well, I'll just have to be a tame cartoonist . . .'[2]

Much of his energy had been dissipated in the struggle to maintain his representation in the pages of the *News Chronicle*, and to insist on the publication of his better cartoons in the shape and size he had intended for them. A less combative artist might have been content to regard his mere professional survival as adequate reward for this effort. But Vicky, whose sense of injustice extended in certain circumstances to himself, required a memorial to his discarded fancies, fallen comrades in the battle for space and for freedom of comment.

The Editor Regrets, published in 1947, is a book of thirty-odd cartoons turned down by Gerald Barry, introduced by Barry himself. 'On the contrary,' he began, 'I regret nothing . . . Not even the alternate cossetting and bullying in which I have had to indulge until he has become the best daily newspaper cartoonist in Britain.' This blurb, with its submerged braggadocio, was a fine example of Barry's skilful give and take. While proclaiming himself the 'chief and most admiring' of Vicky's admirers, he laid out very clearly the several reasons why cartoons sometimes did not make the page. To Vicky's undoubted satisfaction, these included the admission that 'occasionally one may be rejected because it clashes with the policy of the paper'. Here was the evidence of 'suppression' that gave point to the book.

In fact, the success of *The Editor Regrets* was purely gestural: it asserted Vicky's pride and independence, drawing attention to the frustrations of an artistic temperament amid the routines of Fleet Street. But there are no lost masterpieces in this small collection: just a few heavy underlinings of opinions Vicky had made quite plain in his 'allowable' output. Churchill, turning a blind eye to Progress, comes in for the post-war drubbing the *News Chronicle* was disinclined to give him; the Truman administration likewise. Clem Atlas, holding up the globe, found no difficulty in getting published in his later forms; nor did 'The Eagle Has Two Heads', a favourite schema of Vicky's, denoting an undeclared split in policy, usually in America or Germany, whose aquiline emblems laid them ever open to this joke.

WE'RE GOING TO HAVE A BABY, DEAR

71 'We're going to have a baby, dear', in *Aftermath*, London, Alliance Press, 1946

In this dark and foreboding cartoon, the fat industrialist/politician is the only one to have profited from the war. Vicky fears that continued manoeuvring to improve positions in a war-torn Europe will result in further conflict. This drawing was subsequently included in Gerald Barry's compilation *The Editor Regrets* (1947).

Naturally, several 'grims' were rescued from oblivion. Gerald Barry took the opportunity of teasing Vicky about these:

I usually know when one of these 'grim' cartoons is on the way. On presenting himself in my office with his daily offering, he wears an advance look of mingled cunning and despair, as who should say 'You're going to turn me down'. Not believing that in these sad days *News Chronicle* readers share quite his perverse addiction to the saturnine, I usually do. I don't regret this either! Not that some of Vicky's serious cartoons are not first-rate. I will only say that with cartoons as with life, you can't get away with murder as easily as with the custard-pie technique. A successful serious cartoon must be the *perfect* crime, whereas if your aim is accurate you may hit the mark with an indifferent custard pie.

In spite of a faintly objectionable tone, as of a man who may patronise his own creature with impunity, one can feel some sympathy for Barry here as the editor of a daily – especially when

87

TORY H.Q.

SHELTER

HEAVILY DISGUISED VICKY GOES UNDERGROUND TO SEE THE 'PEOPLE IN REVOLT' AGAINST THE ATTLEE DICTATORSHIP —

— HE FINDS SIR WALDRON (STANLEY BOY) SMITHERS WORKING ON A SECRET RADIO TO COMBAT THE EVIL LEFT WING INFLUENCE OF THE B.B.C. —

— AND LORD'B PREPARING A CLANDESTINE PAPER TO FIGHT THE UNI(N)FORMED PRESS —

THE NEW DEMOCRATS

SAME OLD TORIES

— FINALLY HE MEETS THE SMALL BAND OF BRAVE MEN HIDING UNDER A NEW NAME, WHICH WILL STRIKE TERROR IN THE HEARTS OF THE DESPOTS.

72 Untitled, *News Chronicle*, 3 September 1946

Winston Churchill touched a raw nerve and alienated the British electorate in 1945 when he said, 'There can be no doubt that Socialism is irreparably interwoven with totalitarianism and the abject worship of the State . . .', going on to suggest that Socialist Britain could not work without a 'Gestapo'. (It has been suggested that this speech was inspired by Lord Beaverbrook.) In the cartoon the Conservatives regroup from a position of siege but it is the 'same old Tories' with a new standard-bearer – Macmillan – who said, 'Beyond broad principles I would not go . . . The details can be worked out when you are in office . . .'. Sir Waldron Smithers was a robust right-winger, well-known for his defence of 'last ditches'.

one realises the kind of 'grim' to which Vicky was attached. Almost the last thing in *The Editor Regrets* is the cartoon that was also the pay-off to *Aftermath*: an appallingly dispiriting drawing of a toff labelled 'Power Politics' and a skull-faced pregnant woman embodying the Second World War, the caption being 'We're going to have a baby, dear'. Evidently Vicky felt that in

JANUARY : Fuel warnings. Transport House besieged by Labour rebels. Shinwell won't talk. Fog, Rain, and Gales. French Government crisis.

FEBRUARY : Brighter international prospects. Bomb invented which kills only women and children. Gales, Crises in France, Greece, China

MARCH : Unanimously decided in Moscow that Franco is no Gentleman. A million houses just round the corner. Fog. French Government crisis.

APRIL : Bright hopes of healthy scarcity. Successful disposal of unsold surpluses in the United States. Rain. Greek Government crisis

MAY : Cheerful prospects for farmers. A million houses just round the corner. Floods, French and Greek Government crises

JUNE : Strained relations with S. Africa. Don't worry – there'll be no war this month or next month either. Rain. Greek Government crisis

JULY : Settlement near in India. Railway strike. Butlin denounces Government "Holiday-at-Home." Rain. France without Government

AUGUST : Great "Come-to-Britain" tourist drive opens. Trains run late. Thames low, save water appeals. Showers. Greek Government crisis

SEPTEMBER : Threat of new Churchill statue starts armed insurrection in Dover. Million houses just round the corner. Rain. Crisis in India

OCTOBER : Unemployment relieved by announcement of Royal Command Film Show. Gales. Crises in France and Hollywood

NOVEMBER : New medical drug which prevents all diseases causes panic in Harley Street. Showers. French Government crisis

DECEMBER : Only 21 more shopping days to Christmas. Scientist invents Turkey that can't disappear. Frost. French, Greek and Chinese crises

this *danse macabre*, where echoes of Berlin cabarets mingle with a lightly scrambled memory of Daumier, he had said something about the threat of general oblivion that he was not, for the time being, going to better. What gives the composition an extra dimension of unearthliness is the sense of rush in the execution, as though Vicky could not bear a lengthy contemplation of it any more than we. It was emphatically not Gerald Barry's cup of tea.

Few years in Vicky's career would prove as hard to deal with as 1946. Little happened to encourage mirth, but on the other hand, any amelioration of conditions restricted Vicky's freedom to issue entertaining grumbles. 'With all these improvements there will be fewer subjects to be funny about,' as one of his cartoons remarked.[3] In politics he was generally reduced to fending off Tory propaganda, his most effective line being to depict himself as a classic black-clad anarchist researching the matter: 'Heavily disguised Vicky goes underground to see the people in revolt against the Attlee dictatorship . . .' He closed the year with 'Young Vicky's Almanack for 1947', a twelve-frame, month-by-month lunatic prediction of the coming year's events. With just the odd year missed, this idea was to remain a fixture in his calendar wherever he went, a skittish celebration of the fact that yet again he had survived Christmas.[4]

A six-page paper having been reintroduced in the autumn, 1947 began with a paradoxical renewal of the struggle for space, there

73 'Young Vicky's Almanack for 1947', *News Chronicle*, 31 December 1946

It is traditional in the press at year's end to round up and comment on events past and to make predictions for the coming year. Vicky takes the title of his contribution from the popular *Old Moore's Almanack*. This spoof shows Vicky's obsession with the British weather – specifically rain and gales – and includes a repeated gibe at the Labour government's housing programme.

MARK YOU, I TOLD 'EM ALL ALONG THAT FELLA RHODES WASN'T TO BE TRUSTED!

74A   Untitled pocket cartoon under pseudonym 'Smith', *News Chronicle*, 17 April 1947

74B   'Mark you, I told 'em all along that fella Rhodes wasn't to be trusted!', *Daily Express*, 9 October 1965 by Osbert Lancaster

Vicky's front-page pocket cartoons under the pseudonym 'Smith' appeared in March 1947 and lasted until 1949. It had been his own suggestion that the inclusion of such drawings was a good way of matching Osbert Lancaster's success with the style. However, Vicky often found himself short of ideas and re-used a lot from his 'Week-end Fantasia' drawings. This cartoon done with little flair depicts Vicky's stereotyped clubman. Osbert Lancaster, who drew for the *Daily Express* for forty-seven years until his death in 1986, is regarded as the inventor of the pocket cartoon in Britain and the master of that genre.

being more of it to argue over. A new element of anxiety was introduced by the departure of Gerald Barry. As the originator of the idea of a national celebration to mark the centenary of the Great Exhibition of 1851, he was duly entrusted with the task of carrying through to completion what became the Festival of Britain. Vicky was already worried about being 'funny' ('Here's a Vicky joke, dear' – 'Go on, make me laugh' ran one domestic exchange in the 'Fantasia')[5] but his reaction to the departure of his mentor was to take on more work. If he could not be sure of appreciation, he would make himself indispensable.

Worried that Osbert Lancaster was making a success of his pocket cartoons for the *Daily Express*, Vicky suggested that the *News Chronicle* respond in kind. This met with agreement, but also the objection that pocket cartoons signed by Vicky would give an impression of a meagrely staffed and funded paper. Thus it was that when Vicky's front-page miniatures began to appear, in mid-March 1947, they were signed with the deliberately down-beat and unmistakably English name of 'Smith'.

Nobody who looked hard at Smith can have been fooled for long. His responses to the latest daily twists in the story of Austerity were necessarily novel in one sense, but his joke mechanisms were mostly recyclings of Vicky's 'Weekend Fantasia'. Vicky had long ceased to take a pride in his Saturday chore ('It's worse than ever,' he wrote to Lucielle)[6] so it can hardly have given him much pleasure to plunder it for re-runs like the toff picking up a fag-end (later fossilised into Vicky's stock response to a Budget increase in tobacco tax); the slogan 'A woman's place is in the queue', another favourite while the shortages lasted; and the pedestrian with an L-plate, a particular friend of Vicky the lifelong non-motorist. Smith carried on producing only for as long as his creator could bear him. By the autumn of 1948 Vicky was adding the spoof signature just when he felt like it, and the following year the pseudonym died out altogether.[7] Thereafter, and to the end of his career, Vicky never again undertook to provide one-off gag items on a regular basis – except on Saturdays, which kept him busy with topical sillinesses for another decade.

Smith was certainly a tactical error, but he did not hold his master back. Vicky's work gained in strength and variety throughout 1947/8, and one strong reason for this consolidation is not far to seek. In January 1947 Vicky's naturalisation had been formally ratified at last. The ceremony disappointed him. 'I had imagined,' he said, 'a solemn ritual, complete with symbolic gestures and oaths, even perhaps some music. Instead, all there turned out to be was a little dried-up chap who pressed a bible into my hand, stuck his own hand out expectantly and rasped "Two-and-six".'[8]

Victor Weisz, Esquire, was elated nonetheless. Later in the day in Harley Street, he ran into his friend Beecher Moore, the American theatrical director, and a co-director with Alec Clunes of the Arts Theatre Club. Moore was astonished when Vicky slapped him across the chest and cried, 'You foreigner you!'[9] He could never feel nationalistic in a narrow sense ('I grew up as a foreigner in a foreign country')[10] but he did feel completely identified with Englishness. 'I mean, when I talk to you I do not say "they", I say "us",' he told an interviewer. 'There is a sense of humour which I like which was very difficult to acquire at first . . . Another quality which I admire very much is a sort of steadfastness once you've broken the ice with an Englishman. He's a very trustful friend, and I like that too.'[11]

Ironically, the first tangible benefit of citizenship was freedom to travel abroad. Vicky took his summer holiday in Berlin, returning with a reawakened memory of that strange local humour, both stoical and cynical, that he had been at pains to put out of his mind. He made drawings, and brought back topical jokes ('I've just seen a smashing limousine stopping in Zehlendorf, and no American got out!').[12] The trip gave him a fortnight's break from the *Chronicle*, but he left a small stockpile of possible Smiths to be getting on with – he could not bear to be unrepresented.

On his return he was married to Lucielle[13] – the beginning, alas, of a period of increasing strain. His work-load was now enormous: a daily political cartoon, with seldom a day missed; his pocket cartoons; the 'Fantasia', in which he now competed with himself for ideas; his theatrical caricatures; sundry column-breakers to illustrate Parliamentary proceedings and conferences; and the occasional portrait for a profile or a distinguished guest contributor. When his friend Stephen Potter took over the editorship of the *Leader*, Vicky even drew there too. At one point his friends and colleagues intervened to try to stop the treadmill. Tom Baistow, appointed spokesman of the impromptu committee, sought to introduce Vicky to the idea that he was doing too much. He was incensed by the suggestion, repulsing its luckless proposer with a shout of 'You're a *Gauleiter*!', about the worst accusation that readily sprang to mind. A couple of weeks later he had calmed down enough to realise that the message had been kindly meant, but his verdict was unchanged: he must struggle on, for the sake of 'continuity'.[14]

He was right in the sense that his raw material was continually improving. As the political world settled into more recognisable peacetime shapes, personalities emerged in whom Vicky could take a more proprietorial interest. De Gaulle's regal egocentricity

75 *'L'état, c'est moi', News Chronicle,*
8 April 1947

'I am the State,' said Louis XIV, the
French 'Sun King'. A legitimate
statement for a sovereign but one
inappropriate for a politician in a
democracy. De Gaulle had had limited
electoral success as leader of the
Rassemblement du Peuple Francais (RPF
– Assembly of the French People) in
1947, setting himself up as critic of the
Fourth Republic and its constitution.

(*L'État, C'Est Moi'*) was seen blooming as early as April 1947 –
an excellent investment for the Fifties, when the politically
intolerable and physically irresistible General would be one of
Vicky's stars. Another long-runner, R.A. Butler, had begun to
make regular appearances, often in command of a 'What the
Butler Saw' peepshow machine. (Butler made mock-doleful
reference to such a cartoon at the Tories' 1948 Conference in
Llandudno.)[15] Butler's face had not yet ripened into the melting
mass of convexities it later became, and Vicky's version of him
was tentative at first; but he continued to work on Butler, whom
he regarded as a promising closet radical in the Tory camp, and
again was richly rewarded in the following decade.

On the Labour side, Vicky took a by no means purely political
delight in the doings of Hugh Dalton, whose return to the cabinet

76 'What the butler saw', *News Chronicle*, 30 April 1947

R.A. Butler was always regarded as a progressive Tory, so it was fitting that he became chairman of Churchill's innovative Industrial Policy Committee. Here he presents his Industrial Charter to die-hards in a room upon whose walls are hung portraits of past and present Conservative leaders: Churchill, Baldwin, Disraeli and Chamberlain (or rather his umbrella).

WHAT THE BUTLER SAW

VICKY'S NATIONAL GALLERY
(CLEANED PICTURE DEPT.)

77 'Vicky's National Gallery (Cleaned Picture Dept.) "The Laughing Cavalier" is back', *News Chronicle*, 2 June 1948

Hugh Dalton had been appointed Chancellor of the Exchequer and a member of Attlee's unofficial inner cabinet in 1945. His policies were egalitarian, but he had been able to do little to rebalance Britain's post-war economy. He is remembered for being an advocate of cheap money when perhaps this was inappropriate and for his final indiscretion: on his way to make an emergency budget speech in November 1947, he leaked its contents to a London *Star* journalist in the Lobby. A year later, all seemed forgiven – Dalton rejoined the government as Chancellor of the Duchy of Lancaster.

'THE LAUGHING CAVALIER' IS BACK

ICE-COLD WAR

(after the exile occasioned by his famous Budget indiscretion) was celebrated in a rascally reworking of Frans Hals's 'Laughing Cavalier'. Dalton's chuckling countenance spared him a lot of trouble from Vicky. Like Herbert Morrison, whose quiff and wandering eye were his priceless trademarks, Dalton was short on what Vicky characterised as 'the Spirit of Keir Hardie',[16] but his sheer cartoonability staved off the worst of the artist's wrath. Less successful pictorially, but very much closer to Vicky's political centre of gravity, was Aneurin Bevan, whose spreading of panic through Harley Street caused Vicky great delight. He was an utterly convinced supporter of the National Health Service, and teased his dentist about it most devilishly as early as 1946: 'Engel filled a tooth for me and I told him that I'll be back in 1948 – because then we'll [have] the National Health Service and I needn't pay him – I don't think he liked that though.'[17]

Being now on the inside of British society, Vicky could afford to admit to himself that Britons had their faults. The national obsession with sport irked him. He dreaded the onset of the 1948 Olympic Games in London – as did a certain Bishop Carey, who at a youth rally in Hastings burbled: 'I am afraid of the Olympic Games. Some of them will cheat. Dagoes! We won't.'[18] For a time, this became Vicky's text for very proper attacks on British self-righteousness. But it was Germany and America that caused him most concern. Already he feared a renascence of German ambition, and specifically a revival of inadequately weeded-out Nazism. A small blond infant in *Lederhosen* and a Hitler moustache bodied forth his fears; and in his portrayals of traditional Prussians he alluded playfully to the style of George Grosz.

The United States presented a rather special problem to Vicky. His broad attitudes had been set long ago, in the Brecht/Weill world of criminal colonialists and crushed Oriental peoples – a

78 'Ice-cold war', *News Chronicle*, 5 February 1948

Foreign Ministers Bevin (Western Lions) and Molotov (Eastern Bears) defend their goals as General Marshall (US Secretary of State) and Stalin fight for the 'atom' puck. The Marshall Plan was a proposal to coordinate a long-term programme for European economic rehabilitation and to share US atomic and nuclear technology with Britain. It was not well received by the Soviet Union which took it as a manifestation of American imperialism in Europe. The Plan had the effect of highlighting divisions between Eastern and Western bloc alliances.

79 Untitled, *News Chronicle*, 22 March 1948

Vicky inverts his relationship with six world figures – Churchill, Franco, Bevin, Molotov, De Gaulle and Marshall – by representing their (imagined) views of him. This cartoon is one of a number in which Vicky draws himself as if by others.

theme which Korea now kept alive. Vicky harboured an almost physical resentment of America's power. He feared her domination of Western culture, and her devoted pursuit of what he saw as runaway science. Harry Truman he presented as a Walter Mitty figure (the reference was topical)[19] with dreams of settling international disputes the muscular way. Vicky deplored, of course, the 'Anti-Red Smear War'; and while he took at first an impartial view of the Cold War ('Ice Cold War', in February 1948, showed the Western Lions playing the Eastern Bears at ice-hockey), it was the American statesmen who would make most appearances with icicles on their noses.

In Gerald Barry's day, Vicky's freedom to comment on these matters would rarely have been restricted. But Barry's successor, Robin Cruikshank, was one of America's staunchest Fleet Street allies. During the war he had held a senior co-ordinating post in the press corps in Washington,[20] and his wife, who reputedly left Cruikshank in no doubt of her disapproval of Vicky, was herself American. Remembered by one member of his staff as 'a nice chap . . . but hopelessly weak and pussyfooting as an editor',[21] Cruikshank began to come into open conflict with Vicky over his stance on American foreign policy.

Never shy of involving the readers by dramatising his difficulties, Vicky turned the disharmony into cartoon ideas. 'Your cartoonist, sick and tired of being funny, has decided that it's easier

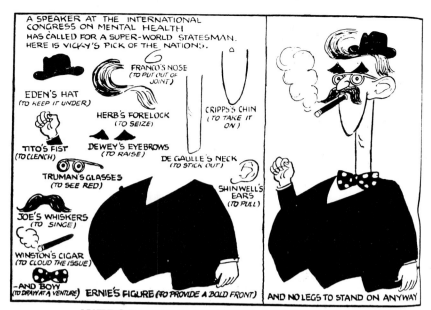

A SPEAKER AT THE INTERNATIONAL CONGRESS ON MENTAL HEALTH HAS CALLED FOR A SUPER-WORLD STATESMAN. HERE IS VICKY'S PICK OF THE NATIONS.

EDEN'S HAT (TO KEEP IT UNDER)

FRANCO'S NOSE (TO PUT OUT OF JOINT)

HERB'S FORELOCK (TO SEIZE)

CRIPPS'S CHIN (TO TAKE IT ON)

TITO'S FIST (TO CLENCH)

DEWEY'S EYEBROWS (TO RAISE)

DE GAULLE'S NECK (TO STICK OUT)

TRUMAN'S GLASSES (TO SEE RED)

SHINWELL'S EARS (TO PULL)

JOE'S WHISKERS (TO SINGE)

WINSTON'S CIGAR (TO CLOUD THE ISSUE)

—AND BOW (TO DRAW AT A VENTURE) ERNIE'S FIGURE (TO PROVIDE A BOLD FRONT)

AND NO LEGS TO STAND ON ANYWAY

INTRODUCING VICKY'S MR WAFFLE

80 'Introducing Vicky's Mr Waffle', *News Chronicle*, 19 August 1948

In his book *Ye Madde Designer* (London, Studio, 1935, p.20) the cartoonist David Low makes a key point about the 'caricature of personality' as he calls it. Generally politicians like to be drawn and often famous idiosyncrasies or 'tabs of identity' are encouraged by those who possess them. Here Vicky has fun with those 'tabs of identity' to compile a statesman. He takes the joke further by commenting on personality traits as well – President Truman's fear of communism, for example.

to be a model', ran one caption, with Vicky posing in a corner while his favourite victims take the opportunity of drawing him as 'Bolshie-Vicky, Fellow-traveller Vicky, un-American Vicky', and so on. An even more pointed record of Vicky's troubles is 'A Cartoonist in Search of New Faces', where it is recorded in so many words that 'The Editor, tired of Vicky's cartoons, has ordered him to find some new faces . . .'[22] The best of them, a Bevin-sized composite figure called Mr Battlee, demonstrates the confidence Vicky now had in his stock Cabinet figures; he could afford to mingle and blend them – and continued to make quite a science of the process, producing in later years such audaciously complex mongrels as 'General Macadenhower'.[23] Vicky's attempt at a generic composite, like 1948's 'Mr Waffle', failed to catch on, though his billing as 'super world-statesman' is an interesting pre-echo of Vicky's greatest hit.

His enthusiasm for the Labour administration (and he was at one with the mass of the public over this) suffered more from the persisting general drabness of life than from any individual measure or policy. Finding an apt quotation closer to home than usual, he brought forth a passage from J.B. Priestley's *The Linden Tree*: '. . . we are trying to do a wonderful thing here. But somehow not in a wonderful way. There is a kind of grey chilly hollowness inside, where there ought to be gaiety, colour, warmth, ambition . . .'[24] The longing for mass uplift (which Gerald Barry, in his way, was hoping to satisfy in 1951) represented a continuing bond between Priestley and Vicky, who supplied a long succession

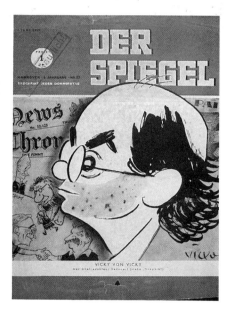

81 '*Vicky von Vicky*', *Der Spiegel*, 2 June 1949

Aged only thirty-six, Vicky is featured in a self-portrait and montage of his work on the front cover of the influential German current affairs magazine *Der Spiegel*. This is a clear indication of the respect he was able to command on the Continent at this time.

82 'In Hollywood: "Who's the guy in the fancy dress?"', *News Chronicle*, 22 September 1949

This drawing is one of five which accompanied Vicky's article, entitled 'Fourteen days that shook Vicky', about his two-week trip to the United States in the company of forty-nine journalists from fourteen countries in September 1949. In it he could not disguise the difficulties he had with the people there and the culture shock he suffered. 'They [are] almost childlike in their efforts to please and to be liked. They are ill-informed about world affairs . . . America is well on the way to becoming a nation on wheels. There is a garage and petrol station on almost every street corner of every town, but hardly a single theatre in any town outside New York.' However he was surprised to find that he liked San Francisco and made a favourable comment freely – 'She is a beautiful city, cultured, cosmopolitan and fascinating.'

IN HOLLYWOOD: 'WHO'S THE GUY IN THE FANCY DRESS?'

of column-breaker caricatures for the Yorkshire sage. Feeling misunderstood by his readers in 1950, Priestley was moved to grunt 'Sometimes I feel that only the glorious Vicky is with me.'[25]

Escaping from similar feelings of his own, Vicky travelled as widely and often as exchange restrictions would permit. From Dublin, Paris and Rome he returned with light, unemphatic pen-and-ink sketches in his Stratford style, and sometimes a brief prose commentary too (of Rome he noted that 'in this city of contrast there seem to be only two classes – the very well dressed and the beggars in rags . . .').[26] And in September 1949, 'having been vaccinated – scrutinised – and finger-printed',[27] Vicky flew off in a Stratocruiser with a party of forty-nine European journalists to discover America. It was a very important trip for him, potentially a turning-point in the development of his beliefs. This time he returned with a fuller account of his journey. Its title, amusingly redolent of Bolshevism, was 'Fourteen Days That Shook Vicky'.[28]

It was an even-handed report. The cigar-smoking businessmen of America all looked alike to Vicky, whether in California, Texas, Detroit or New York; and talking to them 'made me see that our own conservatives are a pack of pink revolutionaries'. In Texas he was bitten by 'the largest mosquito in the world'. He detested Los Angeles, a 'city without pedestrians', and formed the impression that there was 'hardly a single theatre in any town

98

ELECTION STAKES

SAME OLD TORY PARTY

LOVE ME—LOVE MY HORSE

83 'Love me – love my horse', *News Chronicle*, 3 October 1949

Clement Attlee had to call a General Election before July 1950 (this date marked the end of the constitutional maximum of five years for a government). Key ministers – Morrison, Cripps and Bevin – were ailing and although many middle-ground voters accepted Labour's achievements, there was a question-mark over how far continued wartime controls would be acceptable to the electorate. However, in Labour's favour was the fear that a Conservative victory would mean a return to the high unemployment of the pre-war era. Churchill is shown here leading a carthorse to the election start line, when perhaps he needs a thoroughbred.

outside New York'. On the other hand, he 'fell in love with San Francisco at first sight'; shook hands with President Truman (complimenting him, it was later revealed, on resembling Vicky's caricature of him more closely than the perpetrator expected); and found 'most heartening of all . . . the sight of the newest sky-scraper, which is to house the United Nations. One can almost see it grow under one's eyes . . .'[29] This was the same structure that would appear in Vicky's later cartoons as a gravestone.

All in all, Vicky was content to give an impression of America that cannot have greatly deepened the alarm of his editor, Cruik-shank. Vicky's quarrel was always with governments, never with peoples. His visit, in any case, was unmistakably more successful than the next he made, to Germany, where he failed to entice Konrad Adenauer into sitting for him; fell foul of the Bonn bureaucrats ('among them a gentleman who had to be addressed as Dr Dr Brandt'); and was chilled again by the Germans in the mass ('they are industrious, callous, virile and self-pitying').[30] The more he saw of Germany, the more convinced Vicky became that he had been a Berliner – a different species altogether.

Late in 1949, a cartoon called 'Love Me – Love My Horse', with Churchill leading 'the same old Tory party', signalled that election-time was approaching again. A similar scheme, with a dog taking the party's role, had served Vicky well in 1945.[31] But now he was in less hopeful mood. When Attlee issued an anti-climactic call to the nation, he was portrayed as wringing a stran-

99

84 'Cartoonists' Forum', *News Chronicle*, 13 January 1950

Vicky uses the device of guest cartoonists to present an editor-pleasing cartoon. Through his Tory cartoonist, 'Stunt', he reminds his readers of Churchill's 'Gestapo' speech from 1945, while 'Pinky' (the Labour cartoonist) portrays the government in a kindly light. Although Vicky was conscious of compromising himself by producing this kind of cartoon, he took the idea further. On 16 January 1950 he introduced his Liberal cartoonist, 'Midway'.

gled 'peep' from a heraldic trumpet. (Hugh Gaitskell and Edward Heath, likewise orators of limited passion, met the same fate.)[32] Vicky well knew that administering public kicks to the infuriatingly undemonstrative premier was a waste of time, but he did it just the same – on the extreme off-chance that Labour might abruptly lose patience and replace him with a firebrand: Aneurin Bevan, as it might have been.

Despite all exasperations, it was clear that Vicky would be recommending a Labour vote in the polls announced for 23 February 1950; and equally clear that the *News Chronicle*, as ever, would endorse the Liberals. If Vicky had been intransigent, or his editor courageous, there would have been a splendid clash of opinions. But a gentlemanly compromise was arranged. 'True to tradition,' ran the caption introducing it, 'Vicky hands over his pen to guest cartoonists of all parties, who will deal with the burning issues of the Election . . .' Vicky's 'guests' were his own inventions: 'Stunt, the famous mirth-provoking Tory artist', and 'Pinky, the official Transport House cartoonist'. The spoof cartoons they produced did little to obscure Vicky's own allegiances, but they did mute his views and put a little insulating distance between cartoon and leader-column. Three days later, Vicky repaired a rather glaring omission by introducing 'the brilliant Young Liberal, Midway'. It was, as a contemporary observer

SHADOW AND SUBSTANCE

remarked, 'an excellent compromise with an awkward situation, but it was nevertheless a compromise'.[33] Once free of the *Chronicle*, Vicky never allowed himself to be put into such a position again.

He had in any case made a loud contribution already to the Election debate, and in his own voice. *Up The Poll!*, subtitled 'The Sap's Guide to the General Election', is one of the best-known pieces of comic propaganda in post-war British politics. Its text was the work of Olga Katzin (later Olga Miller), alias 'Sagittarius' of the *New Statesman*, a good friend of Vicky's and one of his liveliest sparring-partners in the sphere of café-continental debate which occupied, along with chess, his scant leisure time. 'Sagittarius' had delighted the newly-married Vicky and Lucielle by giving them for a wedding-present a handsome stair-carpet and stair-rods. She and Vicky had already collaborated successfully in 1947 with *Let Cowards Flinch*, an elegantly produced satire of Labour's post-war 'Revolution', clothing Attlee's Cabinet in the Jacobin togs of 1789. Taking its title from the Labour anthem ('Though cowards flinch and traitors sneer/We'll keep the red flag flying here!'), *Cowards* deplored the prevalence of Oxonians and Etonians in the top Cabinet posts; foresaw the victory of the traditional 'digestive' processes of politics over radicalism ('The Labour Dispensation still permits/Speech to the Upper Chamber . . .'); and concluded with the couplet: 'And Labour's Government with pride will claim,/"The more we change, the more we are the same!"'' Vicky responded by adapt-

85 'Shadow and substance', in *Up the Poll! – the Sap's Guide to the General Election* by 'Sagittarius', London, Turnstile Press, 1950

Morrison, Cripps, Bevin and Attlee stand with shadows not their own but Churchill's. The caption is teasingly ambiguous. Who has substance – which side is shadowy?

ing his normally serious loose-line style very persuasively to a comic 'period feel'.

Up The Poll! takes none of the earlier satire back, and even adds a few swipes (Bevin is twinned with Churchill as Tweedledum and Tweedledee, their foreign policies indistinguishable). At the same time, a powerful plea for a Labour vote is uttered, while at a third level the book as a whole is offered with a mocking veneer of neutrality. 'Even the most superficial study of these pages will, it is earnestly hoped, prove invaluable to the inexperienced elector both in helping him to choose his Party – and to keep the Party clean.' Vicky deploys this time his jolly, spur-of-the-moment style – the one that had served 'Smith' and the 'Fantasia' well, and was now increasingly invading his daily political cartoons, driving out the remnants of Low-like formality. The growing economy of this new manner (into which a strong dash of Winnington had been successfully incorporated) showed up particularly well in the treatment of Attlee's face, which Vicky, taking the plainness of the man's personality literally, had reduced to half a dozen lines, two dots, and a moustache. The most famous page in the book took sparsity to its limit: headed 'Conservative Party Policy', it was a blank sheet, signed 'Woolton'[34] at the bottom.

It was as well for Vicky's morale that he had contributed so wholeheartedly to the electoral preparations, for on the day itself – his first opportunity fully to participate in British democracy – he found himself unable to influence the outcome: he had been left off the voting register. He spent the day, according to a cartoon immortalising his agony, seeing so many Xs everywhere that he ended up filling in the football pools.[35]

The election left Labour still in office, but virtually paralysed by a majority that started in single figures and shrank. Vicky, aping the backstairs negotiation for minority support in the Commons (and possibly anxious to disguise as a running idea his pre-election accommodation with Cruikshank and the editorial board) 'called together' his three party cartoonists 'to try to reach a working agreement'. This possibility was destroyed by 'Stunt', the Tory artist, who slung paint at his rivals with a cry of 'You Red!'[36] A perjury verdict had just gone against Alger Hiss in the United States, and the heyday of the Red Scare was on. Vicky drew Senator McCarthy administering a Loyalty Test to the Statue of Liberty: 'You're known to be of foreign extraction and to hold most subversive views'[37] – a description Vicky had now begun to hear applied to himself.

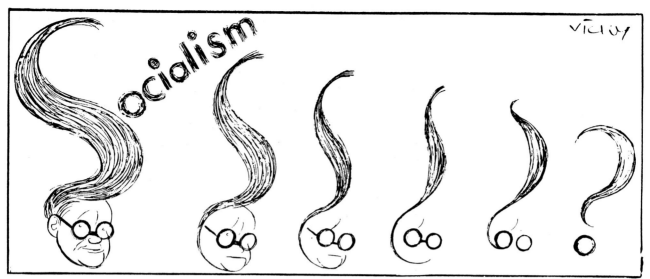

'THE INEVITABILITY OF GRADUALNESS'
—In memory of Sidney Webb.

Labour's precarious position lent an enlivening urgency to Vicky's imaginings. Though by now he had little faith left in the redness of Herbert Morrison's socialism (in an artful abstract sequence, he drew Herbie's famous quiff dwindling from an S-for-Socialism to a question-mark), he respected Morrison's energy in keeping Labour's tiny majority in business, and made much sport of his whipping-in the halt, the lame, the sick and the mad for critical divisions in the House. (It was around this time that Morrison enquired of Vicky why he drew him with such tiny legs. 'To save ink,' Vicky replied.)[38]

But when Sir Stafford Cripps succumbed to illness, a characteristic outburst of dismay greeted the promotion of Hugh Gaitskell. 'Dear Chancellor,' wrote Vicky in his Open Letter, 'they tell me that you are not cartoonable . . .' Having suggested some extremely remote possibilities of image-enhancement – that Gaitskell should present himself, for example, as a second Lloyd George – Vicky left it up to the victim. 'Now what will you do for me?'[39] On this occasion his entreaties were largely rhetorical. Gaitskell soon arrived at his definitive cartoon state, and without benefit of props. It was not to Gaitskell's appearance that Vicky would object, but to his partiality for the crown of the political road. Vicky was forced repeatedly to insist 'Keep Left' (the title of a famous pamphlet of the period),[40] even though it invariably meant drawing motoring scenes, of which Vicky was not fond.

86 '"The inevitability of gradualness" – In memory of Sidney Webb', *News Chronicle*, 22 May 1950

Sidney Webb's presidential address to the Labour Party conference in June 1923 emphasised the Party's attachment to evolutionary socialism and the rejection of extremist elements – specifically communism. Here Vicky suggests that this philosophy, as embodied in Herbert Morrison's winning manifestos of 1945 and 1950, could lead to the Labour Party losing direction.

87 'Parting is such sweet sorrow',
News Chronicle, 10 March 1951

Ernest Bevin was seventy on 9 March
1951. He suffered from serious angina
and had been too ill to accompany
Attlee to Washington in December
1950 to see President Truman. Attlee
now asked him to resign his office.
Within three months Bevin was dead.

PARTING IS SUCH SWEET SORROW

In March 1951 Ernie Bevin too fell fatally ill. Casting himself
outrageously as Juliet, Vicky threw a rose from the balcony to
his 'favourite model' – in the physical rather than political sense.
With Bevin's foreign policy, vis-à-vis America and in the Middle

"AUX ARMES ! WE'RE IN DREADFUL DANGER OF PEACE ..!"

East, Vicky had found much to quarrel. Bevin died a few weeks later, in the same month when Vicky made his first visit to Israel. He was never a Zionist; privately he would favour the idea that Jews should become assimilated wherever they were – which, of course, was relatively easy for a non-religious Jew to say. As Israeli governments became more and more reliant on American financial and philosophical backing, he was increasingly troubled by their stridency; and he had a lively sense of the injustices that had been visited upon the Arab world (French policy in Algeria would bring out a rash of 'grims'). But in 1951 it was too soon to consider such possibilities. 'Above all,' Vicky wrote, 'I have seen children laugh – children who will never know the inside of a ghetto.'[41] The sketch-impressions he brought back were published in the *Jewish Chronicle* as well as Vicky's own paper. In his *Jewish Chronicle* text he went out of his way to stress the physical various-

88 '*Aux Armes!* We're in dreadful danger of peace . . .!', *Evening Standard*, 15 February 1962

The French colony of Algeria experienced many atrocities and terror campaigns in its fight for independence during the years 1954–62. In July 1958 De Gaulle launched an attack on FLN (*Front de Libération National*) strongholds and the indigenous Moslems vowed war to the death. The OAS (*Organisation de l'Armée Secrète*) then began a bombing campaign both in Algeria and in Paris. These acts of terrorism alienated the French public from any attachment they may have had to Algeria.

89 Untitled, *News Chronicle*,
23 April 1951

Aneurin (Nye) Bevan, leader of the so-
called radical wing of the Labour Party
was responsible for the National
Health Service Bill of 1946 which
provided free medical treatment for
all. Subsequent concern over Britain's
capacity to pay for its rearmament
programme led Hugh Gaitskell,
Chancellor of the Exchequer, to
propose putting a charge on dentures
and spectacles. Bevan resigned in
protest. He was supported by Harold
Wilson, President of the Board of
Trade, and John Freeman,
Parliamentary Secretary to the
Minister of Supply, both of whom also
resigned. It is curious that Vicky did
not depict Gaitskell in the rowing
boat, but this probably refers to
Bevan's resentment at being passed
over when Morrison accepted the offer
of Bevin's old job at the Foreign
Office.

ness of the Israelis: 'I have seen Jews of every colour . . .'[42] He
could not have borne it if his own people had constructed a racially
monolithic notion of its own destiny. His fondest memories were
of Haifa, where work momentarily caught up with him: he met
the *Punch* cartoonist David Langdon in the street.

Back in London it was a year of ruptures. Aneurin Bevan, followed by Harold Wilson, resigned from the Cabinet over the
introduction of health charges designed to finance defence spending. In a design that became a favourite, always subtly varied in
detail, Vicky saw Bevan and Morrison rowing a boat so
vigorously in opposite directions that the craft split in two. (He
subsequently preferred to exploit such situations before the final
sundering: an intact boat being rowed in two directions at once
created a greater tension and sense of anomaly.) A month later,
Vicky was paying health charges himself. In hospital for an operation, he pictured himself at the mercy of surgeons still seething
over his Harley Street cartoons at the time of the Health Bill.
The operation itself was a straightforward one. Like the Labour
Party, Vicky had suffered a hernia.

A fortnight later he was back at the *Chronicle*, continuing his
new pocket-size series ('New Cries of London', with rhyming

VICKY laughs at himself

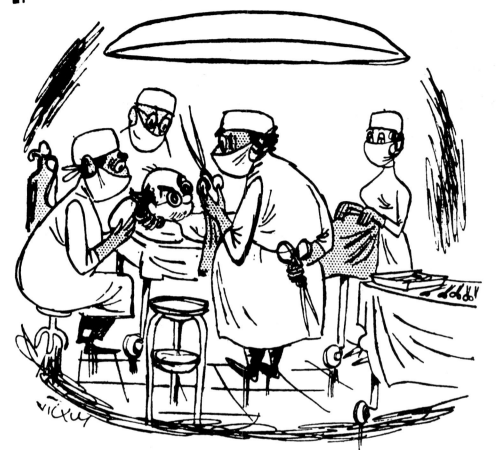

D'you re-member that funny car-toon you did about Harley Street, eh?

Vicky went to hospital on Saturday for an operation. Yesterday's re-port: Patient doing well

90 'D'you remember that funny cartoon you did about Harley Street, eh?', *News Chronicle*, 29 May 1951

The establishment of the National Health Service was very controversial as far as doctors were concerned, particularly in the initial stages. They feared for their independence but soon up to 90 per cent agreed that the NHS was a good and fair way of redistributing medical services throughout the whole country. Vicky's cartoons had been directed against those who were not in favour of a national service and who wished to maintain their private practices. This cartoon's editorial line was 'Vicky laughs at himself' – he was in hospital for a hernia operation.

91 Untitled, *News Chronicle*, 27 October 1951

The Conservative election victory in October 1951 marked the beginning of thirteen continuous years in office for the Tories. As the old guard leave – Gaitskell, Attlee and Morrison (in tears) – Vicky prepares to meet the personalities who will people his cartoons in the future. He is very anxious; the chains indicate he will have to work hard at capturing likenesses. Nearly all carry name cards – Churchill heads the queue, behind him Anthony Eden and Lord Woolton. Brendan Bracken is seventh in line and a triumphant Beaverbrook brings up the rear. The sign Vicky has prepared refers to a phrase Churchill used on 8 October 1951, 'The difference between our outlook and the Socialist outlook is the difference between the ladder and the queue.'

texts by 'Sagittarius'),[43] and beating Labour's resolve into shape in time for the now inescapable early election. Labour's Cabinet were ruthlessly cast as 'Six Characters in Search of a Policy'.[44] Gaitskell, already emerging as a compromiser, advised Attlee in a Grand Prix scenario to keep 'right on the middle of the road'. Back came the 'guest cartoonists' to spare the blushes of editor Cruikshank. 'Pinky' declared himself a Bevanite. 'Stunt' issued his instruction to 'throw out those wicked Socialists', while Vicky stood in the corner of the frame mutely appealing to his readers.

Alas, it was in vain. The Conservative majority was not large, but large enough. Even as Winston Churchill was forming his government, Vicky drew himself chained to his drawing-board, in tears, a bottle of 'venom' at the ready.[45]

Vicky in Opposition 6

During September 1945 Vicky produced a 'Weekend Fantasia' in which a learned judge requested the guidance of the court with the query 'What *is* a banana?' It is a measure of the unchanging colourlessness of the Austerity age that the joke could be repeated exactly, and with equal topicality, seven years later, at the end of 1952. In spite of all the Attlee government had managed to do, the British public was still suffering a numbness, a moral fatigue, from which, some might argue, it has yet to make a full recovery.

For Vicky it had been a period of consolidation and camaraderie. The atmosphere among the confrères at the *News Chronicle* was cosy – even 'dozy', to use James Cameron's word.[1] Cameron himself was about to be added to the merrily turbulent office crowd, bringing to Vicky's life one of its most important friendships. Between Cameron's political convictions and Vicky's, one mutual friend observed, there was not a cigarette-paper's width.[2] The same, sadly, did not go for the senior staff-men. The arrival of Robert Reid as Features Editor added weight to the anti-Vicky lobby, for Reid was a facts man. He was not on Vicky's wavelength and chose not to tune in.

On the positive side, Vicky had for the first time in his daily-paper career a wholly Conservative government to oppose. Having got over his ritual complaint about the Cabinet (which he claimed 'runs to a pattern both in features and dress'),[3] he found them a highly productive set of targets. Immediately below the level of Churchill, the figure-head, or rather hat-rack – Vicky had taken to piling a tower of symbolic headgear upon the venerable leader – a subtly contentious interplay could be discerned between the two neo-Edwardians, Eden and Macmillan (commonly shown together as 'The Western Brothers'), and Rab Butler, still suspected of being a 'progressive Tory'.

More provoking still was the infusion of new blood from across the Atlantic. A year in advance of the US elections, a character called Dulles had come to Vicky's notice – to be introduced with heavy irony as 'John Foster Dulles, Optician – our specialists will make you recognise almost anything – EVEN Chiang Kai-Shek.'

92A 'Vicky's Week-end Fantasia', *News Chronicle*, 22 September 1945

92B 'Vicky's Week-end Fantasia', *News Chronicle*, 29 November 1952

The effect of continuing austerity and wartime controls is clearly seen in two frames of these 'Week-end Fantasia' cartoons. Although drawn over seven years apart, Vicky's judge enquires in both, 'What is a banana?'.

93 '"One man in his time plays many parts" – *As You Like It*', *Daily Mirror*, 30 November 1954 (detail)

Sir Winston Churchill wears all the hats belonging to his long career in the public eye. He was first elected to Parliament as Tory MP for Oldham in 1900 at the age of twenty-six, before joining the Liberals in 1904 and establishing a reputation as a reforming minister. During the 1930s, again allied to the Conservatives, he was in the political wilderness, having resigned from the Shadow Cabinet in protest at his party's support of self-government in India. However he continued to make his voice heard from the back benches, warning Chamberlain and Baldwin of the growing Nazi menace. When Chamberlain resigned in 1940 he advised the King to ask Churchill to form a government. Now able to demonstrate his skills as a leader and orator, Churchill did not retire until 1955.

94 Untitled, *New Statesman*, 25 April 1959

Vicky prepared this collage as a memorial to John Foster Dulles who, as Secretary of State in the Eisenhower administration for six years from 1953, had dominated not only foreign policy but Western strategy as a whole. He was rigidly opposed to negotiation with the USSR and saw the developing world (particularly China) through the distorted lenses of ideological anti-communism. His policy of 'brinkmanship' – a diplomatic technique of advancing to the verge of war without actually fighting – and the use of the phrase 'massive retaliation' (referring to the use of nuclear weapons) when describing American responses to Soviet aggression, alarmed American liberals and Europeans alike.

Later Vicky would turn the controversy round, focusing not so much on America's endorsement of Nationalist China as on her persistent refusal to recognise Mao's vast Communist nation. Vicky, interpreting this as a stubbornly maintained myopia of Dulles's own, eventually rounded off the ophthalmic theme by equipping him with brick-wall lenses.

The Secretary of State on his first appearances resembled his classic Vicky manifestation hardly at all. The version of him that ultimately evolved was as much a stereotype as a caricature. In the case of certain victims – George Brown would be another such – one tended to accept Vicky's version without registering the objection that the original human model actually looked rather different. It was as if the emblematic rendition of the character, the badge representing him, became for the purposes of his role in Vicky's international cast more important than any accurate record of his features. Like David Low before him, Vicky affected to believe in any case that the personages he drew would gradually learn to resemble his versions of them anyway. It was the kind of remark that interviewers were sure to treasure.

Once he had the measure of a political figure, Vicky was capable of reaching well into the territory of hallucination for his

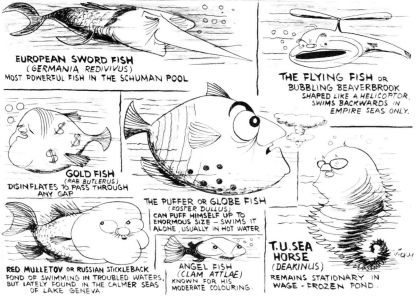

EUROPEAN SWORD FISH
(GERMANIA REDIVIVUS)
MOST POWERFUL FISH IN THE SCHUMAN POOL

THE FLYING FISH OR
BUBBLING BEAVERBROOK
SHAPED LIKE A HELICOPTOR.
SWIMS BACKWARDS IN
EMPIRE SEAS ONLY.

GOLD FISH
(RAB BUTLERUS)
DISINFLATES TO PASS THROUGH
ANY GAP

THE PUFFER OR GLOBE FISH
(FOSTER DULLUS)
CAN PUFF HIMSELF UP TO
ENORMOUS SIZE – SWIMS IT
ALONE, USUALLY IN HOT WATER

RED MULLETOV OR RUSSIAN STICKLEBACK
FOND OF SWIMMING IN TROUBLED WATERS,
BUT LATELY FOUND IN THE CALMER SEAS
OF LAKE GENEVA

ANGEL FISH
(CLAM ATTLAE)
KNOWN FOR HIS
MODERATE COLOURING.

T.U. SEA
HORSE
(DEAKINUS)
REMAINS STATIONARY IN
WAGE-FROZEN POND.

THE NATIONAL AQUARIUM EXHIBITION OPENS IN LONDON TO-DAY.

metaphorical 'likenesses'. Cabinet ministers could be turned into motor-cars: at Motor Show time a whole range could be displayed, with the simple outlines of Clem Attlee's face suiting the treatment particularly well. On dull days in the early 1950s, Vicky extended the genre, with spotters' guides to fish, wild animals and birds, all of them disclosing the features of well-known politicians. It was an exercise in pushing public faces to the very limits of recognisability, the joke being embellished with the Latin appellations of the sub-species and descriptions of their habits.

95 'The national aquarium exhibition opens in London today', *Daily Mirror*, 10 June 1954

Vicky has fun with the personalities currently inhabiting the world stage. An evergreen Adenauer is seen as the most powerful politician in Western Europe. (In 1950 Robert Schuman propounded the 'Schuman Plan' for pooling the coal and steel resources of Western Europe.) Newspaper-owner Beaverbrook had campaigned for Empire Free Trade in 1929 and was the Minister responsible for much-needed aircraft production in the early 1940s. As Chancellor of the Exchequer, R.A. Butler was the architect of 'Credit Squeeze' budgets. John Foster Dulles was an inflexible man, often rash in his tactical dealings with world leaders. Vyacheslav Molotov, Foreign Minister in the Malenkov government, latterly became involved in peace initiatives. Clement Attlee, a retiring man, was not one to subscribe to Churchill's maxim that 'in politics . . . it pays to advertise'. Arthur Deakin became Chairman of the TUC in 1951 and believed in organisation rather than agitation. ('TU Sea Horse' refers to fellow-cartoonist David Low's invention of the TUC carthorse in 1945.)

Foreign Minister Eden attempts reconciliation as relations between Britain and Egypt become strained over the stationing of 10,000 British troops in the Suez Canal zone. Increasingly Egypt came to view this occupation as an indignity until finally in October 1951 she denounced the 1936 Anglo-Egyptian treaty although it still had five years to run. The British lion and a pastiche of an Egyptian animal god glare at each other in this frieze, with the dissolute King Farouk flanking the seated goddess. In Shakespeare's play, Mark Antony's infatuation with Cleopatra, the Queen of Egypt, causes him to be lured into battle against overwhelming odds.

Interestingly, the one British political figure Vicky found it hard to integrate into these merriments was Aneurin Bevan. Even Vicky's standard image of Bevan was unsatisfactory: its neck was too thick. In his Introduction to Vicky's first major collection of post-war work, *Stabs in the Back*, Robin Cruikshank made a sporting attempt at a justification of this, suggesting that the figure 'has the air of being carved out of stone. One can imagine Vicky finding it on a desert island and wondering what strange god it typified.' It is certainly true that some suggestion of an Easter Island statue hangs about the bull-necked Bevan. But Cruikshank rather spoilt things when he went on to claim that 'the artist seems to be saying that for good or evil Bevan is a monolithic figure that stands outside the main stream of our political life'. How Cruikshank must have wished Vicky did believe this. On the contrary, Bevan stood centrally in the stream of Vicky's hopes, and demonstrated not the slightest potential for evil, in spite of a couple of sulphurous resignations, until 1957. If he was monolithic, it was because the cartoonist saw in him the heroic muscularity of the mining community; it was another example

ANTHONY AND CLEOPATRA—

(ACT I, SCENE II)

– one of the last – of Vicky's attempts to offer praise through muscular bulk. Over the years, Bevan gradually lost his sublime goitre, and became a human, identifiable first through his tumbling lock of hair. A certain uneasiness persisted. Vicky had made a big investment in Bevan. His happiest drawings of the man are platform sketches done from life at conferences.

Vicky's work was gaining all the time in acuity. His very first post-election cartoon showed Eden facing the problem of Suez, though only the fellow-prophets among his readers will have noted the clairvoyance of that. He qualified now for international assignments. With the political writer Vernon Bartlett, he visited Paris late in 1951 to sit in on a session of the United Nations assembly, and here he suffered curious rebuff. Having drawn a sketch of the Secretary of State, Dean Acheson, he approached him with a request to sign it (Vicky's early Berlin training in these small acts of effrontery had paid off). But Acheson's reply was unwelcome. 'No!' he barked. 'Too ugly. Come back with something better.' 'Such a thing has never happened before to Vicky,' the *News Chronicle* reported.

Was it merely the relaxation of space restrictions that caused Cruikshank to surround Vicky with other artists? Or was he preparing a second line of defence? In Ronald Searle he secured a brilliant stylist for feature illustrations. The Australian Arthur Horner arrived fully mature with a nonchalant style that particularly pleased the readers in his 'Colonel Pewter' strip. The addition of Sprod in 1953 meant that at last someone was giving full-time attention to the pocket cartoon, a genre Vicky had more or less relinquished.

There was no animosity between Vicky and the new men,[4] but their presence put an added strain on a sensibility already battered by the task of defending his work against editorial niggling. Vicky was sleeping badly, even for him. During the heatwave of July 1952 he blamed his insomnia on the temperature. Escaping to Italy for a holiday he blamed it on the noise in the 'land of *fortissimo*'. His stay in Rapallo offered one consolation in the form of a meeting with Max Beerbohm; Vicky's portrait of the great caricaturist became his *New Statesman* obituary drawing four years later.[5]

Most of September Vicky spent in Moscow, having 'made it clear . . . to the Soviet authorities that he would go only as an unbiased, independent observer'.[6] He turned the experience into a book, *Meet the Russians*, which contains some amusing asides ('after a week there it seemed quite natural to be shaved by a

97 Dean Acheson, *News Chronicle*, 14 November 1951

Dean Acheson was Secretary of State in the Truman administration from 1949 to 1953 and was instrumental in the formation of the North Atlantic Treaty Organisation (NATO). After Vicky had drawn this sketch at the United Nations Assembly in Paris, he asked Acheson to sign it. Acheson refused, saying 'No! Too ugly. Come back with something better'.

98A 'Old peasant', in *Meet the Russians*, London, Max Reinhardt, 1953

98B 'Perfume shop on Gorky Street', in *Meet the Russians*, London, Max Reinhardt, 1953

This book is a record of a three-week visit Vicky made to Moscow in September 1952 at the invitation of the British Society for Cultural Relations with the USSR. His own captions to these two drawings are 'The face of Russia has changed – but this old Russian peasant could have stepped out of the pages of a Tolstoy novel' and 'There are quite a number of perfume shops in Moscow. The favourite perfumes are called Red Moscow, The Kremlin, Magnolia and White Lilac'.

woman barber') and some mild scepticism about Stalin ('Father knows best'), but whose broad purpose was to reassure a shivering Cold War public that their ideological 'enemies' were neither robots nor monsters.

Vicky did not neglect to research his own trade while in the Russian capital.

> I told my colleagues that quite often in Britain, a Cabinet Minister would ask for the original of a cartoon attacking him. Would this, I asked, be possible in the Soviet Union? One artist revealed in reply that a few weeks previously he had used a *Krokodil* cartoon to attack the director of a factory which was turning out shoddy goods. Two days after my cartoon appeared he was sacked. Do you think this man asked me for the original of the cartoon?

In spite of this rather chilling evidence, one is left with the distinct feeling that Vicky's European sensibility was more at home in a society where 'the appetite for the arts is enormous and general' than he had been among the cigars and giant mosquitoes of America.

Back in Britain, the change in the national mood which Gerald

Barry's Festival of Britain had ultimately failed to effect was now being accomplished in advance by the Coronation. Vicky took as little part in this as possible. On behalf of the *Chronicle* he made a tour of inspection of London's decorations, giving them a fairly emphatic thumbs down.[7] On the day, he wore a Union flag and raised a glass – but only in cartoon form. He had made sure he was in Switzerland for the week of celebration. No doubt some acquaintances saw such absences as boycotts, displays of ostentatious outsiderishness on Vicky's part. But they were perfectly consistent with his thought and background. A Jew at Christmas, he was in matters royal a natural republican (and very sensitive to symptoms of regality in the world's presidents, as his treatment of De Gaulle would indicate). He had literally no use for royalty, whose appearance in cartoons was in any case still protected by a powerful if unenforceable taboo. When in the 1970s a collection was published highlighting 'the cartoonists' view of royalty', there was nothing of Vicky's apparently to be found, save a coat of arms casting Harold Macmillan and Selwyn Lloyd slightly irrelevantly as the Lion and the Unicorn.[8] (A barbed cartoon contrasting Prince Philip's wild-life conservation interests with his shooting holidays seems to have been overlooked.)[9]

So 1953 was more notable to Vicky as the twentieth anniversary of Hitler's accession to power, his memories of which he supplied

WHISTLERS

Sir,

It seems to me that London is fast becoming the city of tuneless whistlers. Wherever I go — in streets, buses, tubes etc. — people, young and old, whistle loudly, seemingly unconsciously, unrecognisable notes. The worst offenders are the office boys, who, these days, are driving me nearly crazy in Bouverie Street.

VICKY

99 Whistlers, *News Chronicle*, 21 February 1953

Vicky had a loathing of street noise in general but was particularly disturbed by whistling. He often drew cartoons of workmen digging up the road (perhaps outside his studio). Sometimes they are even shown to be competing with aircraft noise and helicopters.

100 Untitled, *News Chronicle*,
26 June 1953

During the summer of 1953, five MPs
– Charles Orr-Ewing, John Rodgers,
John Profumo, Lady Tweedsmuir and
Ian Harvey – made attempts to
introduce the concept of 'sponsored
television' (commercial television as
we now know it) to encourage
competition with the BBC for TV
airtime. The general public were
resistant to the idea, judging by the
letters published in the *News Chronicle*
at the time. Vicky was mindful that
spoon-fed opinions make for
indifference.

to the *Chronicle* in a poignant article.[10] He was getting ever unhappier with his role on the paper. Arthur Horner remembered him as comically edgy at this time. One day Vicky picked up the ringing telephone with such force that he cracked his own tooth. 'You've just broken my tooth!' he yelled at the caller, and slammed the receiver down again.[11] The sound of whistling plagued him unbearably. It was an era of popular song when virtuoso whistlers like Ronnie Ronalde were all the rage, and their imitators made Vicky's life a misery. He wrote a letter on the subject which the *News Chronicle* reproduced in its handwritten form. 'The worst offenders,' it concluded, 'are the office boys, who, these days, are driving me nearly crazy in Bouverie Street.' This neurotic aversion became so fixed in Vicky that, according to his third wife, he would get off a bus and walk rather than tolerate an amateur *siffleur*.[12]

Moods were turning sour. When A.J. Cummings in a major policy article declared Liberalism to be 'a moderating influence on the class war', Vicky lost patience. In a cartoon called 'Vicky Today Declares Where He Stands', he stood on his head alongside his drawing-board, where Bevan appeared in the same posture. To the debate about 'sponsored TV' (Vicky was against television from the start, seeing it as a further inducement to political apathy among the British public), he contributed a series of mocking 'sponsored cartoons', to which he put an end 'after reading his fan mail'. In doing so, he took the opportunity of satirising that mail itself, with its illiteracies, naiveties and obligatory signatures by 'Disgusted' and 'Always a Tory'. Vicky was visibly angry.

The old team was breaking up. Ian Mackay, the industrial correspondent turned essayist, had died suddenly, at the end of a Labour Conference in Morecambe. Vicky immortalised him (and his tastes for Shakespeare and wondrously florid ties) on the cover of a memorial collection called *The Real Mackay*. Then in September 1953, Richard Winnington died of cancer. 'I shall miss my room-mate badly,' wrote Vicky in his obituary. 'Above all, through his drawings shone an absolute integrity.'[13] There was a nudge for Cruikshank in this, for it was the daily defence of his own integrity that occupied Vicky's energies during his remaining weeks at the *News Chronicle*. The number of readers' letters published in praise of him suggests a campaign to keep him sweet, but it did not work. More and more often Vicky's ideas proved unacceptable to Cruikshank, though according to *World Press News* only three were flatly refused.[14] It had become clear that a new clause inserted in Vicky's new contract the previous

June, to the effect that only the editor himself would have the right to turn down Vicky's cartoon, and even then only when the cartoon would be 'damaging to the paper', had done nothing but formalise the antagonism between Vicky and Cruikshank.

It was on 1 December 1953 that Vicky's *News Chronicle* career came to an end. Rumour stated, and the editorial next to Vicky's space confirms, that his last rejected cartoon concerned Kenya, and the court inquiry into allegations that British soldiers had been offered cash payments for each Mau-Mau suspect they killed. It was nearly a fortnight before Vicky's absence was explained to the readers. When an editorial statement did appear, its communiqué-like ministerial tone ('Of late Vicky had not always been able to see eye to eye with us on a number of things')[15] was widely derided as both unctuous and hypocritical. 'A model of smugness,' said Tom Driberg MP in *Reynolds News*. 'Does a great Liberal newspaper insist on total conformity by all its contributors with a line which is, in any case, sometimes blurred?' The editorial, he surmised, 'must have been composed over a cup of nourishing cocoa' (an allusion to the controlling interest of the Cadbury family, who were said to run 'The Cocoa Press'). 'What this means,' Driberg continued remorselessly, 'is that Vicky was too Radical for the reactionary commercial interests which, ultimately, control the policy of the *News Chronicle* as of all capitalist newspapers.'[16] Vicky himself read this expression of solidarity

101 'After A.J. Cummings, to-day Vicky declares where *he* stands', *News Chronicle*, 9 March 1953

On 3 March 1953 A.J. Cummings (writer of the 'Spotlight' column in the *News Chronicle*) had made what Vicky considered to be a public statement of that paper's political stance. Vicky is clearly upset and annoyed and shows himself allied to Bevan. Vicky Jnr. looks worried. (Vicky left the *News Chronicle* at the end of 1953.)

102 *The Real Mackay*, London, News Chronicle Publications, 1953

This cartoon is the dust jacket for a volume of collected diary pieces and essays written by Ian Mackay between the years 1945 and 1952 for the *News Chronicle*. Mackay had a larger-than-life personality and was well respected for his writing style and his deep knowledge of diverse subjects.

103 The Mandrake Club, *Picture Post*, 31 March 1951

Vicky plays chess at the Mandrake Club in Soho. His brother Oscar sits to his left. Heinrich Fraenkel, writing as 'Assiac' in his book *The Delights of Chess*, describes Vicky as 'an ardent and imaginative player even though his moves on the chess board are never quite as bold as the strokes of his brush on the drawing-board'.

somewhat later, for as Driberg revealed, 'Meanwhile, he is visiting India.' Vicky had fled to the bosom of the 'grim', out of reach of editors who might discourage him from drawing it.

He never participated as fully in the life of any other newspaper.

104 Untitled, *Evening Standard*, 18 October 1960

There was outrage when the *News Chronicle* and the *Star* newspapers were sold by the Cadbury family to Lord Rothermere's Associated Newspapers in October 1960. Throughout its long history (114 years) the paper, founded as the *Daily News*, had been identified with the Liberal Party and had never been run primarily for commercial gain. Staff and readers were astounded to learn literally overnight that it had been sold to a publisher of substantially different political views. The sale provoked a successful agitation for a Royal Commission to enquire into concentration of ownership of the press.

Good fellowship he did find again at the *New Statesman*, and in his social life he always belonged to several unofficial coffee-house debating societies, and the confederacy of chess which met in the cellar gloom of the Mandrake Club. He was even persuaded into the Savile Club, where David Low and Stephen Potter were members. But he never rediscovered, nor did he probably seek, what at the *News Chronicle* he had enjoyed for fourteen years, that day-to-day bantering office life in which he figured as just one in a gallery of characters. Henceforth he was a star performer, and a little lonelier in his eminence. The *Chronicle* itself struggled on, to expire at the end of the decade. Interference, weak editing, the squeezing out of the old Liberalism, even the television age – many reasons have been angrily adduced for the paper's demise. The old hands always identified Vicky's departure as the point where the rot became unstoppable.

The *Manchester Guardian*, which had not prevented Low from making his own severe comment on the 'five-bob-a-head' scheme for dead Kenyans, was first with the news that Vicky was to join the *Daily Mirror*.[17] He had had several exploratory meetings with Hugh Cudlipp, the Editorial Director, and had agreed terms which the gossips adjudged to be very advantageous indeed. There were envious whispers of a £10,000 salary, but the better-informed speculations of the press-watching magazines suggest that Vicky began at about £100 per week. What is known of

"HERE HE COMES, BOYS!"
Yes, Vicky the brilliant cartoonist has arrived. From today his work will appear regularly in the "Daily Mirror."

105 'Here he comes, boys!', *Daily Mirror*, 2 February 1954

Future 'victims' lie in wait for Vicky as he walks nonchalantly down the street towards the offices of the *Daily Mirror*, whistling(!). Bevan (with bouquet), Attlee and Morrison (behind a 'Welcome' mat) look pleased. Malenkov and Molotov (with dove of peace) do not look too aggressive but the others look positively antagonistic, and the witch-hunting Senator Joe McCarthy rides his anti-communist broomstick.

119

later contracts suggests that this figure had risen to £8000 or so per annum by 1958 – considerable sums at a time when the housekeeping allowance for a poor-to-middling family was no more than £5 a week. But Vicky did not become rich. He had no notion of investment, and did not believe in owning property. He paid rent on his flat in Welbeck Street, which he shared with two budgerigars (gifts from the Governor of Malta), and a lively Yugoslav girl called Aurelia Kugli – nicknamed Zlata, which roughly translates as 'Goldie'. Dark, heavy-featured, taller and bulkier than Vicky, she was a forceful character who had been involved in the wartime partisan movement in her native country. They lived together happily for nearly eight years before making the mistake of marrying in December 1958.[8] Their partnership lasted only a matter of months after that, a sad repeat of the pattern Vicky had experienced with Lucielle – to whom he continued to pay voluntary maintenance throughout. With these obligations, and his mother to support, Vicky would privately say that £40 a week had gone out before he even started living.[19]

He stayed with the *Daily Mirror* a few months short of five years. His work there has been seriously underrated. He patently underrated it himself, for he chose to include it in only one collection, *Vicky's World*, and even there he supplied an admixture of contributions from the *New Statesman* and the *Evening Standard*. Maybe the rather damply regretful manner of his parting from the *Mirror* in 1958 cast something of a retrospective pall over his output there.

Vicky always claimed that his cartoons were 'technically not right' at the *Mirror*. 'I use a pen, not a brush. It's fine, and I found my stuff was fighting with big black headlines in the *Mirror*, and it didn't come over. A cartoon needs grey space around it . . .'[20] There was some truth in this, but Vicky emphasised it by way of an amiable rationalisation, best for all concerned. It was an excuse, in fact, which had lain ready to hand ever since the day he left the *News Chronicle*, when the *Manchester Guardian* observed: 'Admirers of Vicky's art will hope that, to compete with the heavy black headlines about him, he does not have to coarsen his drawing or abandon any of his subtlety on his new paper.'[21] In the event, Vicky profited by these dangers. Grey space, certainly, was lacking in the *Mirror*'s pages, but its absence strengthened his style. His inking became more emphatic, his outlines more declamatory, his lettering definitively bold. Considered as art-work in isolation, Vicky's *Mirror* cartoons are highly successful in the mass, and there are individual items which unquestionably number among his very best.

The reasons for his dissatisfaction with the paper actually had more to do with professional vanity than with technique. The fact was that the huge *Mirror* readership – five million copies sold daily – did not naturally include the influential coteries Vicky had grown accustomed to addressing. 'How many of you read the *Daily Mirror*?' Harold Wilson asked a meeting of senior businessmen in March 1954. 'More of you, probably, than will admit it.'[22] The fact that the remark was made in the course of a recommendation of one of his cartoons can have brought Vicky little comfort. He was realising all too soon that if his views were to penetrate into the lobbies and boardrooms, clubs and government offices, the *Daily Mirror* was simply not the natural conveyance.

An expensive advertising launch was arranged for the new man, and Vicky lent himself to a series of trailers featuring alliterative bottles of 'Venom' and 'Vitriol'. He was being pre-sold as a character assassin. The political commentator 'Cassandra' (William Connor) produced a feature ('Danger! Vicky At Work') assuring readers that 'no one is safe', and warning them not to assume that Vicky would always imprison himself in a habitual rectangle like other cartoonists. 'He shoves his cell around . . . A Vicky cartoon may be as long as the garden path one day and as squat as a barrel the next.'[23] Cassandra had been detailed to 'help' Vicky through his early months, but as he later recalled: '"Helping" Vicky was like teaching Margot Fonteyn to dance, and this particular ballet master soon put himself on the retired list.'[24]

Other members of staff, possibly encouraged by some editorial hint that Vicky thrived on public dissension, collided heavily with their new colleague. The reporter Charles Curran, a former Tory candidate, did so after only a month, objecting in a patronising open letter ('Dear Vicky . . . yours more in sorrow than in anger')[25] to the allegation that prices in the shops were shooting up. Vicky replied at once in a cartoon naming Curran – but not nearly so testily as he did the following year in a confrontation with the *Mirror*'s leading sports writer, Peter Wilson. Wilson was a good reporter, but when working under his legendary billing as 'The Man They Can't Gag', he needed to fulfil a quota of obligatory rages over matters of principle. Vicky qualified as one such by producing a cartoon called 'South Africa's Other "Test"', in which the South African leader Strydom, in hunnish horned helmet, swung a club marked 'Strydom's growing racial persecution'. Wilson, remarkably, contrived to see in this 'one of the most offensive cartoons that has ever spoilt my breakfast', one which

SOUTH AFRICA'S OTHER 'TEST'

106 'South Africa's other "test"', *Daily Mirror*, 18 August 1955

J.G. Strydom [Strijdom] was South African Prime Minister from 1954 until shortly before his death in 1958. He had two main political objectives – complete native apartheid and the setting-up of an Afrikaner Republic outside the Commonwealth. When the *Daily Mirror*'s sports writer, Peter Wilson, vented his indignant rage over this cartoon, Vicky countered with a written reply which ended 'If you had to earn your living as a political commentator you would die of starvation'.

'tends to involve a bunch of perfectly decent young cricketers with a vile, Nazi-like, cruel and repressive policy which no sportsman could admire'.[26] Vicky's reply forbore to widen the debate by attacking the curious idea of sportsmen's sanctified immunity from political responsibility. Instead he contented himself by pointing out that no reflection on cricketers had been made at all. 'Nobody, not even you, has ever suggested that . . . when I depict Mr Dulles playing tennis, I am attacking the American players at Wimbledon.' Evidently there was no love lost between the two contributors. Reminding Wilson that 'some time ago you attacked me in your column as a "long-haired character with whom I see eye-to-eye about as often as two cross-eyed gents"' (a piece of writing in which Wilson added lameness to the theme of disability), Vicky signed off: 'If you had to earn your living as a political commentator you would die of starvation.'[27] He was still a strong counterpuncher – and he had caught on very well to the flavour of 1950s *Mirror* polemic.

Relief from the vulgarities of public knockabout came in the form of Vicky's weekly association with the *New Statesman*. A clause in his last doomed contract with the *Chronicle* (which should have run till 1956) had given him the necessary release to work at Great Turnstile, and he simply carried over the arrangement into his *Mirror* contract. At first Vicky drew little else besides the portrait accompanying the week's *New Statesman* Profile, but these 'impressions' succeeded well enough to establish Vicky immediately as an attraction. They also did much to make an

107 Front cover, *New Statesman*, 12 May 1956 and dust jacket for *Critic's London Diary, from the* New Statesman *1931–1956* by Kingsley Martin, London, Secker & Warburg, 1960

This cartoon celebrates Kingsley Martin's silver jubilee as editor of the *New Statesman*. Appointed on 1 January 1931, he remained in the post until December 1960, during which time the paper became a kind of Bible for many left-leaning intellectually minded people. Vicky here makes the most of Martin's forelock, which stuck straight up from his forehead. Politicians, past and present, queue up to pay tribute with flowers, cigars and in one case a cactus. Those who are dead are in outline only – Ramsay MacDonald, Chamberlain, Hitler, Mussolini, Ernest Bevin and Stalin – above the clouds. The others – De Gaulle, Lord Goddard (Lord Chief Justice), Montgomery, Morrison, Franco, Strydom, Adenauer, Senator Joe McCarthy, Chiang Kai-Shek, Syngman Rhee, Dulles, Beaverbrook, Gaitskell, Eden and Churchill – are very much alive.

A 'writer' outside a Post office

beggar

Bombay

institution of the Profiles themselves: a popular volume of them, put on sale in 1957, was taken up and republished by the Readers' Union. In his drawings Vicky softens the growing spikiness of his day-to-day work, adopting a rounded, meaty half-tone and an eye for anarchic detail (like the spiralling eyes of Gilbert Harding) which recall Max Beerbohm.

Vicky knew the *Statesman*'s editor, Kingsley Martin, well and had already drawn him in a friendly spirit. Martin was a traveller and a foreign-affairs man at heart. He also had a deep love of India, which Vicky could now share with first-hand knowledge. His 'Indian Notebook' drawings appeared very early in his *Statesman* tenure – on which the seal was set in November 1954 by 'The Portrait', a full-page eightieth-birthday tribute to Winston Churchill, carrying Vicky's apologies to Holbein, Rembrandt, Modigliani, Toulouse-Lautrec, Van Gogh, Millais and Picasso. A parodistic *tour-de-force* in which Vicky's mischievous enjoyment is everywhere apparent (and in which he cunningly avoided having to make any specifically political acknowledgement of Churchill's achievements), this page was reprinted by lithography and sold to delighted readers for one-and-sixpence. The original went to Winston himself, and given what we know of the fate of the Graham Sutherland portrait that prompted this spoof, there can be small doubt that the Churchills, man and wife, preferred the Vicky version.

108 'From Vicky's Indian Notebook', *New Statesman*, 20 March 1954

These drawings of a scribe who writes letters or fills up forms for the illiterate and a beggar woman were done in December 1953 during the trip Vicky made to India following his resignation from the *News Chronicle*. Vicky visited Delhi and Bombay, bringing back a notebook filled with sketches of street life. (See also **55**.)

109 'The portrait', *New Statesman*, 27 November 1954

This cartoon was subtitled, 'With Vicky's apologies to Holbein, Rembrandt, Modigliani, Toulouse-Lautrec, Van Gogh, Millais and Picasso.' The *New Statesman* sold offprints. Graham Sutherland's portrait of Churchill, commissioned by Parliament as a tribute, depicted the statesman as a frail old man and caused great controversy. Members of the Churchill family disliked it and eventually – so it emerged years later – the picture was destroyed.

THE PORTRAIT

Where *Mirror* readers sometimes needed a tip-off, *New Statesman* subscribers required little elucidation of symbols. Vicky was free to share with them the benefits of his more esoteric reading (including on a few telling occasions the plays of Samuel Beckett). Certain of his repeating genres, like the strap-shaped reworkings of the Bayeux Tapestry, looked particularly handsome on the *New Statesman*'s compact page. But marginal restriction of Vicky's allusiveness in the *Mirror* did him no harm. It concentrated his fire. He plugged away indefatigably at Dulles, exaggerating still further the grumpy-tortoise jut of his neck. So many flint-hearted guises did Dulles go through – as Cold Warrior, Snowman, Penguin, Abominable No-Man, Brink-man and Engineer (Dulles had once nourished an ambition to drive trains) – that finally the *Telegraph* blew up and attacked Vicky for his 'vendetta' against 'a man of outstanding integrity, intelligence and experience'.

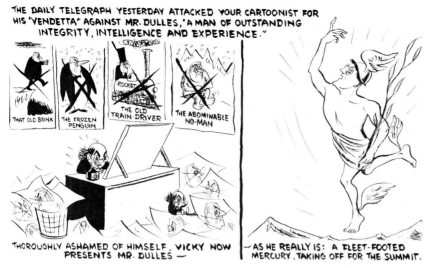

THE DAILY TELEGRAPH YESTERDAY ATTACKED YOUR CARTOONIST FOR HIS "VENDETTA" AGAINST MR. DULLES, "A MAN OF OUTSTANDING INTEGRITY, INTELLIGENCE AND EXPERIENCE."

THAT OLD BRINK · THE FROZEN PENGUIN · THE OLD TRAIN·DRIVER · THE ABOMINABLE NO-MAN

THOROUGHLY ASHAMED OF HIMSELF, VICKY NOW PRESENTS MR. DULLES —

— AS HE REALLY IS: A FLEET·FOOTED MERCURY, TAKING OFF FOR THE SUMMIT.

110 Untitled, *Daily Mirror*, 14 March 1958

Vicky Jnr. wipes away tears as Vicky sweats to produce a portrait of Dulles that would be acceptable to *Daily Telegraph* readers. On 13 March 1955 in his column 'Way of the World', Peter Simple had written a vitriolic piece against Vicky's cartoon depiction of Dulles. Simple praised Dulles as 'a man of firm principles whose hesitations and caution are attributable to an extraordinary concern that the interests of America and the free world shall not be placed into jeopardy'.

In portraying Dulles, by way of reply, as a 'fleet-footed Mercury, taking off for the Summit', Vicky was actually giving the Secretary by some previous standards a quite lightly ironic going-over. (Even Harold Macmillan had been moved to say of Dulles that 'his speech was slow but it easily kept pace with his thought'.)[28] In Vicky's eyes Dulles was a poisonous relic of America's isolationism, a man with a taste for the apocalyptic and a suicidal vision of 'rolling back Communism'. He was also a remorseless Iago who would extinguish whatever childlike virtues might survive in the bosom of President Eisenhower. Ike was an innocent in politics and Vicky drew him with the chuckling, eager face of a baby and an enormous domed skull (resembling Vicky's habitual 'Moonmen', and perhaps derived from them after some

'HELLO OMAHA. HELLO OMAHA. HOLD EVERYTHING – WE'VE LOST THE BUTTON!'

111 'Hello Omaha. Hello Omaha. Hold everything – we've lost the button!', *New Statesman*, 3 May 1958

US forces hunt the nuclear 'button' as Eisenhower plays a relaxed round of golf. Throughout his presidency, the US government was preoccupied with foreign policy and the campaign against communism. Such extremism often placed 'Ike' in an invidious position, throwing his political inexperience into high relief.

'I say, he's playing quite an unheard of opening gambit . . .', *Daily Mirror*, 23 April 1958

1958 marked Khrushchev's triumph over the doctrine of collective leadership in the USSR, when in March he became both Prime Minister and First Secretary. The Soviet Union had already achieved a psychological advantage over the USA on the technological front the previous year, with the production of the first intercontinental ballistic missile and the first earth satellite, 'Sputnik'. Khrushchev was now able to use a 'peaceful co-existence' strategy as a tool to indicate greater or lesser *rapprochement* at any given moment. Adenauer, Macmillan, Lloyd, Dulles and Eisenhower are clearly mystified, while De Gaulle distances himself from the American-dominated NATO.

accidental resemblance was noted). There was no suggestion that the cranium was occupied by a commensurately giant brain. Dominated by Dulles, Ike spent most of his time in Vicky's cartoons with a golf club in his hand, addressing a globe that was either too large to shift or terrifyingly small, depending on whether Vicky wished to stress the President's appalling *de facto* fire-power or his lack of personal driving-force.

That Vicky was so openly identified with a strong anti-American tendency in the Labour Party tended to encourage the accusation that he was therefore pro-Russian. In the sense that he was against those who were automatically anti-Russian, it was true. But right-wing newspapers pressed the charge much further. 'Which British newspaper's cartoons do you think the Communists most appreciate in enslaved Czechoslovakia?' asked the *Sunday Dispatch*, Vicky's old employer. 'The *Daily Worker*'s? No, the *Daily Mirror*'s.'[29] The article went on to describe how a Vicky cartoon showing Churchill and Eden being followed suspiciously be Senator McCarthy and Edgar Hoover of the FBI had been reprinted in *Young Front*, the Czech paper for Communist youth. 'Who is Vicky? asked the *Dispatch*, providing the answer in phrases that were left to speak for themselves: 'refugee', 'Jewish origin', 'Hungarian nationality', 'visited Moscow in 1952'. It was all done very much in the style of Senator McCarthy himself. The *Recorder Weekly* had a go at characterising Vicky's output

"I SAY, HE'S PLAYING QUITE AN UNHEARD OF OPENING GAMBIT..."

VICKY

" YOU SEE, THEY'RE TRYING TO FIND SOME UNDERDEVELOPED
AREAS... "

113 'You see, they're trying to find some underdeveloped areas . . .', *Evening Standard*, 12 May 1961

The peasant group draws the reader's eye, while the labelling on the spacecraft slightly overstates the point. Vicky admired the organisation that was behind the successful launch of cosmonaut Yuri Gagarin (the first man in space) in April, and the flight of the first American astronaut Alan Shepard soon after, but he deplored the high cost.

as a whole. 'He is a Bevanite. His sympathies appear to be with Russia. He is more or less against everybody else except Mr Butler, who might be used to upset the Tories.' Butler found himself in some odd positions in his career, but this was one of the oddest.[30]

What Vicky did have, at the time, was a chess-player's admiration of Russia's strategy. It was the Vicky who in 1953 had beaten the famous C.H.O'D. Alexander in a televised demonstration of simultaneous chess (Alexander played sixteen opponents)[31] who was compelled to admire Nikita Khrushchev's timing of his offers, his protests, his timetables for possible Summits. Khrushchev became 'Grandmaster K', whose Western opponents usually figured as a crowd of squabbling tyros scratching their chins. It was not how things ought to be, but how they were. Vicky

127

Eden (at the wheel) sitting beside Guy Mollet (Premier of France) drives on regardless of the developing conflict in Suez. In November 1956, Eden ordered British and French forces to occupy the Suez Canal zone ahead of the invading Israeli Army. This action was condemned by the United Nations and caused a prolonged controversy in Britain which did not subside when a withdrawal was ordered. Eden resigned on 9 January 1957.

YOU HAVE BEEN WARNED

admired the technique. What really irked Conservative commentators, however, was his preparedness to draw the occasional item of political instruction from the Soviet experience. When Russia became the 'first nation in space', the event struck Vicky as remarkable not so much as a scientific triumph (he deeply deplored the disproportionate expenditure, and drew starving families under the satellite-strewn skies) but rather as a demonstration of the efficacy of state planning. The kind of Conservative he had most detested since wartime, when he had first identified the breed, was the 'anti-planner' whose vaunted libertarian loyalty to free market forces disguised a simple determination to ensure his pockets continued to be lined.

The test of Vicky's objectivity in matters of Russian policy came of course in November 1957, when the world was faced with simultaneous crises in Hungary and Suez. That it was the Russian obliteration of the Hungarian uprising that brought the better work out of Vicky allayed a lot of people's doubts about him, and opened up the period of his greatest fame. The Anglo-French invasion of Suez disgusted but did not surprise him. Throughout the year he had nagged at Eden, reminding him in one outsize cartoon of his own 1951 dictum that 'There is no alternative to

" FASCIST AND REACTIONARY ELEMENTS HAVE BEEN CRUSHED..."
— SOVIET CONTROLLED ⋈ BUDAPEST RADIO

115 '"Fascist and reactionary elements have been crushed . . ." – Soviet-controlled Budapest radio', *Daily Mirror*, 8 November 1956

The control by Soviet troops of Hungarian demonstrators who were demanding better wages and liberty from Soviet domination shocked the world. The reality of Soviet power was underlined by the fact that the West was not able to respond to Imre Nagy's appeals for help.

the rule of law. The U.N. is the only way.' When Eden finally overruled himself, there was little left for Vicky to do but pick up the pieces and wait for Eden to go. Hungary was a much more bitter disappointment – a sudden, possibly permanent end to Vicky's hopes of persuading the Western world that the Bear, after all, was huggable. In a large drawing ('Fascist and reactionary elements have been crushed') by which he finally proved that a version of his 'grim' style could match the public mood to perfection, he showed the simple people of Hungary, to whose nationhood he owed a good deal, in all the sorrow and humiliation of their defeat. Two pages of a special edition of *Picture Post*, 'Cry Hungary', were devoted to a reproduction of the drawing.[32] The *Mirror*'s political editor, Sydney (later Baron) Jacobson, paid tribute to it again in a broadly splashed piece proclaiming Vicky, unilaterally, 'Cartoonist of the Year'.[33] It was a needless stunt, as Vicky had already achieved primacy in his own quiet way.

The *Mirror* job was a hard slog, six solid days a week including a 'Saturday Satire' in the tradition of the 'Week-end Fantasia'. From editorial intervention, however, Vicky was entirely free; this was a condition of his contract, and it was just as well. He seldom agreed with the *Mirror*'s temporising, 'tactical' Labour line. Much more to his liking was the political stance of *Tribune*, as readers of that organ knew. 'There's only one Socialist in the *Mirror* building,' one of them wrote, 'and that's Vicky.' But *Tribune* could never have afforded him – and there he really would have been preaching to the converted, a feeling that already bothered him at the half-Left *Mirror*.

Labour, he was convinced, was losing its identity. The famous composite 'Mr Butskell',[34] whom Vicky drew at first with acknowledgement to its inventor, *The Economist*, was only one symptom of a general drift towards the centre, leaving Tory and Labour virtually interchangeable in parts of their policy. An amalgamation of the party conferences was suggested by Vicky. This sort of criticism was much more damaging to Labour than to the Conservatives, who had obvious vote-catching reasons for claiming that, in Harold Watkinson's phrase, 'in Britain today every single one of us belongs to the working classes' (a scenario Vicky loved to picture, with the Tory cabinet all in cloth caps, mufflers and string-bound trousers). What embarrassed Vicky was that the Labour Party seemed on the whole less keen than the Tories to make this claim of solidarity with the workers.

He blamed Hugh Gaitskell: stylistically, for his lack of proletarian fire, and in policy terms above all for a stance on defence that seemed to Vicky to ignore the clear call for 'moral leadership' that was coming from the rank-and-file.[35] They wanted an end to the H-bomb, and so did he. The unavoidable confrontation

116 'Nah then – wot abaht this for our new image, Mates?', *New Statesman*, 20 July 1962

Reginald Maudling, Enoch Powell, Iain Macleod, Prime Minister Macmillan, Lord Hailsham (ringing his bell), R.A. Butler, Duncan Sandys, Lord Home and Henry Brooke look faintly glum in the uniforms of the working class. After eleven years of Tory rule, the future for the Conservative government did not seem as secure as it had. In a desperate effort to revitalise an unpopular government Macmillan sacked seven Cabinet ministers – Selwyn Lloyd, Lord Kilmuir, John Maclay, Harold Watkinson, Lord Mills, Charles Hill and David Eccles – on a single day (13 July 1962). The 'unflappable' image was gone for ever.

"NAH THEN, WOT ABAHT THIS FOR OUR NEW IMAGE, MATES?"

130

117 '. . . but *I* went naked into the conference room – and won, Nye . . .', *Daily Mirror*, 17 October 1957

Vicky misplaced his trust in Bevan as far as disarmament was concerned. His sober attitude is clear in this realistic non-caricature portrait. Bevan had said on 3 October 1957, in a speech at the Labour Party conference against a motion proposing unilateral nuclear disarmament by the UK, 'If you carry this resolution and follow out all its implications and do not run away from it you will send a Foreign Minister, whoever he may be, naked into the conference chamber.' Vicky contrasts Bevan with Gandhi – the embodiment of non-violence.

'. . . BUT I WENT NAKED INTO THE CONFERENCE ROOM– AND WON, NYE . . .'

happened in 1957. In his 'Almanack' for that year, making all the most unlikely predictions, he had forecast that 'Vicky and *Tribune* [will] attack Mr Bevan'[36] – which is precisely what happened. Bevan's speech to the Labour Conference, reasoning that to ban the H-bomb would be to send a Labour Foreign Secretary 'naked into the conference chamber', occasioned Vicky as intense an anguish as any political event could that did not involve bloodshed and privation. Characteristically he invoked Gandhi, who had gone naked and won. In the longer term, two developments resulted from this climax of disillusion. First, Vicky's campaign against Gaitskell was intensified, to the point where some Labour supporters felt it bordered on cruelty. Secondly, Vicky became one of the founding group that met to form the Campaign for Nuclear Disarmament. He fell out with the *Mirror* over the Bomb. Cudlipp's editorial directly opposed an adjacent cartoon which depicted him as the proprietor of a paper boasting 'the Biggest Daily Sale in the Universe'. Epithets like 'hysterical' and 'escapist' flew back and forth.[37]

Vicky's time at the *Mirror* was already coming to a natural end.

VICKY'S OUTLINE OF A SHORT HISTORY OF THE MODERN WORLD

| 1940 | 1945 | 1950 | 1955 | 195? |
| STRENGTH THROUGH JOY | JOY THROUGH PEACE | PEACE THROUGH STRENGTH | DEFENCE THROUGH DETERRENTS | ANNIHILATION THROUGH ACCIDENT |

118 'Vicky's outline of a short history of the modern world', *Daily Mirror*, 4 March 1955

Mankind's progression from the terror of Hitler through amnesty and the Cold War to armageddon in only fifteen years could be Vicky's last statement. When asked in 1960 what his final cartoon might be, he said 'It would certainly be an anti-hanging, anti-H bomb, anti-war cartoon.'

He had said, and continued to say, exactly what he wished, but not to the people he most wished to hear it. Now he was prepared to trade in his national audience for the direct and urgent impact he would make upon the capital in London's *Evening Standard*. If there was one unique flavour he had brought to the *Mirror*, it was a European outlook for which the paper in other periods has not been renowned. Vicky compelled his millions of readers to recognise that De Gaulle and Adenauer, in particular, were considerable if unlikeable men with some legitimate national interests to promote and some un-English ways of promoting them. In French politics Vicky was expert enough to be an active participant. He had been taken on by Jean-Jacques Servan-Schreiber in the early days of the magazine *L'Express*, accepting the job mainly out of friendship for the Paris-based journalist K.S. Karol.[38] It was Karol who kept Vicky informed about the latest French political battles, and made suggestions for the cartoons – which arrived by plane, completely identifiable as Vicky productions save for the signature. He drew as 'Pierrot', as it was feared that French readers would not take kindly to being admonished by a foreigner, especially a British-based one. Philippe Grumbach, editor-in-chief of *L'Express*, also telephoned suggestions, but Vicky took a privately sceptical view of Grumbach's politics and always took Karol's counsel first.[39] On 15 May 1958, by which time his identity was in the open, Vicky addressed an appeal to *L'Express* readers, voicing his dismay at the French people's preoccupation with the Algerian problem to the exclusion of the H-bomb menace. This four-column manifesto, unlike anything Vicky produced for British consumption, concluded with a lament over the fact that France, 'once the most civilised and humanist country in the world', was now preparing to become a member of the '*Club du Suicide Nucléaire*'.[40]

132

LE DESSIN DE PIERROT

« Pour sa part, le gouvernement a donné l'exemple. »
(Guy Mollet, 9 septembre 1956.)

119 '"*Pour sa part, le gouvernement a donné l'exemple.*" – Guy Mollet, *9 septembre, 1956', L'Express,* 14 September 1956

The conflict in Algeria and the stories of atrocities by French troops there gradually turned world opinion against France. Neither side could win the war and there were no French politicians who could bring themselves to admit that the solution was exile for the Moslem population (*pieds noirs*, so-called 'black feet') and independence for Algeria. Amid accusations that he was not doing enough, Prime Minister Guy Mollet (leader of a minority government) attempted to find a way to bring fighting to an end and here he gives a '1st prize' to himself for his efforts. The captions reads, 'For its part, the government has set an example'. (Vicky's signature on this cartoon is very like his 'Smith' signature (see **74A**)).

Vicky loved France, but preferred a detached intellectual view of her politics. He was happy absorbing theory in the Parisian circles of Pierre Mendès-France, whom he saw when Nye Bevan exchanged visits with the French socialist leader,[41] but grass-roots practice across the Channel greatly alarmed him. During Mendès-France's election campaign of late 1955, he visited the rural hustings of Normandy in the company of K.S. Karol. Vicky, Karol reported, was 'much shocked' by the violent atmosphere of the meeting he attended. A lifelong city-dweller with no taste for a country *bagarre*, he fled the raucous and misnamed 'small farmers' and returned to Paris at top speed.[42]

For Germany Vicky now had little time. He had campaigned tirelessly against the rehabilitation of Alfried Krupp, the steel magnate and arms manufacturer, but watched him change from a war criminal to a capitalist prince again, the richest man in Europe. Adenauer, the German Chancellor ('a vain, headstrong authoritarian'),[43] he saw as a throwback to the *Junker* era or perhaps something worse: he used to tell a joke in which a German *Hausfrau*, asked how things had changed since the war, replied, 'No change. We still have the greatest army in Europe, we still have the greatest industry in Europe, we still have the same kind of leaders running the country. Mind you, I was surprised to see how old the Fuehrer looked – and he's shaved off his moustache, too . . .'[44]

When in the 1950s a reparations system was instituted, Vicky became entitled to state compensation for loss of property on his exile from Germany, and conceivably for damage to health as well. But on the relevant forms he was required to state whether

CORRECTED AND RE-DRAWN
BY FAMOUS GUEST-ARTIST
K. ADENAUER

MADE IN FRANCE

U.S. TIE

MADE IN ENGLAND

MADE IN GERMANY

"HERR DE GAULLE IS NO NATIONALIST. HE IN NO WAY CORRESPONDS WITH THE PICTURE OF HIM GIVEN BY THE PRESS IN THE LAST FEW MONTHS." — DR. ADENAUER, WEST GERMAN CHANCELLOR

120 ' "Herr De Gaulle is no nationalist. He in no way corresponds with the picture of him given by the press in the last few months" – Dr Adenauer, West German Chancellor', *Daily Mirror*, 18 September 1958

The statesman who claimed he was the embodiment of France is shown here as Joan of Arc, Napoleon, Louis XIV and finally as that most familiar symbol – the Eiffel Tower. The bond between Adenauer and Washington had been removed with the death of Dulles. Adenauer was suspicious of Eisenhower's attempts to find agreement with Khrushchev, and he did not like Macmillan. Adenauer is ready to find a new friend in De Gaulle and wears the symbol of the Free French to show his intentions.

or not he had been a member of a long list of organisations ranging from the German Communist Party to the League of Democratic Women. Vicky had not been a member of any of them, but felt that it was not up to him to pass another political test. He refused the offer,[45] continued to pay his British taxes to the very fullest, and was hard to persuade to put in for any legitimate expenses. Vicky always wanted to pay his way. A vestige of the refugee mentality hovered about him. Back in *News Chronicle* days he had taken to carrying a large roll of banknotes in his pocket – some £50, a tremendous amount at that time – as if to protect himself against a sudden onrush of social chaos and deprivation. He became a target in Fleet Street pubs like The Clachan, where panhandlers made a soft touch of him.[46]

He could stand it. He was now comfortably off. Indeed, to get the job he wanted he was prepared to take a cut in salary. Vicky's last cartoon for the *Mirror*, No. 1313 by their reckoning, was radioed down from the Tory Conference in Blackpool. He took a fortnight off, and spent the rest of his life working for the empire of Lord Beaverbrook.[47]

The Age of Supermac

'Vicky Next Week,' promised the *Evening Standard* on the last day of October 1958. In his illustration, Vicky stepped purposefully out of a Trojan Horse. He knew where he was going, and the *Standard* knew what it was getting: a cartoonist who was currently garnering votes for the Labour Party in their pamphlet 'The Future Labour Offers You'.[1] It was not his first offence. 'The Men Who Failed', a Party booklet that launched Labour's counter-attack after Eden's electoral success of 1955, had been little more than a miniature cartoon collection, all the work of Vicky. *Tribune* pamphlets linked him to the even farther Left. Vicky might not belong officially to Labour's crew, but he had nailed a very red flag to the mast. Now the *Standard* was waving it, teasingly, in front of the readers.[2]

To William Maxwell Aitken, Lord Beaverbrook, Vicky's arrival represented the climax of a policy he had cheerfully pursued since 1927, when David Low joined his staff. Beaverbrook favoured leftwardly-inclined cartoonists, and for a number of

121 'All present? – Then let battle commence . . .', *Evening Standard*, 3 November 1958

With his popularity poll already at rock bottom and his ink bottle of poison at the ready, Vicky welcomes Selwyn Lloyd, Beaverbrook, Hailsham, Sandys, Macmillan, Butler, Bevan, Gaitskell, Dulles, Chiang Kai-Shek, De Gaulle, Eisenhower, Nasser, Khrushchev and Mao Tse-Tung. The *Evening Standard*'s advance publicity billed Vicky as 'the great political cartoonist who uses his pen like a rapier'. The space allocated to this first cartoon in the 'Londoner's Diary' was 12.5 cm high by 24 cm wide (five columns). The gauntlet had been thrown down.

ALL PRESENT?—THEN LET BATTLE COMMENCE . . .

connected reasons. Cultivation of his own notoriety was certainly one. He knew that history loves a paradox, and he was not above planting one here and there. He enjoyed the enigmatic, even dangerous aura conferred on him among his fellow Conservatives by his cranky tolerance of the views of the 'other side'. As a Canadian, he shared with the New Zealander Low in particular, but also with Vicky the European Jew, an outsider's impatience with Britain's slow political metabolism. His taste for action was respected by Vicky, who seldom had a good word to say for the letter of the Beaver's political recommendations, but missed him when he wasn't there. In 1948, when Beaverbrook returned after six month's absence abroad, Vicky even went so far as to devote a whole cartoon to welcoming him back.[3] Both men distrusted unanimity. One of the few remarks Beaverbrook is reliably reported to have addressed to his new employee (for Beaverbrook was old now and they seldom met)[4] was 'Readers have got to be annoyed'.[5] In this he was not disappointed.

Vicky took over from Jimmy Friell, a cartoonist who had come from further left again – the *Daily Worker*. Not wishing to put Friell completely out of a job, he arranged that Saturdays should be left free for his predecessor to deal with, a huge relief after so many hundreds of effortful 'Fantasias' and 'Satires'. He also supplied no Wednesday cartoon, which left him potentially with quite a comfortable timetable. As the *Evening Standard* was not a national but a London paper (running third, too, in the circulation battle behind the *News* and *Star*),[6] Vicky's contract, drawn up by Managing Editor Charles Wintour in August 1958, specified a salary of £6000 – quite modest by his recent standards, but still high. Vicky was to enjoy 'complete freedom in the selection and treatment of subject matter for your cartoons and in the expression therein of a policy in which you believe'. Most of the press world believed that Vicky had hereby secured a guaranteed right of publication, but it was not strictly so. Another clause, routinely covering the Editor's right to amend any wording considered defamatory, added that 'the Editor further retains the right to reject your cartoons, but such will be exercised with discretion, and not because of the political content'. Vicky also retained the right to work for the *New Statesman*.[7]

He was scheduled to begin his new job on 1 February 1959, or 1 January if release from the *Mirror* came. In the event, Cudlipp waived all objections, and Vicky cried 'Let battle commence' on 3 November 1958. Milton Shulman had told 590,000 purchasers:

He is against Dulles and the non-recognition of China, the personality cult of Macmillan, the racial riots in Little Rock and Notting Hill, Russian repression of the Hungarian revolt, the terror and counter-terror in Cyprus. He is for better old-age pensions, Summit talks, a more aggressive left-wing Labour Party and unilateral nuclear disarmament. *Evening Standard* readers are in for a stimulating time.[8]

Vicky proved it within one week. 'Introducing: SUPERMAC' ushered in his most famous creation, the one by which his immediate posterity would remember him – and by which Harold Macmillan would be remembered too. It was the name that survived. Pictorially, Supermac derived from Superman, the American comic-strip character, into whose fantasy flying-suit the Edwardian Prime Minister, with his now trimmed walrus moustache, wings of white hair and drooping eyes, so very inappropriately fitted. But the idea arose from the newly published humorous handbook *Supermanship*, as Vicky indicated with his 'apologies to Stephen Potter'.[9] The cartoon's subtitle, 'How to Try to Continue to Stay Top without Actually Having Been There', is in Potter's characteristic idiom; and the idea can be seen

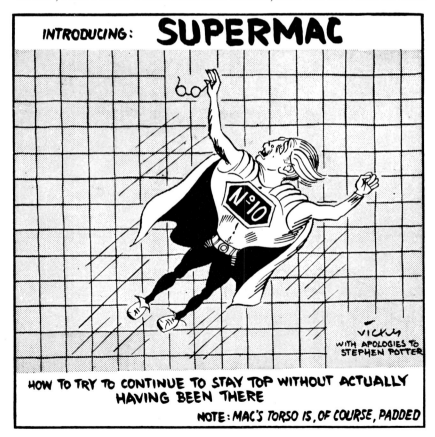

122 'Introducing: Supermac', *Evening Standard*, 6 November 1958

'Supermac' was Vicky's most successful creation and is the best remembered, although it did backfire on him. It was devised at a time when Harold Macmillan held almost hypnotic sway over his Government and the public. Aneurin Bevan had previously called him 'Macwonder'; now Vicky, also intending satire, drew Macmillan as an ageing Superman. Unfortunately the sobriquet became one of Macmillan's assets in the General Election of 1959. (Stephen Potter's book, published in 1958, was called *Supermanship, or, How to Continue to Stay Top without Actually Falling Apart*.)

THE ENTERTAINER

123 'The entertainer', *Evening Standard*, 11 December 1958

The Entertainer (produced in 1957) is a play by the 'angry young man' John Osborne in which the main character, a seedy worn-out music-hall artist, pretends that he is still important. This character was Vicky's way of compensating for the unwelcome success of 'Supermac'. Macmillan's words show him to be uncaring and out of touch with reality. Instead of the traditional cinema queue, the busker has the unemployed as his captive audience.

incubating in Vicky's mind in a *New Statesman* cartoon of the previous week, where political leaders are seen with currently topical reading matter. Macmillan reads *Supermanship*.

'Note: Mac's torso is, of course, padded', warned the inaugural cartoon; but this was easily forgotten by a public who had long been on the lookout for a good label to attach to the Premier. Supermac suited the purpose perfectly, by permitting two opinions of Macmillan to be held at the same time. He was a quaint old personage, to be sure, whose style proclaimed him to be historically unfitted to be in charge of affairs in an age of spy-planes and sputniks; but he was also an actor (with American connections) who played up to this tweedy perception of himself quite consciously, thereby hiding a private personality that was probably quite racy. Supermac satisfied both visions, encouraging a belief in the leader's secret powers while making the most of

" WHEN YOU BECOME PRIME MINISTER, HOWEVER UNEXPECTEDLY,
EVERYTHING BECOMES A LITTLE LARGER THAN LIFE "

— MR MACMILLAN, October 22. 1957.

his air of mothballed grandeur.

Vicky realised his mistake very quickly. 'This figure, Supermac, has really boomeranged on me now,' he confessed.[10] Phasing the character quietly out as soon as he could, he turned to older incarnations of Mac, followed by a number of new ones. It is deeply ironic, in fact, that Vicky's Macmillan should be remembered in this one costume alone, for no figure in all Vicky's lifelong gallery of victims appears in anything like the number of guises Harold Macmillan assumes. To realise how many roles and shapes the list entails is to gain some idea of Vicky's amazingly restless powers of re-invention. He had begun pairing Macmillan with Eden as the Western Brothers a decade before. As he came to solo prominence, Vicky's Mac then fell out of synchronisation with the real-life model, who had drastically cut back his walrus moustaches while Vicky retained them, guarding the integrity of

124 'Introducing: Minimac. "When you become Prime Minister, however unexpectedly, everything becomes a little larger than life" – Mr Macmillan, October 22, 1957', *Evening Standard*, 27 February 1963

In this photomontage, Macmillan is shown reaching the end of his political career. More an elder statesman than an effective political leader, he should be beginning to acknowledge his loss of power. But Macmillan held on because he was determined that at almost any cost R.A. Butler should not succeed him as Party leader. This Micawberesque tactic of waiting for something to turn up damaged Conservative Party unity.

his metaphorical vision at all costs. Macmillan was a character who lived and spoke, as it were, with walrus moustaches in mind.

Then as Macmillan rose to power, beginning to display an unlooked-for ruthlessness, Vicky cast him as the wielder of 'Mac's Axe'. Later came Mac the Knife, responsible for pruning the Welfare State and murdering the ambitions of rivals; and The Entertainer, a check-suited Edwardian music-hall artiste with a policy of diverting public attention from unpleasant realities. Finally, in his political decline, he would dwindle to 'Minimac', a tiny inadequate figure pasted on a huge photograph of the House of Commons chamber. These were Mac's regular roles.

But in between times, he had been bullied into an unbelievable variety of characterisations and accoutrements. He had been Mr Macawber, MacGladstone and MacLaocoon, MacGas the advertising symbol and Machameleon the adaptor to all circumstances. In the animal kingdom he had also starred as a sea-lion, a walrus, a bull, a lamb, a lion and a unicorn, MacPie, (a bird), a duck, a dog, a monkey (and an organ-grinder), half a pantomime horse and the White Rabbit. He had acquired the shapelier forms of Britannia, Cinderella, the Statue of Liberty, a dowager, a scolding mother, a Victorian wallflower in a ball-gown under the mistletoe, a Miss World contestant, a striptease artiste, a lady in a kilt, Cleopatra and the Blue Angel. He had played Bottom, Claudius, Oliver Twist, King Lear, Liberace, Prince Monolulu the racing tipster, Sir Francis Drake, King Harold, and the Prodigal Son. By profession he had been shopkeeper, surgeon, cyclist, cave-man, burglar, zither-player, mountaineer, sea-captain; a Boy Scout, a beatnik, a Beefeater, a hitch-hiker, a tramp (both in and out of the plays of Samuel Beckett), a policeman, a couturier, a ventriloquist, a magician, a stilt-walker, a boxing referee, a huntsman, fisherman (MacFishy) and crack shot; a motorist, a skier, a guardsman, a strict-tempo dancer, and an 'unflappable' reader of Trollope. Nor did he disdain to appear as a car; the figurehead on another car, and on a ship; Uccello's St George; reincarnations of Balfour, Disraeli and Churchill; a director of the Great Western Railway (which indeed he had been); Charlie Chaplin in *City Lights*; a Henry Moore statue, with holes; a guttering candle; Queen Victoria, Bunyan's Pilgrim, Nelson with two blind eyes and the Stag at Bay. Has there ever been another cartoonist gifted with the sheer manic energy required to imagine a pin-striped politician into such a cascade of phantasmagoric forms? The list is by no means complete.

Yet it was Supermac who was remembered. Vicky preannounced his arrival on television the night before, in a BBC programme called 'Press Conference', where he was 'in bubbling form'.[11] He paid a generous passing tribute to David Low, who didn't own a TV (nor did Vicky) but, on receiving reports, sent a good luck note to the *Standard* – 'not that you will need anything but your own talent for it is obvious that you are going to have a long and prosperous tenure'.[12] Vicky certainly seemed confident. On the broadcast he said: 'I told an editor, if readers do not complain, you have not got a cartoonist! My job is to tread on people's toes.'

The *Standard* readers started to register pain almost at once. Vicky's first cartoon, signalling merely the commencement of hostilities, was received in the letters column as 'the most vulgar and repulsive production I have ever seen'.[13] By December, adjacent editorial columns were chipping in on points of principle. 'No, No, Vicky,' admonished a headline, opposite Vicky's representation of The Entertainer serenading a dole queue. 'If the situation were really as Vicky presents it in his cartoon on this page, Mr Gaitskell would be a happy man – confident of winning the next General Election.' Emphasising Vicky's freedom of comment, the text called its result 'a flow of cartoons that are always stimulating but sometimes also wrong-headed. So it is today.'[14]

So it would be every day, for some Londoners. Vicky comforted himself with the thought that 'not all *Evening Standard* readers are Tories. I mean, the *Evening Standard* is read by many people of radical opinions.'[15] But it was the Tories who commanded most of the space set aside for correspondence, and as the 1959 Election approached, they became increasingly incensed with Vicky's output. Many of the letters came from the comfortable suburbs, and some from addresses like the Athenaeum or the Cowdray Club, which must have brought Vicky the satisfaction of knowing that he was now penetrating those plushy social interstices where before he had been unknown. But it would have taken a more unearthly character than Vicky was to accept some of the abuse with equanimity. A good deal of it aimed straightforwardly at removing him from his job: hence the title of his first collection of *Evening Standard* cartoons, published in defiantly red rectangular paperback – *Vicky Must Go!* The rest ranged from the sanctimonious ('Your cartoonist Vicky has a God-given gift in the art of drawing. May I suggest he gives it up until the bitterness and hatred of his soul is removed by reading St John's Gospel') to the xenophobic ('This dreadful unmanly un-English propaganda marked Vicky'). When the date of the election was

'AH, WELL DONE, SIR! AND WHAT A JOLLY GOOD LIKENESS OF THAT FELLER GAITSKELL!'

125 'Ah, well done, sir! And what a jolly good likeness of that feller Gaitskell!', *Evening Standard*, 26 May 1959

A Toryfied Vicky, sporting a Churchillian cigar and signing with the victory salute, exalts Macmillan as St George. This cartoon is something of a blunt instrument with its use of stereotypes of right-wing bias. *Vicky Must Go!* (1960) was the title of Vicky's first anthology.

announced in early September, the barrage intensified. 'Is this person a natural-born British subject?' asked a disingenuous reader from Knightsbridge. 'If so, I suggest he joins the gang of fellow-travellers who smear and belittle their country at every opportunity while taking advantage of everything it has to offer.'

Vicky never protested. Confrontation with his readers' prejudices was an openly advertised attraction of his style. He had never been shy of putting himself in the political frame, participating in the argument, addressing the viewer directly or offering explanation to them through his favourite intermediary, the little sidekick 'Vicky Jnr.'.[16] He never hid behind his work: he was in it. Nevertheless the *Standard* at one point felt it had to step in and defend its contributor – an unusual measure. Three weeks

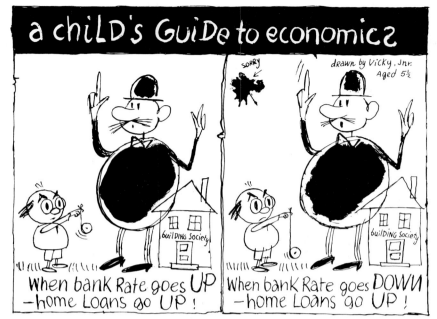

a chiLD's GuiDe to economics

SORRY

drawn by Vicky, Jnr.
Aged 5½

When bank Rate goes UP
—home Loans go UP!

When bank Rate goes DOWN
—home Loans go UP!

126 'A child's guide to economics', *Evening Standard*, 10 June 1965

The Budget of April 1965, one of the toughest in years, was designed to resist the inflationary trend in Britain's economy. The aim of the Chancellor of the Exchequer, James Callaghan, was to reduce domestic consumer spending. Vicky uses the device of a child questioning the stability of the current state of affairs, much as in the story of the 'Emperor's New Clothes', to criticise the effectiveness of this policy.

before the election, a front-page statement was issued,[17] making a three-point apologia for Vicky on grounds of '1. The quality of his work . . . 2. His attack on apathy . . . 3. His right to be heard.' Vicky was, the declaration ran, 'the best cartoonist in Britain today. That is the verdict published in the current edition of *Newsweek*,[18] the influential American news magazine . . . The *Evening Standard* publishes these cartoons with full confidence that its readers will uphold its judgment and support this demonstration of free speech in action.'

This was fairly backs-to-the-wall stuff. If Labour had won the election, Vicky's career might have taken a different turn. Instead,

127 'Introducing: Electrovic, the first robot-cartoonist', *Daily Mirror*, 18 May 1956

Members of the Conservative Government led by Anthony Eden are shown as faceless clones. Vicky made a point of satirising rigidity and bigotry whatever the politics.

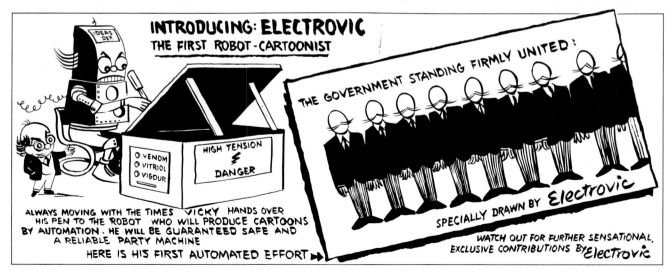

INTRODUCING: ELECTROVIC
THE FIRST ROBOT-CARTOONIST

IDEAS DEPT.

○ VENOM
○ VITRIOL
○ VIGOUR

HIGH TENSION
⚡ DANGER

ALWAYS MOVING WITH THE TIMES VICKY HANDS OVER
HIS PEN TO THE ROBOT WHO WILL PRODUCE CARTOONS
BY AUTOMATION. HE WILL BE GUARANTEED SAFE AND
A RELIABLE PARTY MACHINE
HERE IS HIS FIRST AUTOMATED EFFORT ▶▶

THE GOVERNMENT STANDING FIRMLY UNITED:

SPECIALLY DRAWN BY Electrovic

WATCH OUT FOR FURTHER SENSATIONAL,
EXCLUSIVE CONTRIBUTIONS BY Electrovic

128 'Moscow Tapestry: 1959', *New Statesman*, 7 March 1959

The visit of Macmillan (sporting the famous white fur hat) and Selwyn Lloyd to Moscow for talks with Khrushchev was seen as careful stage management and as a diversionary tactic amid speculation in Britain about the date of the next General Election. However, the background to the visit was more wide-reaching and one of tension and alarm: Khrushchev had suggested the previous November that Berlin should become a demilitarised free city in the territory of the German Democratic Republic, and should inherit from the Soviets all rights to control access. De Gaulle, Eisenhower and Adenauer advise 'no' to everything and on the British party's return are still saying 'no compromise'.

the Conservatives won with a majority of almost 100 over all parties, and everyone's anxiety was for the time being allayed. 'Poor old Vicky,' crowed a reader, 'he did try so hard!'[19] Vicky attributed the win to Macmillan's 'Hat-Trick', his ice-breaking journey to Moscow the previous February, for which he had worn an eye-(and cartoon-)catching white fur hat. Vicky should have been on the trip himself, but the Soviet embassy for reasons which remained mysterious failed to lay on a visa for him. An early-edition *Evening Standard* leader questioning this oversight brought a hasty reparation of the omission, but by then Vicky had missed the plane.[20]

The production of different editions of the day's paper was a large new factor in Vicky's life. Like all daily-press contributors he was used to revising and replacing his work at the last minute when events dictated, but what for others was an emergency procedure now became the rule. He frequently had two cartoons published in a day, and even sometimes three. His routine was firmly fixed. He listened to the radio news at 6.30 a.m., having usually been awake and worrying since five o'clock. From his rented flat, now at 22 Upper Wimpole Street, he then walked to a 'Quality Inn' opposite Broadcasting House in Portland Place, arriving well before eight. Over his invariable breakfast and a lot of coffee (never tea), he attacked the morning papers then took a taxi to Shoe Lane, EC4, there to produce his first idea of the day. Early in the week, he generally had a small stockpile of possibilities to hand, prepared over the weekend to take in to the *New Statesman*'s editorial conference. Here, in a kind of theatrical treat for his colleagues, he would unveil his portfolio of drafts one by one, carefully saving till last what he knew to be the *pièce de résistance*. Some of the superfluous notions might then be recycled later in the week for the *Standard*'s use, leaving the *Statesman* team with the pleasurable and sometimes justified impression that they had taken the cream.[21]

But day by day, new political developments, or dissatisfaction with his cartoon already in print, would always stimulate Vicky to renewed production at the *Evening Standard*. He would stay at his drawing-board in his top-floor studio, a lace curtain over the glass door-panel guarding his privacy, until the day's possibilities, and no doubt Vicky himself, were exhausted. His cartoon for the next day's early editions had to be away by 3 p.m.; but he would often spend the following morning changing the subject

129 Untitled, *New Statesman*, 14 May 1960

In May 1960 the Paris summit conference collapsed in disarray. A United States U-2 reconnaisance plane piloted by Gary Powers had been shot down over the USSR causing ill-feeling on both sides. Khrushchev exploited the tension by waiting until the meeting was assembled before demanding an apology from President Eisenhower. This was not given and the meeting was adjourned.

130 '"Thus speaketh the Lord of hosts, saying, Execute true judgment, and shew mercy . . ." – Zechariah, 7, 9', *Evening Standard*, 26 May 1960

Adolf Eichmann had been one of the Nazi leaders responsible for carrying out Hitler's 'final solution' to the Jewish problem in Europe – a euphemism for mass extermination. At the end of the Second World War he had been captured by the US Army but escaped to South America. In 1960 he was traced by Israeli agents to Argentina, where he had been living incognito, and was abducted. Tried in Israel in 1962, he was found guilty of crimes against humanity and hanged.

" THUS SPEAKETH THE LORD OF HOSTS , SAYING , EXECUTE TRUE JUDGMENT, AND SHEW MERCY .... "   — ZECHARIAH , 7 , 9 .

for the benefit of the afternoon editions. From Easter 1961 on, when Vicky could no longer bear to pretend that Wednesday's news was undeserving of comment, this became a five-days-a-week obligation – the most punishing that he had yet set himself.

In 1960 Vicky's personal ideas and preferences took a series of knocks. He was present in Paris when the longed-for Summit talks collapsed, Khrushchev walking out over the U-2 spy-plane incident. The *News Chronicle* ceased publication, which distressed Vicky greatly (though the simultaneous demise of the *Star* did strengthen the *Standard*'s position in the market). The trial of Adolf Eichmann reanimated horrors that were never far away from Vicky's mind, and over which he grieved through the medium of a strange, cloaked figure embodying stricken humanity (ill-drawn by Vicky's best standards, with its overlong and oddly angled arm upraised to its face, this was another of those conventions signalling that Vicky was working at the very limit of what a newspaper cartoon could say).[22] There was nothing conventional about Vicky's feelings – he felt 'real, deep, emotional grief' over injustices and cruelty – but they froze his will to 'perform'. In direst moments he invoked his humanitarian tableaux as a Christian might the cross.

146

I FIND YOU 'NOT GUILTY' OF CONTINUOUSLY FLOUTING PARTY CONFERENCE DECISIONS . . .

In July, Aneurin Bevan died, saluted by Vicky with a quotation from his own *In Place of Fear*: 'The pulse of progress beats differently for different parts of the world . . . we must recognise that fact and realise that once we stood where they now stand.'[23] This was the broad historical compassion on which Vicky insisted, and to which the Labour Party seemed less and less capable of giving expression, preoccupied as it was with local squabbles. Only a few days before, a directive had gone out from the Parliamentary party to 'refrain from personal attacks on the leader'. Vicky intensified his, accusing Gaitskell roundly of flouting party conference decisions and then finding himself not guilty of the charge – a cartoon to which Vicky appended the sardonic note 'N.B. THIS IS NOT A PERSONAL ATTACK'. As far as Gaitskell's wife Dora could see, however, such comments were indistinguishable from *ad hominem* affronts, and at a reception she accused Vicky of stabbing Labour in the back and called him,

131 'I find you "Not guilty" of continuously flouting party conference decisions . . .', *Evening Standard*, 19 December 1960

At the 1960 Labour Party annual conference the left wing, led by Nye Bevan, identified themselves with the Campaign for Nuclear Disarmament and carried a motion in its favour. The Labour Party in the main remained committed to NATO and this issue rapidly became one which the leader Hugh Gaitskell was determined to resolve. He used his 'Fight, fight and fight again' speech to argue that rejection of a defence policy as a whole meant withdrawal from NATO, and he spent the next year working, successfully, to get the motion reversed.

132 Untitled, *New Statesman*, 16 April 1960

Anxiety about and disapproval of British manufacturing and testing of nuclear weapons first found a clear voice early in 1958 when the Campaign for Nuclear Disarmament (CND) was formed. The mobilisation of nationally known and optimistic intellectuals associated with the *New Statesman* played a crucial role in the movement's birth. At the first meeting were, amongst others (left to right in the cartoon), John Collins, Canon of St Paul's (in whose house at Amen Court the meeting was held), J.B. Priestley, Bertrand Russell, Michael Foot, Kingsley Martin and Vicky. The Easter protest marches CND organised from the Atomic Weapons Research Establishment at Aldermaston to London became an annual event. Vicky draws himself as hopeful that perhaps one day the political leaders of the world – Khrushchev, Macmillan, Eisenhower and De Gaulle – will join such a march. (De Gaulle has adapted his placard to show the symbol of the Free French.)

reportedly, a 'filthy little Hungarian'.[24] Vicky left quietly in the company of Kingsley Martin. Vicky claimed a high regard for the abilities of Gaitskell, 'but I've always somehow believed that he's not the right leader for what I believe a socialist Labour Party should be'.[25] His campaign continued.

The Granada TV programme 'What the Papers Say' named Vicky 'Cartoonist of the Year' for 1960. The newly-formed Cartoonists' Club added a similar title, but he turned down their 'Jester' award on a 'matter of principle', presumably not wishing further to ritualise the processes of competition among his fellow-professionals. Vicky was in an exceptionally outward-looking internationalist phase at this time. He had always associated himself with causes, even going so far as to draw a Christmas card for the Movement for Colonial Freedom in 1955.[26] Now, amid the rising spirit of 'protest', he became identified with a number of pressure groups. Together with Sybil Thorndike, Frank Pakenham (later Lord Longford) and the Bishop of Southwark, Mervyn Stockwood, he issued appeals on behalf of the UK Committee for Algerian Refugees, whose publicity campaign used his drawings.[27] Along with Canon Collins, Anthony Greenwood MP, the Countess of Lucan and J.B. Priestley, he formed a deputation which lobbied the Russian ambassador, Mr Soldatov, protesting against the resumption of Russian nuclear tests.[28] Vicky was also an enthusiastic Aldermaston marcher for the CND. Puzzled by some of the banners carried, which struck him as having little or nothing to do with disarmament, he used to joke that the next

148

"LOOK! I'M SAVING WHITE CIVILISATION ..."

year he would turn up with a sign reading 'Bismarck Must Go!', just to add to the amiable confusion.[29] During the Commonwealth Conference of 1961, he also sat on the pavement outside Lancaster House as part of a protest against apartheid in South Africa. A legal dispute over money was going on at the time between Vicky and his second wife Lucielle. 'He will now have to get back to his drawing-board,' wrote her lawyer with a lawyer's chuckle, 'in order to make up for the arrears of maintenance he has had to pay you!'[30] But Vicky never deserted his drawing-board for long.

He sold many of his originals, usually to the politicians who appeared in them, but the profits he turned over to charity – in one instance by a particularly direct method. Sir Gerald Nabarro MP, the maverick Tory and boss of the No-Nail Box Company, always bought any cartoon he figured in (he acquired twenty altogether)[31] a fact which Vicky exploited. Even in a cartoon depict-

133 'Look! I'm saving white civilisation . . .', *Evening Standard*, 24 March 1960
Since 1948, the South African Nationalist Party under a series of Prime Ministers – Malan, Strijdom and Verwoerd – had created an independent republic outside the Commonwealth and a state based on apartheid. Following the massacre, by South African police on 21 March 1960, of eighty-three unarmed Africans and the wounding of over three hundred more (all of whom were peaceably demonstrating against the pass laws), Sharpeville became a household word. Vicky's horror at the event is plain in his drawing. Verwoerd wades up to his knees in blood, his suit and hands are stained.

149

ing the Tories' entire front- and back-bench personnel as rhinos, an idea promoted by Ionesco's then controversial play *Rhinoceros*, the top-hatted Nabarro was allowed to remain in human form, and duly applied to Vicky for the original.[32] Vicky always agreed to such requests, but charged an inflated price and insisted that Nabarro leave the 'payee' space blank on his cheque. By this means, Vicky was able to convert Nabarro into an active supporter of political charities he would otherwise never have dreamed of funding.

Most of the money went to Oxfam, always Vicky's favourite charity, and the reason why his drawings of the victims of repression and malnutrition came to be known as his 'Oxfam style'. Contemporary advertisements for the Oxford Committee for Famine Relief, however, used drawings by another hand, and it is interesting to note how much less alarming than Vicky's were drawings of the starving which allowed themselves the luxury of a smooth rhythmic line.[33] The propagandist unloveliness of the limbs Vicky drew made colleagues shake their heads and turn

134 Sir Alec Douglas-Home, May 1967

In May 1967, the William Ware Galleries in London organised an exhibition and sale of original cartoons in aid of Oxfam. Many cartoons by Vicky were on sale together with those by such contemporaries as Emmwood, Jak, Papas and Giles. Vicky's old political adversary, Sir Alec Douglas-Home, opened the exhibition and, as if to prove that political wounds heal over, he purchased a drawing, entitled 'The Knack', of himself lying back on the House of Commons front benches. (The film *The Knack* (1965), directed by Richard Lester and starring Michael Crawford, Ray Brooks and Rita Tushingham, was at the time an innovative film about contemporary London. It was based on the original play by Ann Jellicoe.)

IS IT WELL WITH THE CHILD ?

135 'Is it well with the child?', *Daily Mirror*, 10 December 1957

Vicky was a life-long supporter of OXFAM (the Oxford Committee for Famine Relief) and campaigned in the way he knew best. For this cartoon, Vicky wrote the legend, 'Two-thirds of the world's children suffer the effects of malnutrition, disease and ignorance, to-morrow is the eleventh anniversary of the United Nations Children's Fund which depends entirely on voluntary contributions from governments and private sources.'

the page – but his was the likelier style to move a reader to remedial action.

Evening Standard readers still seemed easier to move in other directions. Some merely complained of Vicky's 'disrespectful' approach, as though respectful cartoons were what they had been accustomed to. Others were abusive ('that, to my mind, unspeakable little creature who calls himself Vicky' . . . 'the bloodiest pen in Fleet Street'), and to these Vicky sent a stereotyped reply. Xenophobia was still on the increase. 'I have long felt that you should pack off that dabbler in British politics, your foreign imported cartoonist, to his own native country, where he can try guying his own leaders and get himself liquidated for his pains,'[34] wrote a man from Finchley. In some readers, Vicky inspired an almost physical revulsion ('I personally always pass over – with a shudder – the page where his effort appears') to which the religious were especially prone: 'Eisenhower, Dulles, De Gaulle and Adenauer have one thing in common: they are practising Christians. Vicky's sour cartoons of these fine men are disgusting. His signature crouches in the corner like some malevolent spider.' Some readers were so extreme in their own malevolence that, as the *Standard* Editor Charles Wintour shrewdly calculated, they must inevitably provoke a backlash in Vicky's favour. In other circumstances, one letter from a doctor in Harrow, reacting to Vicky's assertion that the death penalty 'blemishes Justice', might have qualified as unpublishable. 'When I see a cartoon such as Vicky put in on November 11,' the man wrote, 'I feel sorry Hitler did not get hold of him before he reached this country.' Vicky, an editorial note confirmed a few days later, 'had no objection to the publication of [the] letter, which was one of many expressing the same point of view. Publication, which should never be taken to mean editorial approval, has stimulated an avalanche of letters in support of Vicky.'[35]

Stylistically, Vicky's drawings were now paring themselves down to their essential wit. Working at speed in his self-imposed determination to keep abreast of events, he was gradually forsaking the elaborate backdrops and populous supporting casts he had once relished. On particularly fraught days now he sometimes gave an impression of haste – but haste translated into the agitation of his characters. Vibration-lines indicating violent movement – of buildings, towns, even planets, as well as people – are highly characteristic of this excited, hard-pressed phase in his work. Legs had long been reduced to angular sticks, feet to pod-like triangles. There is a feeling of headlong dash in the pen-work, and more

white space: exhilarating but dangerous.

Amid the extraordinary political upheavals of 1963, Vicky reached his fiftieth birthday. Britain had recently been refused entry into the European Common Market; Hugh Gaitskell had died; Harold Wilson had been elected leader of the Labour Party. The *New Statesman* celebrated its Jubilee with a number featuring sixteen Vicky portraits on the cover.[36] (Week by week, in addition to his Profile drawings and political cartoons inside the paper, Vicky was now producing a small front-page drawing to head the 'Contents' column: this was known in the *Statesman*'s local jargon as the 'ear'.) A week later, it was Vicky's own Jubilee. At a dinner presided over by Max Aitken, son of the Beaver and chairman of the Board of Beaverbrook Newspapers, tribute was paid to Vicky by the Beaverbrook cartoonists – Giles and Osbert Lancaster, Cummings and Jak. Carl Giles presented a cartoon of Vicky facing a Tory firing-squad. A slight air of falsity attended the celebration, for Cummings detested Vicky's political line and did not much care for him personally,[37] while Vicky and Jak,

136 'A tribute from one master cartoonist to another', *Evening Standard*, 26 April 1963 by Giles

At a dinner in honour of Vicky's fiftieth birthday, Sir Max Aitken presented Vicky with this Giles cartoon. Giles drew a diminutive Vicky standing on a soapbox in front of a daubed hammer and sickle to indicate his political leanings (the paintbrush and pot of whitewash lie nearby). He faces a line of people who would dearly like to be rid of him. Selwyn Lloyd stands in the middle brandishing a blunderbuss, with a Giles granny on the far left of the group.

PEOPLE MEETING MR. SELWYN LLOYD FOR THE FIRST TIME PROBABLY DO NOT FEEL HIS IMPACT BECAUSE OF HIS GOOD LOOKS, HIS GOOD MANNERS, HIS IMMENSE BUT UN-EXTRAVAGANT CHARM...

MEN OF IMPACT – Nº1

137 'Men of Impact – No. 1', *Evening Standard*, 19 May 1961

In reality, Selwyn Lloyd was short in stature, small in nose and mouth and had an ordinary chin. Vicky invented a completely new nose for him and here makes him truly a dwarf. As Chancellor of the Exchequer Lloyd was heavily reliant on Macmillan's goodwill (as the huge portrait behind implies) and in July 1962 was one of the victims in the 'Night of the Long Knives' when seven Cabinet ministers were sacked at a stroke.

Standard colleagues, were more or less openly incompatible, maintaining long, wordless feuds that ran into periods of years.[38]

To cap this unlikely junketing, the senior Conservative ex-Minister Selwyn Lloyd (dismissed nine months before in Macmillan's Cabinet purge) turned up with his own cartoon of Vicky, whom he depicted, not altogether ineptly, as a horned devil. To judge by the history of Vicky's versions of Selwyn Lloyd, this may very well have been the first evidence of competence he had personally observed in the man, who for years had been the target of one of Vicky's most implacable campaigns of sarcasm. 'I had difficulty with Mr Selwyn Lloyd,' he once admitted. 'I was in the end accused of almost having invented him. I tried to portray this rather timid little man, although he is not a little man at all, and probably not very timid either. I may have got it wrong, got him wrong, I don't know. I've always believed that politicians grow more like the drawings than they are in real life.'[39] In Lloyd's case the adaptation was largely a nasal matter. The feature Vicky had chosen to exaggerate in him was a nose which he strangely extruded as if to suggest that the organ was about to turn itself inside out – a process which dragged up Lloyd's top lip to expose a set of moronically questing teeth. It was a persuasive image which, like many of Vicky's finest inventions, somehow got clean away from reality and took the public with it.

With his girlfriend Ingelore Lew, a young and stylish fashion-buyer of German-Jewish origin who worked for Marks & Spencer, Vicky took an early summer holiday in Ischia. Though an enthusiastic sun-worshipper, and always a grateful escapee from the British climate, he was not very good at holidays. Addicted as he was to news, he began to fret as soon as his morning fix of information was withdrawn. On occasion he had been known to give up and come home early. Now it happened again. 'In Ischia he had promised not to look at a newspaper,' the *Evening Standard* reported. 'All went well for a day and then he saw the headline "Profumo Crisis". He tried to forget it, but every time he saw a perfume shop – *Profumeria* in Italian – he worried. By the weekend he could stand it no longer. He flew back.'[40]

Vicky could not bear to miss a crisis that might bring a government down. John Profumo, Secretary of State for War, had resigned from Parliament just before Vicky's departure, but only now were the reverberations of the event shaking the Establishment. 'Today is the crucial debate in Parliament,' Vicky wrote excitedly to Inge on 17 June.[41] 'I'm now sure Macmillan will get through but he'll retire within three months from now.' Vicky had a marvellously fine-tuned judgement of political probabilities. Macmillan actually lasted four more months. About the sexual background to the Profumo case Vicky had little to say. This was an area of scandal in which the British peculiarly revelled, though selectively (they were prepared to overlook, for example, the philanderings of Lloyd George); but Vicky still inclined to the continental view, dear above all to the French, that the individual sexual morality of political leaders was to a very large degree no business of the public's. Moreover Vicky was too highly-sexed himself to gloat over another man's enslavement to his hormones. So while his *Statesman* colleague 'Trog' (Wally Fawkes) cornered the market in shady ladies, establishing a small but uproarious tradition of call-girl jokes ('There's no doubt in

my mind, sweetie, life was better under the Conservatives'),[42] Vicky held back. His 'ear' drawing of Profumo tended to stress the nobility of a sufferer; and his one reported attempt at scurrility, Macmillan as Richard III crying 'My kingdom for a whore!', was turned down by Kingsley Martin's successor as *New Statesman* Editor, John Freeman.[43]

The world was changing faster than Vicky professionally cared to see. In only one respect was he conservative, and that was in wishing to be left in peace with the characters he had 'worn in'. Now, within the space of a few weeks, Macmillan resigned and John F. Kennedy was assassinated. For the first event, Vicky was ready. Lord Home, now to become Prime Minister as Sir Alec Douglas-Home, had grown familiar as Foreign Secretary, and would continue to appear as a cross between a skeleton and a matchstick man (a guise which happened to suit his reputed habit of making economic calculations with the aid of matches). Naturally, *Evening Standard* readers pronounced Vicky's portrayal of the new leader as 'satanic'; and indeed, the widely held view that Home was completely innocuous was not shared by Vicky who subscribed to the *Statesman*'s characterisation of him as the 'Cold War Earl'.[44] He treated life, public and private, the Profile-writer opined, 'with the competent complacency which, in his view, it deserves'. There was nothing much to appeal to Vicky in such a personality.

As for the Kennedy shooting, he was shocked by the event but not devastated as he might have been by the particular loss to politics the President's death entailed. Flying from New York to Los Angeles to cover the Democratic Convention of July 1960, Vicky had found himself sitting next to the then Senator Kennedy, whose company he shared for a full six hours. Several sketches were made. 'You've made me look rather old,' Kennedy said, signing one of them. 'This handsome young American face,' Vicky reported, 'with the charming Lindberghian, toothy smile is dominated by strange, cold unsmiling eyes which seem too old. It was *this* expression I concentrated on and he spotted it.'[45] In Vicky's vocabulary, 'Lindberghian' was not an altogether complimentary adjective, for it denoted not just the glamour of the aviator but the extreme pro-German isolationism of the political orator Lindbergh later became. Vicky was looking through Kennedy to his father Joe, an anti-British Catholic with his own isolationist connections. The lineage was worrying, and Vicky had never been able to forget it.

While Beatlemania raged and Shakespearians celebrated 1964's

138 Untitled, *New Statesman*, 29 November 1963

This full page of sketches of John F. Kennedy accompanied an article written by Karl E. Meyer entitled 'History as Tragedy'. President Kennedy's term of office had been cut short by his assassination, on 22 November 1963, in Dallas, Texas. In July 1960, Vicky had spent six hours sitting next to Kennedy on a plane travelling from New York to Los Angeles for the Democratic Convention. He noticed 'the handsome boyish features of Senator Kennedy', but also his cold eyes that seemed older than his years.

157

SALUTE TO GIACOMETTI AT THE TATE

139 · Untitled, *New Statesman*, 23 July 1965

Vicky finds another way of depicting Sir Alec Douglas-Home. Maudling, Heath and Macleod look at his gnarled and emaciated body displayed in the style of the Swiss sculptor and painter, Alberto Giacometti. The cartoon appeared the day after Douglas-Home resigned the leadership of the Conservative Party.

Quatercentenary of the Bard, the political world entered numbly upon another election year, in Britain and America. The *Standard* roused themselves again to anticipatory wrath, but by now it was tinged with a bitter resignation. It was hard to believe in Douglas-Home's chances of victory. 'When Harold Wilson gains power, the obvious choice for a life peerage must be Vicky. Don't sack him, it's too late,' grunted one correspondent, almost equivocally. Another, looking more rationally to the future, asked: 'What on earth is Vicky going to do if, with the kind assistance of the *Evening Standard*, Labour comes to power at the next General Election? Surely he could not possibly ridicule with truth and fairness Mr Wilson as he does Sir Alec Douglas-Home nor agitate against a Labour government as he does against the present one?' This, for once, was a question worth asking, but there could as yet be no answer to it. Vicky contented himself with chronicling the slow submersion of Tory hopes. In the *New Statesman* he drew a scene from Beckett's *Endgame*, with Douglas-Home and Selwyn Lloyd imprisoned in their dustbins. 'Finished, it's finished, nearly

"...WE HAVE NOT YET FOUND A WAY OF TALKING TO THE YOUNGER GENERATION" — MR. MAUDLING ON JULY 6.

TOP OF THE POPS: TWISTIN' AND SHOUTIN'

The Whitehall Beatles

EXCLUSIVE PICTURE OF BRITAIN'S SENSATIONAL NEW VOCAL GROUP REHEARSING FOR THEIR FIRST APPEARANCE AT BLACKPOOL NEXT MONTH.

140 'Exclusive picture of Britain's sensational new vocal group rehearsing for their first appearance at Blackpool next month', *Evening Standard*, 12 September 1963

In 1962 the twin themes of modernisation and European cooperation were used as pegs on which to hang the flagging image of the Conservative Party. De Gaulle's veto in 1963 put paid to the second, and the first – expenditure on roads, universities and technological research – never provoked the expected public response. In the run-up to the General Election, Macleod, Maudling, Butler and drummer Hailsham present their own version of up-to-the-minute unity by masquerading as the pop group, The Beatles.

finished, it must be nearly finished,' they chanted. 'Mac the Knife' made one surprise reappearance, when Iain Macleod, the former Tory Chairman, spilt the beans in the *Spectator* about Macmillan's determination that Rab Butler should not succeed him. It was one of the last cartoons in Vicky's last, punningly titled collection, *Home and Abroad*.[46]

On Polling Day, Vicky left his wife-to-be Inge, as was his habit,

'FINISHED, IT'S FINISHED, NEARLY FINISHED, IT MUST BE NEARLY FINISHED.' — SAMUEL BECKETT, ENDGAME

141 '"Finished, it's finished, nearly finished, it must be nearly finished" – Samuel Beckett, *Endgame*', *New Statesman*, 31 July 1964

Edward Heath was the victor in the voting for a Conservative Party leader to replace Douglas-Home on 27 July 1964. Douglas-Home and Selwyn Lloyd await the outcome in the dustbins of 'Nagg' and 'Nell' – the senile parents from *Endgame*. Vicky uses 'Hamm''s opening phrase from that play – an observation on the inevitable passing of time – to show that all are just waiting for this particular political episode to come to an end.

142 '"On the sidewalk Sunday morning lies a body oozing life. Someone's sneaking round the corner. Is that someone Mac the Knife?" – *The Threepenny Opera*', *New Statesman*, 1 February 1958

Early in 1958 Macmillan decided that the time had come for an expansionist economic policy. The Conservatives had just lost the Rochdale by-election, coming third behind the Liberals who had run a close second to the surprise Labour victor. Vicky feared that the Welfare State would be butchered by the Government to finance this expansion and would soon be without life.

an illustrated note on the breakfast table. 'Hope that you had a really good rest,' it read, 'so that you can face the day and all its arduous duties.' A vigorously X'd ballot paper completed this graphic reminder. Every vote did indeed count. The headline on next morning's *Evening Standard* was 'Wilson Makes It – Only By Four.'[47]

Drawing to a Close   *8*

On 24 October 1964 – the Labour government was just a week old – Vicky was married for the fourth time. Dr Johnson's phrase 'triumph of hope over experience' might have been invented for him, the more pointedly so since the pattern of his new alliance was just the same as ever. He had lived with Ingelore Lew for a couple of years already, and now the relationship would have to survive the strain of its solemnisation. Aurelia Weisz, Zlata, had divorced Vicky the previous June,[1] naming Inge as his partner in adultery. 'I'm so terribly sorry that you should be dragged into

143   Wedding day, 1964

At the Marylebone Registry Office in London, on Saturday 24 October 1964, Vicky married for the fourth time. Ingelore Lew was an independent woman with her own career as a designer for Marks & Spencer, and the only wife to have active Jewish connections.

Here's my Heart — dear Ingelein,
but be my own sweet Valentine.

We're not in his Horoscope, haha!

Jerry,
It worked

144A 'Here is my heart – dear Ingelein, and be my own sweet Valentine', unpublished, no date

144B '*We*'re not in his Horoscope, ha ha!', unpublished, no date

Each morning Vicky wrote and illustrated in colour a letter to Inge. These letters remain the only record of their life together. They are very domestic in nature – shopping, washing up, details of the weather forecast – but hint at a darker side; sleep and health problems. Valentine's Day and birthdays were always picked out for special attention. Vicky's twin problems – the devil (illness) and the ghost (insomnia) – wage war over his head while he glumly reads the currently fashionable *Queen* magazine. At one point (referring to Inge's sleeping problems), he wrote in a morning letter, 'Now there are two unquiet spirits spooking around at night.'

this,' Vicky told Inge in an early-morning note. 'I so wanted to avoid all unpleasantness – but now, I'm afraid, it'll be just that.' His sketch showed Inge with a halo, and himself as a blue-chinned malefactor in the dock, pleading 'Not Guilty!' to the judge. The alimony payable to Zlata meant that he was now disbursing to two former wives at once, neither of whom had known, while married to him, what he earned.

The only one of Vicky's wives with active Jewish and Israeli connections, Inge was a slim, smart, career woman, about the same height as Vicky and equally self-lacerating in her conscientiousness. Her flair had at last made a comfortable home of the flat at 22 Upper Wimpole Street, which in Zlata's time had been, in that lady's own opinion, 'freezing, like a cellar'.[2] The morning notes tell of domestic responsibilities shared (Laundry Day, the Saturday shopping) and shirked (Vicky cooked well but seldom washed up. Inge's halo made frequent in-house reappearances).

They ate out a good deal, being especially fond of the White Elephant Club, run by Vicky's old friend Stella Richman,[3] and the Hungarian restaurant the Gay Hussar, whose proprietor, Victor Sassie, had been smitten with Inge for years. Along with

admiration, however, came an insight into her complicatedly des-
pairing nature. Inge was, Sassie felt, 'one of those people who
never survived the war. Her mind was shattered by what the Germans had done to the Jews. She was very conscious of being German as much as she was Jewish . . . She didn't feel she had the
right to live, somehow . . . She didn't want to participate. She
was disillusioned to the point of extinction.'[4]

It is noticeable that in the morning messages which are now
the only record of their life together, Vicky works just as hard
to raise his wife's morale as he does to apologise for the humps
and hollows in his own – which is saying a good deal, since Vicky
was now complaining of a number of ailments, not all of them
acscribed to the hypochondria he had seemingly 'caught' from
his brother Oscar. His lumbago was almost certainly an occupa-
tional legacy, his delicate stomach the result of worry. His head-
aches (drawn as little goblins with hammers, or in bad cases a
whole girder atop the head) might have arisen from any combination of eye-strain, tension, three and a half decades of accumulated
concentration, or an internal war between the barbiturates he took
at night and the pep pills that sometimes enlivened his day. He
had once been an eighty-cigarettes-a-day man, but under the
simultaneous instructions of doctor and dentist, he had given up
overnight in a startling display of will-power. He drank wine with
meals, preceded eccentrically by brandy, of which he was con-
tinentally fond.[5]

Sleep was a problem to both partners. They kept three beds
– yours, mine, ours – to accommodate the mood of the moment,
sometimes bestowing or receiving 'night visits' for which Vicky
expressed gratitude in the morning. Their sexual compatibility
was apparently intermittent. Vicky sometimes apologised for his
bad performance, emotional or physical; and there is one enigmatic drawing, of Vicky and Inge strolling on the seashore followed at a distance by a woman in a pullover, which might
indicate that Inge was not as convinced in her sexual orientation
as Vicky was. 'I'm so glad it all went better than we had feared
and I know it'll lead me to a better understanding of you', was
Vicky's inscription. (A lesbian involvement had reputedly figured
in the break-up of his marriage to Zlata).[6]

With his marriage to the *Evening Standard* Vicky always pronounced himself perfectly content, in spite of the readers, who
were now clamouring for a post-Election role-reversal: 'Now
that we have a Socialist government, could we have a Tory cartoonist?' Charles Wintour felt unable to oblige. As for Vicky,

145   Untitled, *New Statesman*,
25 December 1964

Harold Wilson, who had been Prime
Minister for only ten weeks, looks
over his shoulder to his recently
defeated challenger Alec Douglas-
Home, now transmuted into a Dalek.
(A Dalek was a mutated alien inside a
high-technology wheelchair able to
project lethal rays. Writer Terry
Nation named it, for the TV series *Dr
Who*, after an encyclopaedia volume
covering DAL-LEK.) Current
rumours were that Wilson would be
calling a spring election (his party's
present majority was very slim); this
being so, Home is armed and ready.
He has already 'exterminated' other
rivals, now only one remains.

his immediate problems were aesthetic rather than political. He
could not produce, either in cartoon form or as straight sketch
portraiture, a version of the new Prime Minister which satisfied
him. This was a very old problem. As long ago as 1950, in Milton
Shulman's book *How to be a Celebrity*, which he had illustrated,
Vicky had asserted that 'Harold Wilson, President of the Board
of Trade, is practically hopeless from a cartoonist's point of view.
There is nothing in his face that is remotely abnormal.' Vicky
wished, reported Shulman, that Wilson would 'grow a beard or
something. And then he added a remark which showed how far
Wilson had really sunk in the artistic scheme of things. "I still
have to stick a label on him," he said, as if confessing some secret
crime.' Of course, there was no danger of his having to resort
to such humiliating expedients in 1964. Yet the Wilson Vicky
was having to settle for – a light-eyed roundhead with gappy
teeth and a quiff dangerously reminiscent of Herbert Morrison
– did not do much more than identify the man. The figure unmistakably embodied Wilson while somehow missing the interesting
things that could be said about his face – things which Vicky

tended to lump together into two fat black smudges underlining the leader's eyes.

Seriously worried over the problem, Vicky discussed it with Tom Baistow, who one day spotted a Trog cartoon that seemed to sum it up. It showed Wilson coming home from work in his habitual Gannex coat, calling 'I'm home, dear' to his wife, and hanging his face on a hat-rack.[7] No wonder Vicky didn't feel he ever got him right, Baistow said; nobody did. Grateful for the thought, Vicky nevertheless still had to work out a way of dealing with Wilson's mask. A political problem underlay his difficulty. Vicky was still unsure how much faith to, almost literally, 'place in' Wilson. On the Prime Minister's record were some items that should have endeared him considerably to Vicky – notably his support for Aneurin Bevan at the time of his Health Charges resignation, and the book Wilson had produced in 1953, *The War on World Poverty: An Appeal to the Conscience of Mankind.* Here was a title that could not have been more appealing to Vicky if he had devised it himself. But since that period Wilson had given evidence of less altruistic concerns. His skill in calculating career moves had outstripped his other talents, and how much of the idealist remained in him now remained to be seen. Vicky wanted to believe in him, but the instinct of his pen, one senses, was predicting disappointment. For the first time, too, Vicky was beginning to deal in leaders who were younger than himself. It is possible that he experienced the guying of his elders as a psychologically essential component of his work; he had never had time to grieve over the father who had deserted him.

Vicky's criticism of Labour, to the probable but unexpressed astonishment of *Evening Standard* readers, began within a few weeks, when a sale of war-planes to South Africa contravened an earlier statement of 'principle'. Wilson acquired 'cat's eyes' with triangular pupils – a small advance. Consolation of a kind for Vicky came in the result of the American Presidential election, won in a landslide by Lyndon Johnson over the unthinkable hard-Right Republican Barry Goldwater. Vicky's Goldwater, a black-clad 'baddie' cowboy, had been a caricatural success, but so had the Stetson-topped Democrat Johnson with his huge ears and leathery jowls.[8] Vicky's instinct about L.B.J. suggested that with his knowledge of Congress, the new President would very likely get more things done there than Kennedy would have managed. This intuition would have proved sound in the matter of America's domestic politics, had Vicky lived long enough to see it worked out. But now the Vietnam War had set in motion yet

146 '"Yes, we are in the closest touch about developments" – The Prime Minister on Tuesday', *New Statesman*, 18 June 1965

President Johnson's hard-line anti-communist views and those of his advisers had resulted in an escalation of the number of US troops in Asia from early 1964 and this continued through the first half of 1965. He believed in the 'domino theory', that the fall of South Vietnam to communist rule would eventually mean the fall of all South-East Asia. Harold Wilson offered no criticism of this policy and is shown to be subservient and poorly clothed in contrast with his rickshaw rider.

'YES, WE ARE IN THE CLOSEST TOUCH ABOUT DEVELOPMENTS'

another of those cycles of military oppression and counterthrust which Vicky so vividly dreaded.

Harold Wilson called on L.B.J. in Washington just as the heaviest fighting was breaking out in Vietnam. To Vicky this was an early test of Wilson's Socialist commitment, recalling the visit Gaitskell had paid to Kennedy at a time when the Americans had just recommenced a programme of H-bomb tests. Gaitskell had failed him, refusing to put over the message that his own Labour Party was on record as condemning all such tests by whatever nation. Now Wilson had a similar but more urgent opportunity. Inevitably, Vicky suffered disillusion once more. Worse would come, but even in 1964, he was drawing L.B.J. in Gannex and pipe, and Wilson in a Stetson, enjoying a 'frank and full exchange of views'.[9] This was not so much agreement as a shameful mutual absorption.

A world the young Vicky had made his own was now slipping away. Winston Churchill and Herbert Morrison, two of the stalwarts of *Chronicle* days, died; Rab Butler, Vicky's putative ally among the Tories (and certainly a reliable bulwark against the hangers and floggers in the party) retired to the House of Lords. Vicky's latest – last – version of the 'Mona Lisa' ('The Smile'), which once had framed the likes of Stalin and Bevan, found itself delineating the less momentous physiognomy of Mr Patrick Gordon-Walker.[10] Great men were passing from the face of the earth. A tremendous loss to Vicky's personal pantheon was the death of Albert Schweitzer, whom he had described, in respect-

THE NEW CABINET

147 'The New Cabinet – "A country neglects its eggheads at its peril . . . it is time we got together" – Lord Hailsham', *New Statesman*, 4 January 1958

Vicky produced his own key for this drawing of the New Year Cabinet, as follows (reading from left to right):

Back row: Minister of Agriculture, Lord Boyd-Orr (animal nutritionist);

Minister of Education, John Osborne; Minister of Labour, T.S. Eliot; Minister of Health, Dame Edith Sitwell; Home Secretary, Malcolm Muggeridge; Lord Chancellor, Bertrand Russell; Minister of Defence, Capt. Liddell Hart (military theorist and historian); Colonial Secretary, Kingsley Martin (*New Statesman* editor); Duchy of Lancaster (Responsible for Information), Vicky.

Front row: Foreign Secretary, A.J.P. Taylor (historian); Prime Minister, Lord Hailsham; Chancellor of the Exchequer, Victor Gollancz (publisher).

Another suggestion, but one which did not appear, was Minister of Supply, Prof. Jacob Bronowski (mathematician and humanist).

fully sketched form, as the 'world's greatest man'.[11] The rising young generation of 1960s 'satirists' sensed in this hero-worship a weakness, a kind of piety, in Vicky. *Queen*, one of the iconic 'trendy' magazines of the decade, made it the basis of a heavy attack on him, denouncing his 'humanitarian' drawings as mawkish utterances revealing Vicky as a 'mindless suppliant for progressive sympathy'.[12] Unlike those great caricaturists whose theme is the follies of mankind, the writer barged on, Vicky also

167

ANOTHER DAY OF
INDIAN SUMMER

148 'Another day of Indian summer', unpublished, no date

Vicky's letters to Inge nearly always contained a weather prediction – 'You can rely on V.W.F.!' (Vicky's Weather Forecasts) – usually with drawings of the sun or perhaps himself as a snowman. Sometimes he did not bother, especially when it was raining – 'You *know* the weather forecast.' This drawing shows Inge as a hedgehog, Vicky as a snail.

failed in his satirical duty when drawing 'international Schweitzer-figures, whom he invariably flatters. His self-portrait "signature" drawing, hinting at the harmless "little man", contrives, by its juxtaposition with the attack in the cartoon, to suggest that he both loves power and rejects it (a characteristic Schweitzer attitude).' The idea that a cartoonist might both love power and reject it seemed to come as a bit of a shock to this theorist, as though this were some strange perversion of Vicky's own – whereas in fact it would serve very well as a shorthand definition of the kind of people almost all cartoonists are, including the great ones with a supposedly detached interest in human folly. It is certainly true that Vicky 'flattered' Schweitzer to the extent of never sending him up (Bertrand Russell, whom he similarly revered, he knew well enough to take to the borders of comic caricature); but it is hard to begrudge Vicky the odd venerable humanitarian in whom to glimpse the possibility of a constructive non-party-political idealism. Privately, he drew himself reading *Queen* while Inge perused the *Spectator* – a satire for home consumption.

Vicky's domestic drawings for Inge, done completely off the cuff, delicately coloured with crayon, and featuring Harold Mac-

168

millan scarcely at all (except as MacChicken), were executed with a charming grace and an inventiveness that matched Vicky's best professional standards – and all were done before his working day began. In this genre he was his own best subject. According to circumstances and the prevailing level of self-criticism, he might metamorphose into a frog, a centipede, a hound in a doghouse, half a pair of lovebirds or snails, Hamlet, King Lear, Shakespeare, a spook, a spaceman, a Scotsman, a spring lamb, a Chinese face on a tin of peaches, or even the nib of his own pen. Inge appeared either as herself, or in a limited range of encouraging metaphorical guises, as flower, or butterfly, or the twin creature of whatever Vicky happened to be that morning. Inge also stood accused of being a floating voter (between Lib and Lab), a reader of James Bond, and a fan of 'The Saint' and 'The Avengers' on TV (Vicky had been obliged to join the TV age).

Together, they might play Scrabble at home, or go out to an orchestral concert. Vicky had grown weary of the theatre, and the triviality of most modern plays positively angered him. Under the influence of Zlata he had gladly turned to concert-going, enduring even the deeply suspect Wagner for Inge's sake. He preferred not to inflict on her the social duties of the famous man's wife, knowing that she would have to put up with a lot of shop-talk. An unavoidable dinner at the Society of Industrial Artists and Designers, of which Vicky was a Fellow, went typically badly, bringing breakfast-time apologies and a drawing of a tableful of faceless men – the 'Society of Insipid Artists', as he captioned them. Most notes ended with a capsule weather forecast, ironically annotated with, for example, a picture of the sun 'drawn from memory', Vicky's favourite weather-joke since 'Weekend Fantasia' days.

Throughout his newspaper career, Vicky had lived in fear of waking with an empty head. He could not see where the next idea was coming from, therefore it might not come. He had described such a feeling to Lucielle back in the 1940s.[13] Reviewing the 1960 two-volume history of *English Political Caricature* by M. Dorothy George, he had put it on record: '[The graphic artist's] one pursuing fear must be the haunting doubt whether tomorrow will bring its life-saving idea. And I am ready to testify that *that* is fear enough.'[14] Now, in his drawings for Inge, he presented himself still as empty-headed, blank-paged, his thought-bubbles mere white spaces. Friends sympathised, but it was hard to take Vicky's protestations seriously. Year after year, he always *did* come up with a daily idea – indeed, if ideas were

149 'The man who never was',
Evening Standard, 23 July 1965

Alec Douglas-Home's year as Prime
Minister was dogged by his
unpopularity with colleagues and lack
of personal impact on the public, who
remained unimpressed by the slogan,
'Life is better under the Conservatives'.
On 15 October 1964 Labour won an
overall majority in the General
Election – albeit only four seats –
which put an end to thirteen years of
Conservative rule. The Tory
leadership issue continued towards
crisis point until Home's disinclination
to retain the leadership if a fight was
involved led him to resign on 22 July
1965. This left the way open for
Edward Heath, who became the first
Conservative Party leader elected by
ballot. This cartoon's caption is that of
a film (released in 1955) about a dead
man carrying false papers who was
dropped into the sea in 1943 by the
British secret service in order to
confuse the Germans.

THE MAN WHO NEVER WAS

in such short supply, why was he so prodigal with them, putting
in replacements when the notion he'd first thought of would have
done? It all felt like part of some self-therapeutic rhetoric on
Vicky's part, an aspect of the self-dramatisation that helped him
carry on.

In August 1965, however, he did force himself to take a three-
week holiday in the Alps, the longest parting from work he had
had since the terrible 'flu bout of twenty years before. In an interview for a book published directly after his death, Vicky mentions
a period 'two or three months ago' when 'I was desperate', and
this was probably it. 'I said to myself, take a year off. There are
pressures, steady pressures. Then it passed.'[15] One can only wish
Vicky had taken his own best advice. The summer break was not
enough. It followed a fraught period consequent upon the resignation of Douglas-Home from the Tory leadership, a departure
Vicky greeted with an acidly barren cartoon of the sepulchrally
grinning stick-man heading for a hugely signposted Exit, over
the caption 'The Man Who Never Was'. The *Standard* readers
responded with a unison burst of paroxysmal outrage. 'Completely disgusting . . . What a contrast between your balanced
appreciation of the man, and the situation, and the cheap stupid
ungraciousness of the cartoon . . . Vicky's cartoon is malicious,
vicious and in gross bad taste . . . this petty little scribbler . . .'[16]
and so on. It was not, perhaps, the cartoon one would have chosen
to illustrate Vicky's subtlety – and yet, in the gesture of the hand,

170

half-waving, half-groping, there is an oddly memorable ambiguity which a lesser artist, had he had the luck to happen on it, might have expunged in favour of something more definite. But Vicky was close to running on instinct alone here. It was a good time to get away.

He returned to an autumn of gathering political gloom. The Wilson problem had been staved off by Vicky's last great thematic series – the neo-Shepard *House at Pooh Corner* drawings. Arising from Wilson's reported habit of humming when he was worried, these cast Wilson as Pooh and George Brown as the uncontentable donkey Eeyore. Such cosiness, however, was difficult to apply to international affairs. A new Indo-Pakistani war was in progress, Russia admitted supplying arms to Hanoi, and Ian Smith was confronting Her Majesty's Government with the possibility of what duly became Rhodesia's Unilateral Declaration of Independence. On top of it all, Vicky faced the imminent danger of the withdrawal from politics, subject to election results, of his last

150 '"Hello, are you stuck?" he asked. "N-no," said Pooh, carelessly. "Just resting and thinking, and humming to myself." – *Winnie the Pooh*', *Evening Standard*, 25 February 1965

Harold Wilson was keen to effect some kind of saving in his Government's defence expenditure. Attempts to do this involved cancelling his predecessor's plans – the Hawker Siddeley 681 short take-off and landing transport plane, the Hawker P1154 supersonic vertical take-off fighter and a fifth Polaris submarine – all of which proved to be unpopular decisions (see also **154**).

THE GREAT FRENCH MIME MARCEL MARCEAU IS NOW APPEARING IN LONDON.

151 'The great French mime Marcel Marceau is now appearing in London', *Evening Standard*, 15 August 1962

De Gaulle's European policy was based on plans for French domination of the 'Six' or 'Little Europe' (Belgium, Germany, France, Italy, Luxembourg and the Netherlands) and complete independence from the United States. He was uncompromising and distinctly cool towards Macmillan's efforts to secure British membership of the EEC because of the British Government's allegiance to Kennedy and the Commonwealth. De Gaulle gave the final 'thumbs down' and said 'Non!' in January 1963.

inexhaustible international figure, Charles de Gaulle. Vicky hated De Gaulle, as a man wholly in thrall to a messianic vision of his own embodiment of power; but he needed him. His loss would deprive Vicky of the last remaining thread leading back to the Gerald Barry years. He had never piped De Gaulle quite as thin as a thread, but it had sometimes been close: the General had appeared as the striped pole on a road-block, a traffic signal (red light only), and a golf club; the slinkiest of mannequins, a giraffe, and a cork in a bottle. Matching Macmillan for a while in his literary and historical range, he had played Joan of Arc, a Roman Emperor, Giant Despair, Cyrano de Bergerac, Napoleon, the Sun King and Marcel Marceau (a cartoon Vicky presented to the great mime himself). Squeezed into the shape of a cactus or Concorde, he was equally recognisable. 'Cher Monsieur Le Président,' pleaded Vicky in his last Open Letter, 'we have lost of late some of our dearest subjects, and are left largely with props such as the pipe, the smile' (Vicky made much of Edward Heath's cupid's-bow lips) 'and the hat. I appeal to you not to resign as this would be the final blow to us.'[17] De Gaulle obliged by defeating François Mittérand for the Presidency in December; but two months later, the final blow fell anyway.

★   ★   ★

When a man commits suicide, the indications that it was inevitable leak back into the memory of his friends – an uncomfortable form of wisdom after the event. Looking back on the man's daily out-put of work it is easy to complain that they should have known all along. One can only say that, at the time, Vicky's work occa-sioned no alarm. Its gradual deterioration went unnoticed by the world at large. Everyone had become accustomed to a sparser texture in the pen-work, amounting now to a bleached look, as of a man who lacked the energy to apply much ink. Half-tones were almost banished, the interest in shades and textures virtually gone. Vicky had been inventing daily for thirty years in Britain, and for most of a decade before that on the Continent. He was very, very tired, and could not sleep. He felt, so he said to James Cameron, that he was losing his capacity for work.[18]

At the start of 1966, Cameron had just been in Vietnam, making a series of exceptionally fine reports. After a hellish return journey lasting several days he subsided into his British bed, only to be awakened at 3 a.m. by a telephone call from Vicky. 'Jimmy,' he said, '*what* are we going to do about *Rhodesia*?'[19] This anecdote circulated long afterward as evidence of Vicky's preposterous and endearing tenacity – his unique insistence that politics not only mattered but could be materially altered by the concern of indi-viduals. But dating as it does from the last weeks of Vicky's life, the story should perhaps take on a more tragic gloss. Here was a man who had sacrificed his sense of self-preservation to the seriousness of his work.

That large proportion of the British public whom Vicky had failed to shake out of a sport-fixated apathy now looked forward to the 1966 World Cup. For Vicky, the social and political scene offered very little future allure. Wilson was in Johnson's pocket. He had failed to get tough with Ian Smith. Even Gaitskell would have described the immigration policy he was settling for as 'shabby'. The 'hard, unpopular decisions' he had promised had turned out to include medals for the Beatles. Vicky felt, he said, as if he now did nothing but criticise Labour.[20] The BBC let him down by banning Peter Watkins's film *The War Game*, with

173

COME AND CHEER THE HILARIOUS SUPER-HUMAN EXPLOITS OF ACE-HERO **BATMAN**

COME AND **HISS** THE VILLAINOUS, WILY ORIENTALS!

SUPPORTED, OF COURSE, BY HIS INTREPID BOY-WONDER ASSISTANT **HAROLD**

152 'Batman the thrill-serial, which has been sweeping America, is starting its London run today', *Evening Standard*, 2 February 1966

President Johnson had announced in his State of the Union message on 12 January that the USA was strong enough to fight brutal and bitter war in Vietnam, pursue its goals in the rest of the world and build a 'Great Society' at home. Wilson as Boy Robin barely clings to the cloak of this 'super-hero'. The idea for this cartoon was suggested by a reader who was at that time Press Officer for Columbia Pictures, the distributors of the film.

whose anti-nuclear aim Vicky deeply sympathised. The social atmosphere was poisoned by the Moors Murders trial, in which tape recordings of the torture of children were brought in evidence. When the stork delivered 1966 in Vicky's cartoon, there was a black hawk among the surrounding doves.[21]

In the first week of January James Cameron joined the *Evening Standard* as 'The Dissenting Voice', something Vicky might have supposed he already was. Still, with Michael Foot already there as book critic, Vicky was truly among friends. He continued courteously to go about his business, sending originals and notes both to the playwright Frank Marcus, whose award-winning drama *The Killing of Sister George* he had converted into a starring vehicle for George Brown, and to the reader who suggested Batman as a possible role for Harold Wilson. It was a bomb-dropping

174

L.B.J. who actually took the part, with Wilson as his boy assistant, Robin.[22]

Readers were up in arms again, over Vicky's treatment of Ian Smith – physiological rather than political this time. 'Vicky's cartoon,' came the thunder from Gillingham, 'deliberately caricatured the drooping and puckered left eye. Perhaps not all your readers are aware that this disfigurement is the result of severe burns sustained while piloting Hurricanes and Spitfires against the Luftwaffe in World War II . . .'[23] Vicky could hardly be expected to modify Smith's physique in salute to his war record, and he did not.

Towards the end of January 1966, he asked his Editor, Charles Wintour, out to lunch. They bought lunch for each other in alternation every three months or so and it happened to be Vicky's turn. In the course of the conversation he said, without emphasis, that whatever happened to him, he had never been so happy as he was on the *Evening Standard*. That was nice to know, Wintour replied. Then Vicky repeated his assurance, this time with underlinings – *whatever* happened he had *never* been so happy. Wintour reaffirmed his pleasure with added warmth. Everyone misses a clue, and Wintour looked back on this exchange as his.[24]

One wonders how close Vicky had come to sharing the sentiments of one Kurt Michael Oppen, whose thoughts appeared at the end of January in the letters column of the *New Statesman*.[25] In reply to Malcolm Muggeridge's article announcing that he loved England, Mr Oppen declared in angry, depressed and ultimately callous terms that he, for one, did not. Inveighing against the climate, the decrepitude and ugliness of British cities, industrial antagonisms, intolerance of non-whites and Jews, and an attitude to work which made it 'not a creative activity but a kind of spiritual death', the correspondent concluded: 'Why, then do I remain? As the French would say: "*Faute de mieux, je couche avec ma femme.*"' It is not even certain that Vicky could say as much. He told Tom Baistow that at one time or other, all four of his wives had denied him access to their bed. Baistow became convinced that Vicky now foresaw the end of yet another marriage.[26]

In mid-February Vicky took a week's break. In the last fortnight his Editor had felt that his cartoons had 'lacked their normal force',[27] and this was an opportunity for him to replenish his energies. But Vicky brooded on this, becoming apprehensive, his wife later said, that he was going to lose his job.[28] On his own, he travelled down to Climping in Sussex, to stay at Bailiffscourt, a quiet, scenic hotel built out of renovated medieval frag-

153 'Just look at the mess you've made, Wilson!', *New Statesman*, 25 February 1966

Denis Healey's Defence White Paper in February 1966 contained a number of controversial decisions – retention of military commitments east of Suez, abandonment of the CVA-01 aircraft carrier (thereby provoking the resignation of Navy Minister, Christopher Mayhew) and the decision to purchase fifty F-111A aircraft from the USA. Edward Heath is not in a position to criticise. The previous Conservative administration also had a history of defence investment and then cancellation – specifically of Blue Streak (in 1960) and Skybolt (in 1962). This drawing would have been selected at the *New Statesman* weekly editorial meeting on Monday, 22 February 1966. As the paper is printed on a Wednesday, ready for sale on Thursday, this is therefore the only cartoon to have been published after Vicky's death.

JUST LOOK AT THE MESS YOU'VE MADE, WILSON!

ments, and an old haunt of his and Inge's. From Bailiffscourt he sent a Valentine to Inge, a day late, sketching the sun – 'drawn from nature (really)' – with one of the new Staedtler-Noris felt-tip pens he was trying out. But by next day the treacherous British climate had closed in on him again. 'Yesterday was sunshine,' he wrote, solitude bringing out a vestigial Germanic tinge in his style,

> today is raining and a biting wind – the sea is angry. I'm going for long walks nevertheless and read. The nights are cold, long and lonely and – rather frightening. There is a new young, unsympathetic French couple (with dog) and a young shy English couple (with baby) and the bearded old man (he's called Professor) who only seems to have lunch here. The food seems to have got much better and I'm sure my tummy is getting bigger. I hope you've settled in back home and don't feel too lonely. Thinking of you and loving you – Vicky.[29]

By the weekend he was home again, bringing his frightening nights with him. In his absence, Hannen Swaffer Awards for journalism had gone to James Cameron as Writer of the Year, and to Michael Foot as Critic. Vicky's closest friends were at the top of their form. On the Sunday night he went to hear Beethoven's Eighth conducted by Klemperer at the Festival Hall.[30]

At the *New Statesman* on Monday, he deposited an 'ear' of Denis Healey and a cartoon in which Edward Heath, standing in a bin

FLEET STREET'S VOLATILE 'CARTOONIST COURAGEOUS' IS DEAD AT 53

Unmistakable: the style of his caricatures

 SUPERMAC HITLER DE GAULLE AND HIMSELF

Vicky's last cartoon

VICKY — cartoonist courageous — died in London yesterday.

He was found dead in a bedroom of his home in Upper Wimpole Street. He was 53.

And last night Londoners were looking at his last cartoon in the Evening Standard, which first published his work when he fled to Britain in 1935.

The last "dig"— a drawing of the Wilson - Kosygin meeting in Moscow.

Vicky, born Victor Weisz, of Hungarian parents in Berlin, started as a political cartoonist in Germany in 1929.

After Hitler's rise to power he came to Britain and quickly became a front-rank cartoonist.

He was with the News Chronicle for 13 years before joining the Daily Mirror and finally the Evening Standard in 1958.

Although he was hailed as a genius and one of the most pungent political commentators, Vicky was always under fire by critics.

'Spite'

In 1955 a Labour M.P. complained in the Commons of a "most ill - natured and spiteful attack"—and, later, Vicky's "Supermac" and Douglas - Home caricatures offended Tory voters.

Vicky married Miss Ingelore Lew in October 1964. It was his second marriage.

—*from the Evening Standard yesterday*

154 Untitled, *Evening Standard*, 23 February 1966

Wilson had arrived in Moscow on 21 February for three days' talks with Soviet leaders, among them Premier Kosygin. Items on the agenda were the difficult and major issues of the spread of nuclear weapons, Vietnam, and possible ways of reducing tension between East and West. Wilson left Britain in the wake of a defence row (see **150**) and General Election speculation. Not far from his mind is how successfully Macmillan improved his image as a world statesman when he visited the USSR in the election year of 1959. This is the last cartoon Vicky ever drew.

of 'Tory Defence Litter', points the finger at Wilson who occupies a smaller 'Labour Defence Litter' bin of his own. It was by any standards an acceptable production: if it had been the first published effort of a new cartoonist, one would have called it promising. But judged against Vicky's work of even a year or so before, it has an exhausted look, as did Vicky on that day. Paul Johnson, who had succeeded Freeman as Editor, asked Vicky if he felt better for his holiday. Vicky said no, he was sleeping only two hours a night. Then he went in to see Mervyn Jones, one of his newer *Statesman* colleagues. He couldn't stay long, he said, as he had to go and do something for the *Standard* on the worsening situation in Nigeria. Seeing how bad Vicky looked, and sensing what manner of cartoon he had in mind, Jones suggested hesitantly that perhaps it might be better if he didn't do a Nigeria cartoon. After all, he could take any old event as his subject, it didn't have to be Nigeria. No one was demanding it of him. 'I demand it of myself,' Vicky said, and those were the last words Jones heard him speak.[31]

No comment on Nigeria appeared. Vicky's cartoon of Tuesday 22 February clothed Healey as Britannia with a 'F-111' trident and an 'East of Suez' shield.[32] By 3 p.m. that day Vicky had gone on to complete a scene in which Harold Wilson sat at the conference table in Moscow (where he now was), facing the Soviet leader Kosygin but thinking of Big Ben approaching the electoral eleventh hour.[33] Vicky returned to Upper Wimpole Street. The previous Friday, the perennial Dr Nicholls had prescribed him some new sleeping tablets, non-barbiturates and 'completely harmless'.[34] But Vicky still had a stock of barbiturates in the form of Tuinals, which he had been taking for years, usually in pairs. When he retired to bed, he took a dose amounting to four times the maximum medicinal dose. Inge was away on business in Manchester. Vicky left her a note on the writing-desk.[35] According to report, it clearly indicated his intention. Inge returned the following morning to find Vicky dead, in an ordinary position of sleep.[36]

★   ★   ★

The news spread so rapidly that Vicky's family was taken cruelly by surprise. Oscar Weisz learnt of his brother's death from a television newsflash. Their sister Elizabeth was in a newsagent's shop when the proprietor crassly pointed out the headline in the *Evening Standard*. She fainted.[37] The *New Statesman* staff were in the print-room preparing the week's edition when they heard. Paul Johnson knocked out his emergency tribute in ninety minutes. In Moscow, Harold Wilson interrupted his preparations for a number of television broadcasts to issue a tribute at midnight local time. 'All of us who have enjoyed his creations,' he said, 'including not least the victims of some of these creations, mourn his passing. British public life will be the poorer for all of us.'[38] The *Spectator*'s Diarist had talked to Vicky just a few days before. 'He told me (not for the first time) that he was haunted by the fear of going on after he had said all that he had to say. At least he did not do that,' wrote Nigel Lawson.[39]

A *Times* obituarist tapped out the opinion that Vicky was 'not a very profound thinker'.[40] His old friend and *Chronicle* colleague Professor Ritchie Calder jumped in to rectify this. 'His childish charm (as a person) and his impish humour (as a cartoonist) concealed an intellectual depth which was often embarrassing to his associates,' Calder wrote, marshalling his thoughts for the entry on Vicky he would eventually write for the *Dictionary of National Biography*. 'How could one cope with a jester who could dissect British humour or plumb British politics far below the depths of the party programmes, or quote incessantly books which one should have read, or ask scientific questions that scientists had

never asked themselves?'[41]

The *Evening Standard* readers had their say. One of their traditions was represented exemplarily by Lord Cardross, who wrote in to say:

> You misjudge your readers if you really think that Vicky will be missed. Your paper was bought in spite of him, not because of him. The only people who will miss the cartoons will be the inhabitants of the tiny little world of Fleet Street, and I suppose it was for their benefit that you put in your self-congratulatory bit about 'best cartoonist of his generation'.[42]

Fortunately there were contrasting views, and some poignant ones. A representative of the Owner-Drivers' Radio Taxi Service wrote to say how popular Mr Weisz had been on his habitual run from Upper Wimpole Street to Shoe Lane.[43] 'Now that this lucid interpreter is no more,' added a lady from west London, 'we realise how much he meant to us. Did *he* ever realise it?'[44]

Such reactions emerged after the inquest, where Vicky was described as a 'depressive person' who would fall into phases of depression suddenly, often pulling out again after about a week. The Westminster Coroner recorded that Vicky had died of barbiturate poisoning self-administered while suffering from depression. Oscar and Elizabeth had tried to disguise the facts of the case from their mother, Isabella Weisz, but this now became impossible. It was another suicide, after nearly forty years – this time the devoted son who had supported her financially and visited her week by week ever since her arrival in Britain. It was

155 Untitled, *Observer*, 4 January 1987 by Trog

The Earl of Stockton, Harold Macmillan, who died on 30 December 1986, arrives in heaven only to meet his old adversary. This admirable cartoon by Wally Fawkes is a fitting tribute to Vicky's influence by a fellow political commentator.

too much for the eighty-four-year-old woman, who fell ill and died within six weeks.

In his will Vicky left £19,719, most of it to Inge.[45] He continued to make money posthumously for Oxfam. From a Memorial Concert at the Festival Hall, where the distinguished Hungarian conductor Georg Solti made a rare appearance as a pianist, proceeds of £1157 7s. 2d. were passed on to the charity.[46] Royalties from the 'Memorial Volume' James Cameron edited the following year went to Oxfam also.[47] An exhibition of 'Vicky and his contemporaries' at a gallery in the Fulham Road was opened by the not yet re-ennobled Sir Alec Douglas-Home. 'Faced with the choice between my TV image and Vicky's,' Home jovially confided, 'I chose the latter.'[48] Those old digestive processes of British politics were slowly metabolising Vicky's reputation. He had been a jolly good show.

One last sadness awaited his friends. In 1975, Inge was found dead from an overdose of drugs. She had a long history of mental illness, the court was told, and had made frequent attempts to kill herself. Every year on the anniversary of the death of her husband, she slipped into a bout of deep depression. This time she had not emerged.[49]

★   ★   ★

What Vicky would have made of the next twenty years of politics is a fascinating and terrible question. He spared himself the completion of the Vietnam horror; the rise and fall of Richard Nixon (whom he had given ample evidence of despising) and performances by subsequent presidents which have made Eisenhower look like a tactical genius; the assassination of the famous by the mad, and the powerful by the fanatical. Had he lived he would have had to face visual evidence of mass starvation such as had never been seen by the world audience since the liberation of the German concentration camps. Neither Israeli policy nor Arab terrorism could have failed to rob him of sleep.

What kind of socialism could he have continued to support? Only the art critic John Berger fully faced this question in the aftermath of Vicky's death. Berger's opinion in 1967 was that Vicky had admitted to himself the ultimate futility of 'legitimate' political action. 'Socialists who want socialism in Britain,' he wrote, 'are now bound to work outside the publicly defined and acknowledged areas of political life; and perhaps, soon, outside the law. The shop steward or the president of a students' union is now potentially a far more politically significant figure than any member of parliament. It seems to me likely that Vicky realised this.' Berger was writing before the somewhat symbolic upheavals of 1968; but substitute 'local councillors' or 'constituency Labour Party officials' for the students and union men and you have an argument that still works. 'Once he became an outsider,' Berger continued (tellingly, because Vicky had trained himself so heroically to be an insider), 'critical and sceptical of the whole political circus, it would have become quite impossible. He was bound to lose either his liberty or his mass public. He would have been reduced to working for a small militant minority ... He needed his mass public, not for his vanity but for his faith.'[50]

Could Vicky have worked for the 'small, militant minority' we have since seen arise? Is the idea of a Social-Democratic Vicky remotely possible? Surely no to both. But one can be sure he would not have picked his way tactically through to a well-defended position. Vicky did not calculate politics, or dispense politics, or even really 'have opinions' on politics. He *felt* politics, an art he taught us all too briefly . Now we have lost it again.

References

CHAPTER I

1. Michael Bateman, *Funny Way To Earn A Living*, pp. 9–12. Where publication details are not quoted in these Notes see Bibliography.
2. BBC Home Service radio broadcast, 'Frankly Speaking', 12 February 1960. About half the thirty-minute programme is preserved in the BBC Sound Archives, the rest is in transcript only.
3. *Ibid.* Vicky's soft-spoken delivery may suggest 'Dennstedt'.
4. *Ibid.*
5. *Ibid.*
6. Oscar Weisz, interview with Peter Birks, 31 May 1978. All three Weisz children anglicised the spelling of their first names on arriving in England. The text follows their example.
7. Quoted in Milton Shulman. *How To Be A Celebrity*, p. 209.
8. Hans Tasiemka, *Freies Volk (Schweiz)*, 26 February 1954. Rolf Nürnberg (Nuernberg), editor of the Sports Section, was the son of the owner of the *12 Uhr Blatt*. A boxing fan, he produced a biography of the heavyweight champion Max Schmeling (1932), whose cover bears Vicky's typical beetle-browed simplification of the boxer's face. An incomplete file of the *12 Uhr Blatt* survives in the State Library of the DDR, East Berlin. On a brief visit in May 1987, R.D. was able to inspect a microfilm run of the paper from August to December 1932, the last months before Hitler's accession to power. During this time Vicky drew chiefly sportsmen (preponderantly boxers), film stars like Garbo and Dietrich, and visiting variety artistes such as Wilson and Keppel (of the British music-hall team Wilson, Keppel and Betty). Vicky's political output was confined to portraits ('Face of the Day: Goering'), and the occasional political cartoon with an art-world slant, e.g. Nazi leaders starring in their own production of '*Was Ihr Wollt*' ('What You Will'). Vicky shared cartooning duties with a less vivid performer called Goltz. He signed himself 'V.Weiss', or, celebrating his involvement in the newspaper world, '*V.Weiss, 12 Uhr Dienst*' ('12 Uhr Service').
9. Vicky to Lucie Gray Weisz, 25 June 1957. 'It is strange how the *Dreigroschen Oper* has suddenly "arrived" after all these years – I remember seeing the first night back in 1928 – Ah, well.'
10. Unsigned, *Der Spiegel*, 2 June 1949, pp. 30–31.
11. Quoted in Uwe M. Schneede, *George Grosz, His Life and Work*, (London, Gordon Fraser, 1979), p. 159.
12. *News Chronicle*, 20 April 1944 (Hitler's birthday).
13. *News Chronicle*, 3 September 1947; 'Vicky in *Wirtschaftswunderland*', *New Statesman*, 14 September 1957.
14. *News Chronicle*, 30 January 1953.
15. Unsigned, *Der Spiegel*, 2 June 1949.
16. 'Pem', *Anglo-Jewish Refugee Information*, April 1966, p. 10.

CHAPTER II

1. Born Wittkowski, son of a dentist. For a time represented MGM in the Balkans.
2. The actress Beatrice Lillie had an apartment in the same building. Adjacent to Vicky's studio was an office where Dr Hans Feld, Alberto Cavalcanti, Robby Lantz and his father Adolf Lantz were attempting to set up a film company (Dr Hans Feld, interview with R.D., 5 May 1987).
3. *Evening Standard*, 14 February 1936.
4. Apparently the only reliable source of European

newspapers was a stall in Piccadilly.

5. Dr Feld had been a guiding light of the famous *Film-Kurier* magazine. In May 1987 he was a guest of honour at the opening of the West Berlin Film Museum.

6. *Headway*, November 1938. Described as 'a caricature drawn from life'.

7. Quoted in Ian Hunter, *Malcolm Muggeridge: A Life* (London, Collins, 1980), p. 115.

8. 'Vicky by Vicky' did not mark the artist's first appearance in his own work. *12 Uhr Blatt*, e.g. for 19 September 1932, under '*Wochenschau*' ('Show of the week'), has Vicky as a film cameraman in tweed cap and plus-fours.

9. Vicky had reportedly signed an animation-film contract in Berlin, and had made stage and costume designs for the Scala Theatre (*Sketch*, 10 November 1937).

10. It was possibly here that a famous Vicky anecdote originated. When a restaurant radio began to play the *Horst Wessel Lied*, Vicky called the waitress over and insisted, 'I cannot hear this tune.' The girl obligingly turned the volume up, whereupon Vicky reiterated his complaint, with a consequent further increase in volume. He finally fled the restaurant, still unaware that 'I cannot' does not usually mean, as the German does, 'I am not

willing to'. (Recounted by Quentin Crewe, *Sunday Mirror*, 6 August 1967.)

11. *Sunday Dispatch*, 5 December 1937. 'Almost in Confidence', by the Marquess of Donegall.

12. Mme Lucie Gray Mondange, interview with R.D., 16 February 1987.

CHAPTER III

1. BBC radio, 'Frankly Speaking', 12 February 1960.

2. 'One of the rare great ones', by Gerald Barry, *Observer* 27 February 1966.

3. *Ibid.*

4. 'Innocents at the Oval', by George Mikes and Vicky, *News Chronicle*, 19 August 1953.

5. *Time and Tide*, 28 December 1940. Gerald Barry wrote to protest against Lady Rhondda's supposed allegation that the *News Chronicle* had been spreading 'alarm and despondency' (which under wartime regulations was a criminal offence). Lady Rhondda replied that the words used had actually been 'gloom and despondency'.

6. The release of 'Wooping' (Willie Wolpe) from the Mooragh camp was reported by the *News Chronicle* on 28 August 1940. In the *Dictionary of National Biography 1961–70* (Oxford University Press, 1981), P.R. Ritchie Calder reported that Vicky 'was frequently denounced as an enemy alien,

subject to drafting into the Pioneer Corps', but did not enlarge upon this. The Home Office state that Vicky had received a work permit and permission to stay in Britain indefinitely, on 14 March 1939. Also, on 31 January 1942 a Home Office directive was issued exempting him from internment and from the special restrictions applicable to enemy aliens under the Aliens Order 1920.

7. Reprinted in Cabell Phillips, *From the Crash to the Blitz* (London, Collier-Macmillan, 1969), p. 257. Cartoon titled 'Fellow Diplomats', 27 February 1938.

8. Vicky to Lucielle Gray, 15 February 1946.

9. James Cameron in *Vicky: A Memorial Volume* (London, Allen Lane, 1967).

10. Vicky to Lucielle Gray, 16 December 1945. 'Low's been doing some lovely stuff from Nuremberg – I think I would have done something different though (not so good of course).'

11. *News Chronicle*, 31 May 1941.

12. *News Chronicle*, 23 June 1941.

13. The first 'Weekend Fantasia' appeared on 16 August 1941.

14. *News Chronicle* report, 27 July 1943. 'Vicky cartoon for Italians': '. . . *non avete da perdere altro che le catene*'. 'The drawing is printed in black and white with the surrounding borders in magenta. On the back is General Eisenhower's proclamation to the Sicilian

people, issued last week.' From 1939 to 1946 the Studio Manager at the Ministry of Information responsible for the visual preparation of Official Propaganda was Edwin J. Embleton MBE, among whose portfolios survive Vicky's versions of the following wartime personalities: Viscount Gort, Admiral Sir Dudley Pound, General Sir Edmund Ironside, Air Chief Marshal Sir Cyril Newall, Lord Chatfield and Lord Nuffield.

15. Quoted in Rotha, *Richard Winnington, Criticism and Caricatures 1943–53*. Also Tom Baistow, interview with R.D., 6 January 1987.
16. *Time and Tide*, 28 January 1939.
17. Born 1905, wartime broadcaster for the Indian Section of the BBC.
18. *Daily Worker*, 20 December 1944.
19. *New Statesman*, 6 January 1945.
20. *News Chronicle*, 19 November 1941.
21. *News Chronicle*, 31 July 1945.
22. Like Vicky, an active promoter of Picasso, some of whose work he showed at his Haymarket gallery.
23. Sir Matthew Smith (1879–1959), much influenced by Matisse and the Fauve movement. Tate Gallery retrospective, 1953.

CHAPTER IV

Unless otherwise specified, material in this chapter is taken from the collection of letters written by Vicky to Lucielle Gray, 1945–6, now preserved at the Brynmor Jones Library of Hull University, Cat. No. DX/166. '173 pages are illustrated' (catalogue note).

1. Published in 1931. Rodney Ackland (born 1908) was often called 'The English Chekhov'. 'His best early plays . . . inhabit a world which recalls the seedy Bohemian gentility of the novels of Jean Rhys' (*Oxford Companion to English Literature*, 1985 edition).
2. 23 November 1945. Some of the early letters carry only an indication of the weekday, but can be dated from internal evidence.
3. 5 December 1945. Vicky's hopes of going to Nuremberg had also been dashed that day. He had put up the idea 'about 3 times . . . without success and am mad'.
4. *News Chronicle*, 20 December 1945. 'The Old Masters Were Once "Garbage" Too.'
5. 16 January 1946. Vicky spelt the name 'Benzindrine'.
6. A patriotic 'Comedy in 4 Acts' by Christine Jope-Slade and Sewell Stokes. Stokes wrote to commiserate with Ackland on the withdrawal of his play, reminding him that it would be remembered long after *Britannia* was forgotten. (Press cutting, n.d., in possession of Lucie Gray Mondange.)

7. Letter in *News Chronicle*, 13 February 1946.
8. *Ibid.*
9. *Tribune*, 29 March 1946. 'Vicky of the *News Chronicle*', by Frederic Mullally.
10. Peter Noble, *Profiles and Personalities*.
11. None of Lucielle's answering letters is preserved.
12. No. 136 Grove Hall Court. 'In the beginning I used to go up to Grove Hall Court in the early afternoon, prepare the dinner and all that and then go to bed. When he was asleep, I'd get up, dress and dash back to my rented room. In the beginning it was wartime and sometimes there were air raids. I used to run down the road gazing at the searchlights, listening to the planes, the bombs. In the end I gave in and went to live at Grove Hall Court – it was just one room.' (Lucie Gray Mondange to R.D., 23 February 1987.)
13. Letter, *ibid*.

CHAPTER V

1. *News Chronicle*, 11 March 1946.
2. No. 98, 1 May 1946.
3. *News Chronicle*, 17 July 1946.
4. This was another of Vicky's traditions that began at the *12 Uhr Blatt*. The edition of 31 December 1932 featured not only Vicky's multi-frame sports round-up of the year, but also a month-by-month

'*Voraussage* [forecast] *für* 1933'.

5. *News Chronicle*, 22 February 1947.
6. No. 56, 15 March 1947.
7. The 'Smith' signature made a late appearance on 23 May 1949. By October, pocket cartoons carried Vicky's own signature.
8. Translated from an unsigned article, *Der Spiegel*, 2 June 1949.
9. Beecher Moore to L.O., 19 September 1986.
10. BBC radio programme 'Born Elsewhere', broadcast 16 February 1964. Transcript.
11. *Ibid.*
12. Vicky article, *News Chronicle*, 3 September 1947. Slightly paraphrased.
13. 20 September 1947.
14. Tom Baistow, interview with R.D., 6 January 1987.
15. *News Chronicle* report, 8 October 1948.
16. The ghost outline of James Keir Hardie (1856–1915), Socialist pioneer, tended to lurk as an accusing presence at the back of Vicky's more chiding tableaux, e.g. 'The Party Spirit', *News Chronicle*, 2 October 1953.
17. No. 65, Vicky to Lucie Gray, 26 March 1946.
18. *News Chronicle*, 17 June 1948.
19. 'The Secret Life of Harry Truman', *News Chronicle*, 24 November 1948. James Thurber's 'The Secret Life of Walter Mitty' first appeared in the *New Yorker* on 18 March 1939, but the Danny Kaye film of the same name was released in 1947, reaching London in 1948.
20. Director of American Division of Ministry of Information 1941–45, Deputy Director-General of British Information Services in U.S., 1941–2.
21. Tom Baistow, quoted in Rotha, *Richard Winnington*, and interview with R.D., 6 January 1987.
22. *News Chronicle*, 25 January 1949.
23. *New Statesman*, 28 March 1959.
24. *News Chronicle*, 27 October 1948.
25. *News Chronicle*, 19 October 1950.
26. *News Chronicle*, 3 May 1949.
27. *News Chronicle*, 6 September 1949.
28. *Ten Days That Shook The World*, eye-witness account of the Russian Revolution (published 1919) by John Reed (1887–1920).
29. *News Chronicle*, 22 September 1949.
30. 'The New Germany Is Much Like The Old', *News Chronicle*, 13 April 1950.
31. 'Love Me, Love My Dog', *News Chronicle*, 23 May 1945: 'Horse', *ibid.*, 3 October 1949.
32. Attlee, Gaitskell, Heath. (Respectively *News Chronicle*, 26 October 1949; *Daily Mirror*, 4 December 1957; *New Statesman* 15 October 1965.)
33. Milton Shulman, *How To Be A Celebrity*, p. 214.
34. Frederick James Marquis, Lord Woolton (1893–1964), Conservative politician. Became Food Minister in 1940, famous for association with exiguous wartime recipes like 'Woolton Pie'. Appointed Minister of Reconstruction, 1944; later a senior coordinator of Tory strategy.
35. *News Chronicle*, 24 February 1950.
36. *News Chronicle*, 7 March 1950
37. *News Chronicle*, 28 March 1950
38. Quiff cartoon, 'The Inevitability of Gradualness, In Memory of Sidney Webb', *News Chronicle*, 22 May 1950. Morrison reviewed Vicky's *Stabs In The Back* for that paper on 27 June 1952: 'One day I said to him, Vicky you old rascal, last week you made me look 90. Next week he did another cartoon in which he made me look 190! It's best to grin and bear it.'
39. *News Chronicle*, 23 October 1950.
40. *Keep Left*: by a Group of Members of Parliament (New Statesman Pamphlet, May 1947). Followed up by *Keeping Left*, January 1950.
41. 'Growing Pains of a Nation', *News Chronicle*, 2 April 1951.
42. '"Vicky's" Sketches From Israel', *Jewish Chronicle*, 27 April 1951.
43. The series began on 7 May 1951.
44. *News Chronicle*, 19 June 1951.
45. *News Chronicle*, 27 October 1951. The Conservatives won 321 seats, Labour 295 and Liberals 6.

CHAPTER VI

1. *Vicky: A Memorial Volume.*
2. Anthony Howard, interview with R.D., 6 January 1987.
3. *News Chronicle*, 7 December 1951.
4. 'Vicky envied Horner greatly, the way he approached his work with total nonchalance and ease.' Aurelia (Zlata) Weisz, interview with Peter Birks, 7 February 1977.
5. 'Land of Fortissimo', *News Chronicle*, 29 July 1952. 'In Memory of Max, 1872–1956', *New Statesman*, 26 May 1956.
6. 'I went to draw people', *News Chronicle*, 1 October 1952.
7. 'Arthur Brittenden's Coronation Diary', *News Chronicle*, 14 May 1953. Among Vicky's comments were: 'What could be worse than those ugly crush gates painted scarlet, green and sickly lavender? . . . Of course, I'm a black and white artist and so have no idea about colours.'
8. Peter Grosvenor (ed.), *We are Amused.*
9. '. . . and may I in this National Nature Week make another appeal for the preservation of wild life . . .', *New Statesman*, 24 May 1963.
10. 'Vicky looks back 20 years', *News Chronicle*, 30 January 1953.
11. Arthur Horner, interview with Peter Birks, 25 August 1976.
12. Aurelia Weisz interview, 7 February 1977.
13. *News Chronicle*, 18 September 1953.
14. *World Press News*, 18 December 1953.
15. *News Chronicle* editorial, 12 December 1953.
16. *Reynolds News*, 13 December 1953.
17. *Manchester Guardian*, 12 December 1953.
18. They were divorced on 8 July 1964.
19. Tom Baistow, interview with R.D., 6 January 1987.
20. BBC 'Frankly Speaking' broadcast, 12 February 1960.
21. *Manchester Guardian*, 12 December 1953.
22. *Daily Mirror*, 26 March 1954. 'Vicky, Jane and Mr Wilson'.
23. *Daily Mirror*, 1 February 1954.
24. *Daily Mirror*, 24 February 1966.
25. *Daily Mirror*, 8 March 1954.
26. *Daily Mirror*, 18 August 1955.
27. *Daily Mirror*, 20 August 1955.
28. Quoted in Piers Brendon, *Ike: The Life and Times of Dwight D. Eisenhower* (London, Secker & Warburg, 1987), p. 231.
29. *Sunday Dispatch*, 1 August 1954.
30. Four cartoons by Vicky were included by Lord Butler in his memoirs, *The Art of the Possible.* He supplied a Foreword to Vicky's collection, *Vicky Must Go!*
31. An account of a losing game played by Vicky against the same Hugh Alexander is given by Heinrich Fraenkel ('Assiac') in *The Delights of Chess* (see Bibliography).
32. 'Cry Hungary' went on sale in late November at two shillings a copy.
33. Vicky's signature on the congratulatory montage was faked, not very well.
34. 'What's in a name?', *Daily Mirror*, 1 March 1954. 'The *Economist* has suggested a composite Chancellor . . .' Butskell was later killed off by Vicky: 'Personal Announcements: Mr Butskell, our composite Chancellor, quietly passed away on April 20, 1955 . . . (No tears!)', *Daily Mirror*, 22 April 1955.
35. 'We're right behind you, comrades', *Daily Mirror*, 28 February 1958.
36. 'Old Vicky's Almanack for 1957', *Daily Mirror*, 1 January 1957.
37. *Daily Mirror*, 20 March 1958.
38. Now of the *Nouvel Observateur.*
39. 'Vicky has foreseen, with his traditional pessimism, that this man will finish on the wrong side of the barricade, and he was right. P. Grumbach works today for Robert Herstant, the French equivalent of R. Murdoch, and none of us is on speaking terms with him.' (K.S. Karol to R.D., 25 April 1987.)
40. 15 May 1958. 'In England the campaign for nuclear disarmament is developing rapidly,' Vicky assured his '*Chers amis*'.
41. On 21 February 1959, there was a meeting of Bevan, Pietro Nenni (leading Italian

socialist) and Mendès-France at Bevan's farm in the Chilterns. A record of the discussion was published as *Rencontres* (Paris, Julliard, 1959). On his way home, Mendès-France attended a *New Statesman* editorial lunch. The photographer Henri Cartier-Bresson was present at both gatherings, and took a fine profile shot of Vicky at the lunch.

42. *New Statesman*, 31 December 1955. Drawings datelined 'St Georges-de-Vièvre, Dec. 1955'.

43. 'Vicky in *Wirtschaftswunderland*', *New Statesman*, 14 September 1957.

44. Cutting in *Daily Mirror* file. Article by Wolf Mankowitz, 29 September 1957.

45. London Diary by 'Critic' (Kingsley Martin), *New Statesman*, 14 May 1955. Vicky is not mentioned by name, but the subject of the piece is 'a personal friend who came here in 1934 and is now a British citizen'. Such a description might also have approximately fitted Heinrich Fraenkel, but when Fraenkel was interviewed (Peter Birks, 9 November 1976), he was 'insistent that I could quote him on one specific thing – that Vicky refused reparations from Germany during the time of the *Wirtschaftswunder* in the 1950s. Vicky was the only person Fraenkel knew who refused reparations' (Birks' notes). This seems to settle the matter.

46. Tom Baistow interview, 6 January 1987.

47. Another factor in Vicky's departure was apparently anti-Semitism among *Daily Mirror* readers: 'rather sordid stuff', commented Lord Cudlipp (conversation with R.D., 10 March 1987).

CHAPTER VII

1. This pamphlet included a cartoon by Vicky, and another by Zec, which the Labour voter was encouraged to pull out and use as a poster. The scheme caused controversy when Lord Hailsham (Quintin Hogg), on behalf of the Tories, declared that it contravened election regulations. Vicky drew himself imprisoned in the stocks (*Evening Standard*, 25 November 1958).

2. 'Vicky wields his pen like a rapier, pricking the pomposities of the politicians on the Left and Right. Especially on the Right.' *Evening Standard*, 31 October 1958.

3. *News Chronicle*, 15 March 1948 ('Lord Beaverbrook has come back invigorated . . .'). See also *News Chronicle*, 23 January 1950 ('Another call, your Lordship') with its spoof telegram to Beaverbrook: 'Please come home stop needed urgently here to supply election laughs stop Vicky.'

4. Beaverbrook once invited Vicky to participate in a country-house weekend, from which he returned unrefreshed. 'But at least Beaverbrook didn't get it all wrong,' Vicky assured his friends. 'He did show us a film.' 'Which film?' his friends enquired. '*The Lost Weekend*,' replied Vicky. (Dr Hans Feld.)

5. Paul Johnson's Diary, *New Statesman*, 14 May 1965.

6. The figures quoted by Ewan Pearson ('Focus on Fleet Street') in *Tribune*, 21 November 1958, were:
   News 1,225,013
   Star 789,485
   Standard 589,706

7. Photostat of Vicky's original contract kindly supplied by Sir Charles Wintour.

8. *Evening Standard*, 31 October 1958. 'Milton Shulman introduces "This Man Vicky"'.

9. Stephen Meredith Potter (1900–69). whose *Supermanship* was the fourth in the instructive series inaugurated in 1947 by *The Theory and Practice of Gamesmanship ; or the Art of Winning Without Actually Cheating*.

10. BBC radio 'Frankly Speaking', 12 February 1960.

11. *Evening Standard* report, 6 November 1958.

12. Low to Vicky, 13 November 1958.

13. *Evening Standard*, 5 November 1958.

14. *Evening Standard*, 11 December 1958.

15. BBC 'Frankly Speaking',

12 February 1960.

16. Vicky Jnr. began to make regular appearances in the *News Chronicle* during 1951. Vicky Snr. invariably addressed him as 'dear'.

17. 'Vicky and the *Evening Standard*', 16 September 1959.

18. *Newsweek*, 14 September 1959. The opinion was actually that of thirty-four-year-old draughtsman, James Ivey, who had been touring Europe, meeting 55 cartoonists in 11 countries. 'When I visited Vicky he told me, "A cartoon is a signed statement of belief and opinion. By-lined columnists are given freedom to state opinions. Why not cartoonists in America?"'

19. *Evening Standard*, 12 October 1959.

20. 'No Visa for Vicky', *Evening Standard*, 20 February 1959.

21. Anthony Howard, interview with R.D., 6 January 1987.

22. The right arm upraised to the suffering head had been a frequent motif, more naturalistically drawn, in the work of Käthe Kollwitz.

23. *Evening Standard*, 7 July 1960. Aneurin Bevan, *In Place of Fear* (London, William Heinemann, 1952).

24. Mervyn Jones, interview with Peter Birks, 9 February 1977.

25. BBC programme, 'World of Books', 1 January 1963.

26. *Daily Mirror* file cutting, 18 November 1955.

27. *New Statesman*, 24 December 1960.

28. *Daily Mirror* file, 6 September 1961.

29. Mervyn Jones, 9 February 1977.

30. Solicitor's correspondence dated 15 March 1961, supplied by Lucie Gray Mondange.

31. *Daily Mirror* report, 28 February 1966.

32. *Evening Standard*, 10 May 1960.

33. E.g. 'The Dead Drive No Tractors', Oxfam advertisement in *New Statesman*, 8 September 1961.

34. Ibid., 1 May 1963. The erroneous presumption here is that Vicky 'belonged' in Hungary.

35. *Evening Standard*, 21 November 1960.

36. *New Statesman*, 19 April 1963.

37. Michael Cummings, interview with Peter Birks, 12 June 1978.

38. Jak (Raymond Jackson), interview with Peter Birks, undated; Sir Charles Wintour, conversation with R.D., 10 March 1987.

39. BBC 'World of Books', 1 January 1963.

40. *Evening Standard*, Londoner's Diary, 11 June 1963. Vicky's cartoon of the day ('Oh dear, *he's* come back too . . .!') depicted himself returning to add the last straw of dismay to Macmillan's crisis burden. In a *Sunday Times* Supplement interview (14 June 1964), George Melly accused Vicky of egotism over this. Vicky replied, 'Well, the *Standard* had said I was off on holiday, and it was a way to say I had decided to come back, but I can see why it irritated you. I do it much less now . . .'

41. Vicky to Inge Lew, 17 June 1963. Letters to and from Ischia had crossed, Vicky's addressed to 'Inge Lew' and hers asking him to address correspondence to 'Mrs Weisz'. A few conventional letters are scattered among Vicky's undated messages to Inge in the Hull University collection.

42. *New Statesman*, 14 June 1963.

43. Item in *Time and Tide*, 27 June 1963.

44. Profile under this title, *New Statesman*, 5 January 1962.

45. Drawing published *Evening Standard*, 11 July 1960. 'When Vicky Met Kennedy', 9 November 1960.

46. Pronounced, to suit the jacket illustration, '*Hume* and Abroad'. 'Mac the Knife', *Evening Standard*, 17 January 1964.

47. *Evening Standard*, 16 October 1964.

CHAPTER VIII

Material from Vicky's notes to Inge is drawn from the collection DX/165 at the Brynmor Jones Library of Hull University.

1. *Daily Mirror*, 8 June 1964.

2. Aurelia Weisz interview, 7 February 1977.

3. Former wife of the actor Alec Clunes. Later Controller of Programmes, London Weekend Television.

4. *Observer* Magazine, 13 February 1983. Article 'From Vicky to Inge', by Eric Silver. Silver was largely responsible for arranging the provision of a safe home for these 'letters'.

5. *Sunday Times* Supplement, 14 June 1964, interview by George Melly.

6. Elizabeth Weisz, interviews with R.D., various dates 1986–7.

7. Trog used the idea again in depicting Leonid Brezhnev, *Punch* 27 June 1973 (see *The World of Trog*, London, Robson Books, 1977).

8. Goldwater used the slogan 'In Your Heart You Know He Is Right'. Michael Ryan (later producer of the Granada TV programme 'What the Papers Say') wrote to Vicky suggesting that Douglas-Home's cadaverous appearance merited the variation 'In Your Heart You Know He Is Dead'. Vicky was amused, but declined the suggestion on grounds of taste. In the event, his Election cartoon for the *New Statesman* (16 October 1964) used the safe but much feebler 'In Your Heart You Know He's Wrong'.

9. *New Statesman*, 11 December 1964.

10. *Evening Standard*, 26 January 1965. Signed 'Leonardo da Vicky'.

11. *Daily Mirror*, 20 September 1955.

12. *Queen*, 20 February 1962.

13. Lucie Gray Mondange, interview with R.D., 16 February 1987.

14. 'To Tweak the Whiskers of the Great', *New Statesman*, 27 February 1960.

15. Michael Bateman, *Funny Way To Earn a Living*, pp. 9–12.

16. Vicky had used the caption 'The Man Who Never Was' before, applying it to Selwyn Lloyd (*Daily Mirror*, 24 February 1958).

17. *Evening Standard*, 1 November 1965.

18. *Vicky: A Memorial Volume*, text by James Cameron. Also tape transcript conversation between Keith Mackenzie and James Cameron, 14 July 1977. (Peter Birks research file.)

19. Charles Wintour, *Pressures on the Press* (London, André Deutsch, 1972).

20. *Vicky: A Memorial Volume*.

21. *Evening Standard*, 31 December 1965.

22. Frank Marcus to L.O., 13 October 1986. Brian Doyle to L.O., 25 September 1986.

23. *Evening Standard*, 21 January 1966.

24. Sir Charles Wintour, conversation with R.D., 10 March 1987.

25. 'I Don't Love England', *New Statesman*, 28 January 1966.

26. Tom Baistow, 6 January 1987.

27. Charles Wintour, interview with Peter Birks, 9 February 1978.

28. Telephone conversation, Mark Roberts with R.D. Mr Roberts was lodging with Inge Weisz at the time of her death, and often discussed Vicky with her.

29. Vicky to Inge Weisz, 15 February 1966.

30. *Vicky: A Memorial Volume*.

31. Mervyn Jones, 9 February 1977.

32. *Evening Standard*, 22 February 1966.

33. *Ibid.*, 23 February 1966. 'On this page – the date was November 3, 1958 – Vicky drew his first cartoon for the *Evening Standard*. Here, with sadness and a deep sense of loss, we print his last.'

34. *Daily Telegraph*, 1 March 1966.

35. *Daily Worker* report, 1 March 1966: 'note clearly indicates his intention'.

36. *Evening News*, 28 February 1966.

37. Elizabeth Weisz, interviews with R.D.

38. *Evening Standard*, 24 February 1966.

39. 'Spectator's Notebook', *Spectator*, 25 February 1966. Nigel Lawson wrote, 'Talking to him was always stimulating, not simply because he felt strongly about the injustices of the world, but also because he was so extraordinarily well-informed about politics.'

40. *The Times*, 24 February 1966.

41. *Ibid.*, 28 February 1966.

42. *Evening Standard*, 1 March 1966.

43. *Ibid.*

44. *Ibid.*

45. *Evening News*, 23 June 1966.

46. *Daily Telegraph*, 11 July 1966.
47. Royalties to the end of June 1967 amounted to £530.13s.9d. (*Evening Standard*, 19 December 1967).
48. *Daily Express*, 3 May 1967.
49. *Evening Standard*, 25 March 1975.
50. *New Society*, 11 May 1967. 'When it was finished', review by Berger of *Vicky: A Memorial Volume*.

Bibliography

Books and Pamphlets by Vicky

This list includes all the books and pamphlets authored by Vicky and volumes to which he contributed. It excludes books using occasional Vicky drawings as illustrations.

I. BOOKS

Schmeling: Geschichte einer Karriere (Berlin-Charlottenburg, Grossberliner Druckerei für Presse und Buchverlag, 1932). By Rolf Nürnberg, cover and illustrations by Vicky.

Outrageous Rhapsodies (London, Herbert Jenkins, 1938). By G.W.L. Day, 25 illustrations by Vicky.

Home Truths (London, John Lane, 1939). By William Douglas-Home, with drawings by Vicky.

We Are Not Amused (London, Cresset Press, 1940). By G.W.L. Day, 50 illustrations by Vicki (sic).

Drawn by Vicky: 100 Cartoons from the News Chronicle (London, The Walding Press, 1944). Foreword by A.J. Cummings.

9 Drawings by Vicky (Scenes in an Indian famine) (London, Modern Literature, 1944). Introduction by Mulk Raj Anand.

Aftermath: Cartoons by Vicky (London, Alliance Press, 1946).

Profiles and Personalities (London, Brownlee, 1946). By Peter Noble, with 4 drawings by Vicky.

Let Cowards Flinch (London, Turnstile Press, 1947). By 'Sagittarius', 30 illustrations by Vicky.

The Editor Regrets: Unpublished Cartoons by Vicky (London, Allan Wingate, 1947). Introduction by Gerald Barry.

Sigh No More, Ladies (London, Herbert Joseph, 1948). By G.W.L. Day, 29 illustrations by Vicky.

Up the Poll! The Sap's Guide to the General Election (London, Turnstile Press, 1950). Verse by 'Sagittarius', 62 illustrations by Vicky.

How to be a Celebrity (London, Reinhardt & Evans, 1950). By Milton Shulman, 28 caricatures by Vicky.

Stabs in the Back (London, Max Reinhardt, 1952). Introduction by R.J. Cruikshank, selected cartoons 1945–52.

The Real Mackay: Being Essays by Ian Mackay (London, News Chronicle Publications, 1953). Edited by Stanley Baron, profile by R.J. Cruikshank, 13 illustrations by Vicky.

Meet the Russians (London, Max Reinhardt, 1953).

New Statesman Profiles (London, Phoenix House, 1957). 46 drawings by Vicky with a note on profiles by Kingsley Martin.

Guilty Men, 1957 (London, Victor Gollancz, 1957). By Michael Foot and Mervyn Jones, 12 cartoons by Vicky.

Pilgrim's Progress in Russia (London, Housman's, 1959). By Emrys Hughes, with 16 cartoons by Vicky.

Vicky's World (London, Secker & Warburg, 1959). Introduction by Malcolm Muggeridge.

The Delights of Chess (London, MacGibbon & Kee, 1960). By 'Assiac', with 7 drawings by Vicky.

Vicky Must Go! (London, Beaverbrook Newspapers, 1960).

This England: Selections from the New Statesman 'This England' 1957–1960 (London, Turnstile Press, 1960). Edited by Audrey Hilton, illustrated by Vicky.

Twists (London, Beaverbrook Newspapers, 1962). Foreword by Randolph S. Churchill.

Home and Abroad (London, Beaverbrook Newspapers, 1964). Foreword by Osbert Lancaster.

This England: Selections from the

'*This England*' *column of the*
New Statesman *1960–65*
(London, Turnstile Press,
1965). Edited by Audrey
Hilton, illustrated by Vicky.
Vicky: A Memorial Volume
(London, Allen Lane, 1967).
With an introduction and
commentary by James
Cameron.
Impressions (unpublished). By
Vicky and Vickers.

2. PAMPHLETS

Austria, 1946 (London, St
Botolph, 1946). By Dr S.W.
Jeger and Maurice Orbach.
Cover by Vicky.
*It Need Not Happen: The
Alternatives to German
Rearmament* (London, Tribune
Pamphlet, 1954). Contribu-
tions by A. Bevan, B. Castle,
R. Crossman, T. Driberg,
I. Mikardo, H. Wilson.

*China and the United Nations: The
Cold Spot in the Diplomatic
Thaw* (London, Union of
Democratic Control, 1955). By
Ben Parkin.
*The Men Who Failed: The Story of
the Westminster Dunces*
(London, Labour Party, 1956).
The Future Labour Offers You
(London, Labour Party, 1959).
Detachable cartoon/poster by
Vicky.

Supplementary bibliography

This list, which is by no means exhaustive, includes books in which Vicky drawings appear.

*The Great Bohunkus: Tributes to
Ian Mackay* (London,
W.H. Allen, 1953). Edited by
Trevor Evans, Foreword by
Lord Beaverbrook.
W.S.C.: A Cartoon Biography
(London, Cassell, 1955).
Compiled by Fred Urquhart.
Hugh Gaitskell, 1906–1963
(London, Thames and Hudson,
1964). Edited by
W.T. Rodgers.
*Harold Wilson: A Pictorial
Biography* (Oxford, Pergamon
Press, 1964). By Michael Foot,
compiled and edited by John
Parker and Eugene Prager.
*George Brown: A Profile and
Pictorial Biography* (Oxford,
Pergamon Press, 1964). By
'Cassandra'.
*Kingsley Martin: Portrait and Self-
Portrait* (London, Barrie &
Jenkins, 1964). Edited by
Mervyn Jones.
*Churchill and Beaverbrook: A Study
in Friendship and Politics*
(London, Eyre &
Spottiswoode, 1966). By

Kenneth Young.
NAB 1: Portrait of a Politician
(London, Maxwell, 1969). By
Gerald Nabarro.
In My Way (London, Victor
Gollancz, 1971). By George
Brown.
*The Art of the Possible: The
Memoirs of Lord Butler* (London,
Hamish Hamilton, 1971).
*Leader Lost: A Biography of Hugh
Gaitskell* (London, Leslie
Frewin, 1972). By Geoffrey
McDermott.
Exploits of a Politician (London,
Barker, 1973). By Gerald
Nabarro.
*Aneurin Bevan: A Biography (Vol.
2, 1945–1960)* (London, Davis-
Poynter, 1973). By Michael
Foot.
'*Swaff*': *The Life and Times of
Hannen Swaffer* (London,
Macdonald, 1974). By Tom
Driberg.
*Film Criticism and Caricatures
1943–53* (London, Paul Elek,
1975). By Richard
Winnington. Selected with an

introduction by Paul Rotha.
Dustjacket caricature of
Winnington by Vicky.
The Diaries of a Cabinet Minister
(London, Hamish Hamilton;
Jonathan Cape, 1975–77). By
Richard Crossman.
*Hugh Gaitskell: A Political
Biography* (London, Jonathan
Cape, 1979). By Philip M.
Williams.
*The Last Edwardian at No. 10: An
Impression of Harold Macmillan*
(London, Quartet, 1980). By
George Hutchinson.
*The Backbench Diaries of Richard
Crossman* (London, Hamish
Hamilton/Jonathan Cape,
1981). Edited by Janet Morgan.
Hugh Dalton (London, Jonathan
Cape, 1985). By Ben Pimlott.
*The Political Diary of Hugh Dalton
1918–40, 1945–60* (London,
Jonathan Cape, 1986). Edited
by Ben Pimlott.
Loyalists and Loners (London,
Collins, 1986). By Michael
Foot.

Picture Sources and Acknowledgements

For assistance in supplying cartoons and/or for permission to reproduce them, the authors wish to thank the following:

Centre for the Study of Cartoons and Caricature, University of Kent at Canterbury: cover, nos. 7A, 7B, 34, 36A, 42B, 42C, 43B, 47, 50A, 52, 53, 54, 55, 66, 70, 71, 75, 77, 84, 85, 86, 87, 88, 89, 93, 94, 95, 96, 98A, 98B, 102, 105, 106, 107, 110, 111, 112, 114, 115, 118, 120, 121, 122, 123, 124, 126, 127, 128, 129, 130, 132, 133, 134, 135, 137, 138, 139, 140, 141, 142, 145, 146, 147, 149, 150, 151, 153, 154

Daily Mail: nos. 25, 37, 42B, 43A, 43B, 44, 46, 48, 49, 50A, 50B, 51, 52, 53, 54, 56, 57, 60, 61, 64, 65, 66, 67, 70, 72, 73, 74A, 75, 76, 77, 78, 79, 80, 82, 83, 84, 86, 87, 89, 90, 91, 92A, 92B, 96, 97, 99, 100, 101, 102

The Syndics of Cambridge University Library: nos. 16, 17, 18, 20, 26, 30, 32, 39, 40, 42A, 43A, 44, 46, 48, 49, 50B, 56, 57, 60, 61, 64, 65, 67, 72, 73, 74A, 76, 78, 79, 80, 82, 83, 90, 91, 92A, 92B, 97, 99, 100, 101, 104, 125, 131, 136

Evening Standard: nos. 13, 14, 36B, 88, 104, 113, 121, 122, 123, 124, 125, 126, 130, 131, 133, 136, 137, 140, 149, 150, 151, 152, 154

New Statesman and Nation: nos. 10, 12, 94, 107, 108, 109, 111, 116, 128, 129, 132, 138, 139, 141, 142, 145, 146, 147, 153

Elizabeth Weisz: nos. 2, 3, 4, 5, 11, 13, 14, 21A, 21B, 23, 24, 28, 31, 41, 58, 143

Syndication International: cover, nos. 33, 36A, 93, 95, 105, 106, 110, 112, 114, 115, 117, 118, 120, 127, 135

The Brynmor Jones Library, University of Hull: nos. 59, 62, 63, 68, 144A, 144B, 148

The British Library, Newspaper Library: nos. 15, 19A, 19B, 25, 51, 117

Rosita Gross: nos. 6, 22A, 22B, 38, 81, 103

The Hans Tasiemka Archives: nos. 8, 9, 33

Rt Hon Michael Foot MP: nos. 1, 155

Peter Johnson: nos. 37, 109

A.R. (Pat) Adams: no. 27

Tom Baistow: no. 36B

BBC Hulton Picture Library: no. 35

Ben Uri Art Society: no. 108

Mark Bryant: no. 69

Moneesha Cameron: no. 45

Brian Doyle: no. 152

L'Express/K.S. Karol: no. 119

Wally Fawkes: no. 155

Hans Feld: no. 16

London Express News and Features Service: no. 74B

Oxfam: no. 113

Private collection: no. 10

Rosemary Say: no. 102

Daily Telegraph: no. 15

John Vickers Theatre Collection: no. 58

The Authors have attempted to trace all copyright holders. Advice of omissions would be appreciated and they will be corrected in future editions.

Index

All numbers refer to pages. Roman numbers refer to text; italic numbers to illustrations.